BIOLOGY REVISION
FOR LEAVING CERTIFICATE

BIOLOGY REVISION
FOR LEAVING CERTIFICATE

PHILIP MURPHY

Gill & Macmillan

Gill & Macmillan Ltd
Hume Avenue
Park West
Dublin 12
with associated companies throughout the world
www.gillmacmillan.ie

© Philip Murphy 2003
Illustrations © Michael Phillips 2003
ISBN-10: 0 7171 3506 3
ISBN-13: 978 0 7171 3506 6
Print origination in Ireland by Carole Lynch

The paper used in this book is made from the wood pulp of managed forests. For every tree felled, at least one tree is planted, thereby renewing natural resources.

All rights reserved.
No part of this publication may be copied,
reproduced or transmitted in any form or by any
means without written permission of the publishers or else
under the terms of any licence permitting limited copying
issued by the Irish Copyright Licensing Agency.

CONTENTS

Introduction ... vi

UNIT 1 – BIOLOGY: THE STUDY OF LIFE
1.1 Scientific Method ... 1
1.2 The Characteristics of Life ... 2
1.3 Nutrition ... 3
1.4 General Principles of Ecology ... 6
1.5 A Study of an Ecosystem ... 16

UNIT 2 – THE CELL
2.1 The Cell Structure ... 17
2.2 Cell Metabolism ... 22
2.3 Cell Continuity ... 37
2.4 Cell Diversity ... 40
2.5 Genetics ... 41

UNIT 3 – THE ORGANISM
3.1 Diversity of Organisms ... 55
3.2 Organisation and Vascular Structures ... 66
3.3 Transport and Nutrition ... 77
3.4 Breathing System and Excretion ... 84
3.5 Responses to Stimuli ... 91
3.6 Reproduction and Growth ... 111

Glossary of Terms ... 128

Past Exam Papers and Marking Schemes ... 143

INTRODUCTION

BIOLOGY SYLLABUS
The new Biology Syllabus is divided into three units consisting of the following sections:

UNIT 1 – BIOLOGY: THE STUDY OF LIFE
1.1 Scientific Method
1.2 The Characteristics of Life
1.3 Nutrition
1.4 General Principles of Ecology
1.5 A Study of an Ecosystem

Mandatory Activities in Unit 1 are:
1. The Development of the Processes of Scientific Method.
2. Qualitative Food Tests for:
    (a) Starch,
    (b) Fat,
    (c) Reducing Sugar,
    (d) Protein.
3. Habitat Study of a Selected Ecosystem.

UNIT 2 – THE CELL
2.1 The Cell Structure
2.2 Cell Metabolism
2.3 Cell Continuity
2.4 Cell Diversity
2.5 Genetics

Mandatory Activities in Unit 2 are:
1. Use of the Light Microscope.
2. Preparation and Examination of Animal and Plant Cells.
3. Investigation of the Effect of pH on Enzyme Activity.
4. Investigation of the Effect of Temperature on Enzyme Activity.
5. Prepare an Enzyme Immobilisation and Examine Its Application.
6. Investigate the Influence of Light Intensity **or** Carbon Dioxide on the Rate of Photosynthesis.
7. Prepare and Show the Production of Alcohol by Yeast.

8. Conduct Any Activity to Demonstrate Osmosis.
9. Investigate the Effect of Heat Denaturation on Enzyme Activity.
10. Isolation of DNA from Plant Tissue.

UNIT 3 – THE ORGANISM
3.1 Diversity of Organisms
3.2 Organisation and Vascular Structures
3.3 Transport and Nutrition
3.4 Breathing System and Excretion
3.5 Responses to Stimuli
3.6 Reproduction and Growth

Mandatory Activities in Unit 3 are:
1. Investigation of the Growth of Leaf Yeast using Agar Plates and Controls.
2. Prepare and Examine Microscopically the Transverse Section of a Dicot. Stem.
3. Dissect, Display and Identify an Ox's **or** a Sheep's Heart.
4. Investigation of the Effect of Exercise on the Breathing Rate **or** Pulse of a Human.
5. Investigation of the Effect of the Growth Regulator IAA on Plant Tissue.
6. Investigation of the Effect of Water, Oxygen and Temperature on Germination.
7. To Show the Digestive Activity during Germination Using Starch Agar **or** Skimmed Milk Plates.

MANDATORY ACTIVITIES

> It is compulsory that all Mandatory Activities are carried out in the Laboratory, or, in the habitat for Ecology Activities. All records of procedures, results, interpretations, sources of error, safety measures etc. are to be available for inspection if required. Your teacher will provide the necessary guidance on the depth and detail expected in each of the Activities.
>
> The Mandatory Activities described in this text should only be used as general guidelines for experimental procedures.

LEAVING CERTIFICATE EXAMINATION

It is proposed that the Examination Paper will be presented in three sections as follows:

1. SECTION A

Answer any Five Questions out of Six: (5 × 20 marks)

Two Questions from Unit 1
Two Questions from Unit 2
Two Questions from Unit 3

2. SECTION B

Answer any Two Questions out of Three: (2 × 30 marks)

> The Questions in this section are based on the Mandatory Activities and the Manipulation of Data.

3. SECTION C

Answer any Four Questions out of Six: (4 × 60 marks)

One Question from Unit 1
Two Questions from Unit 2
Three Questions from Unit 3

The Summary of the Marks Awarded for each Section of the Examination Paper is provided below:

Section	Marks	% of Total
A	100	25%
B	60	15%
C	240	60%
Total	**400**	**100%**

UNIT 1 – BIOLOGY: THE STUDY OF LIFE

1.1 SCIENTIFIC METHOD

In general a scientist develops a theory or hypothesis based on observation. The theory is then tested through experiment to see if it is valid. A scientific investigation or scientific method involves a sequence of steps that may support or refute a theory. It is essential that any scientific method can be repeated independently by any other scientist. The general steps in a scientific investigation are shown in fig. 1.1.

Fig. 1.1 Scientific Method

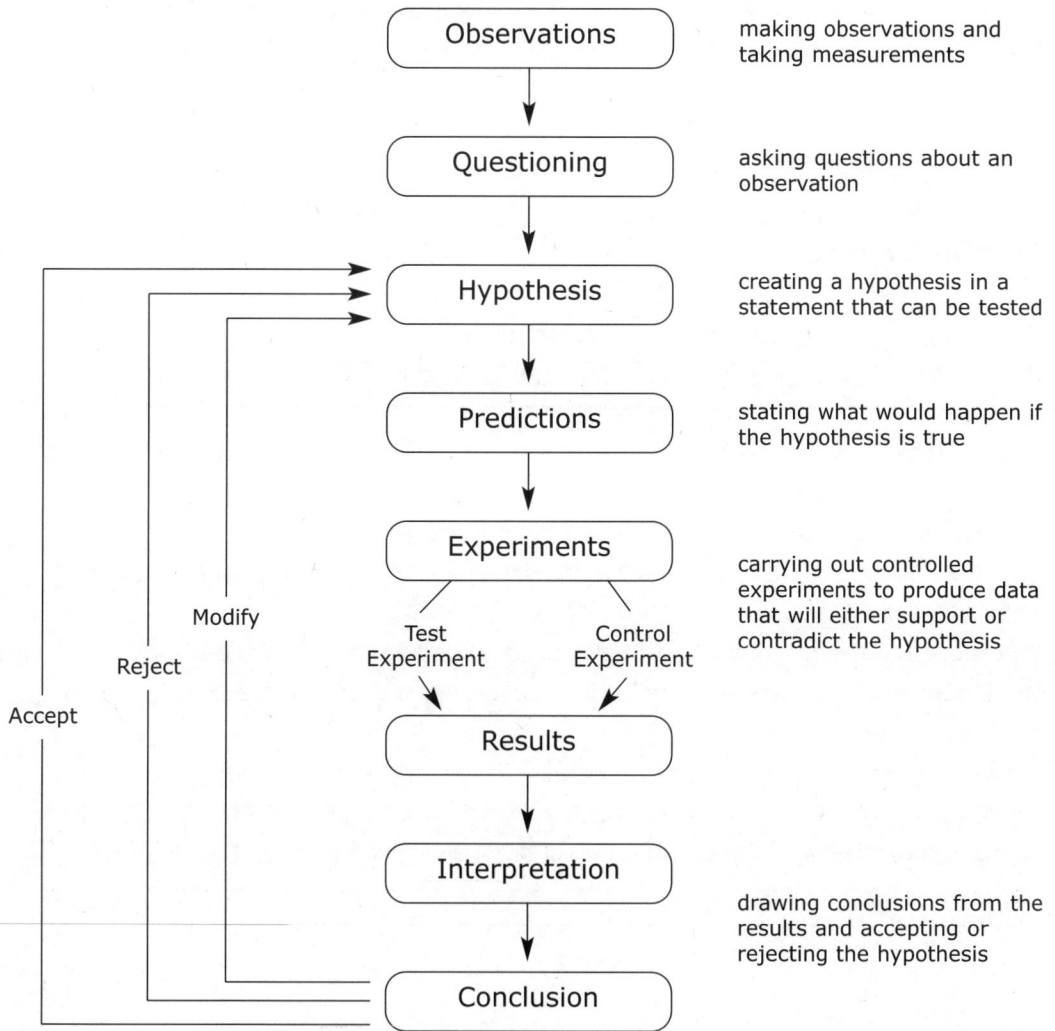

Limitations of Scientific Method
1. Interpretation of results is limited by our present knowledge and abilities.
2. Living organisms are rarely predictable and unknown factors can affect outcomes.
3. Scientists often have theories as to the outcomes of experimentation before the experiment is carried out. These can influence their interpretation of results.
4. Scientific theories are tested to see if they can be proven false. Only one confirmed negative result is needed to disprove a theory even if hundreds of experiments support it.

EXPERIMENTATION
In any biology experiment many conditions or factors (light intensity or temperature for example) can be varied. These factors are known as **variables**. During many experiments when varying one factor the other variables must be kept constant.

Every experiment needs a **control** to compare results. A control is generally the same apparatus as the experiment but without the factor under test being varied.

1.2 THE CHARACTERISTICS OF LIFE

DEFINITION OF LIFE
It is difficult to define life but all living things have two features in common:
1. Metabolism: They carry out chemical reactions to live.
2. Reproduction: All organisms can produce offspring for continuity.

CHARACTERISTICS OF LIFE
There are six characteristics common to all living organisms:
(a) **Respiration**: The chemical release of energy from food which occurs at a cellular level.
(b) **Nutrition**: The means by which an organism obtains its energy to live, and the matter it needs to build its structures.
(c) **Excretion**: The removal of the wastes produced in metabolism from the body.
(d) **Movement**: Animal movements are obvious while plant movements are slow, involving only parts of the plant.
(e) **Growth**: An increase in size due to an increase in solid matter in the body. There is usually an associated increase in complexity of the organism as it grows.
(f) **Reproduction**: The ability to produce new individuals of the same species.

1.3 NUTRITION

> Food is any substance used by living organisms to provide energy, materials for repair and maintenance or to control metabolism.

Most types of food are in the form of large complex **biomolecules**.

> Biomolecules are complex molecules made up of different elements. They are produced originally by plants from simple elements.

The six most common elements in food biomolecules are:
Carbon, Hydrogen, Nitrogen, Oxygen, Phosphorus and Sulphur.

There are four main types of food biomolecules:
(a) **Carbohydrates,**
(b) **Lipids,**
(c) **Protein,**
(d) **Vitamins**.

Carbohydrates

Carbohydrates contain the elements Carbon, Hydrogen and Oxygen.

There are three forms of carbohydrates:
1. Monosaccharides (single units),
2. Disaccharides (double units),
3. Polysaccharides (many units).

Monosaccharides and disaccharides are soluble in water.

Sources of monosaccharides and disaccharides are found in foods such as apples, milk, sugar.

Polysaccharides are insoluble carbohydrates.

Sources of polysaccharides in food are potatoes, rice and flour.

The main **function** of carbohydrate in the diet is to produce energy.

A summary of the different forms of carbohydrates is provided in fig. 1.2.

Fig. 1.2 Summary of Carbohydrate Forms

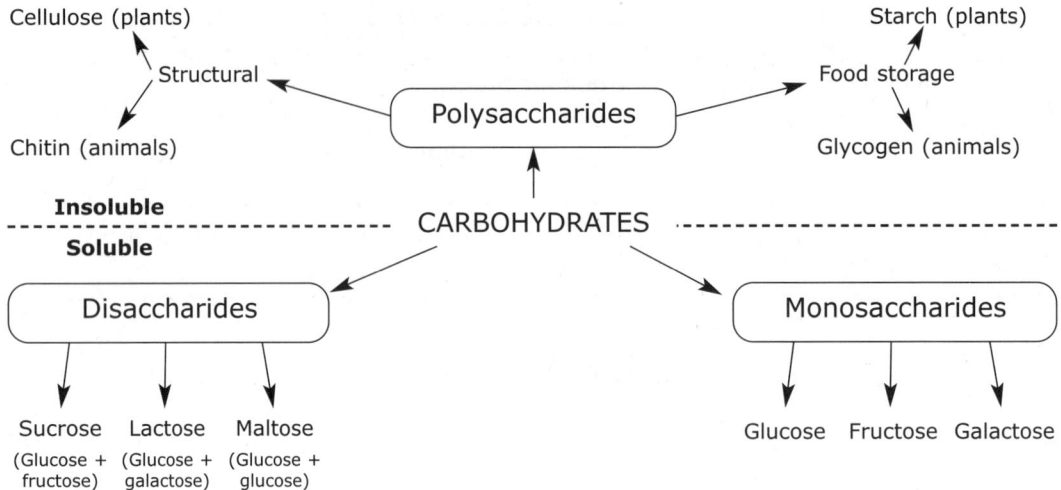

Lipids

Lipids contain the elements Carbon, Hydrogen and Oxygen.

There are two types of lipid, oils which are liquid at room temperature and fats which are solid at room temperature. The smallest unit of a lipid is one molecule of glycerol joined to three fatty acids.

Sources of lipids are red meats, dairy products and vegetable oils.

Main function in diet: Provide Energy and a source of fat-soluble vitamins.

Structural Functions: Phospholipids and lipoproteins form cell membranes. Lipids form a protective layer around some body organs such as the kidneys.

Protein

Protein is made up of the elements Carbon, Hydrogen, Oxygen, Nitrogen and occasionally Sulphur. The smallest units of proteins are **Amino Acids**.

Main function in the diet: Provide materials for maintenance and repair and provide the building blocks for enzymes. Enzymes control chemical reactions in all organisms.

Structural Functions: The protein Keratin forms hair and nails. The protein Myosin forms part of muscle fibres.

Sources of protein include meat, fish, nuts and milk.

Vitamins

Vitamins are complex organic chemicals that must be taken in the diet. They are necessary only in tiny amounts and often used as coenzymes. Vitamins have no energy value and are classified according to their solubility.

Vitamin C is an example of a water soluble vitamin while Vitamin D is fat soluble.

Vitamin	Solubility	Source	Function	Deficiency Disease
C	Water	Citrus fruits	Maintenance of connective tissue	Scurvy, Bleeding gums
D	Fat	Fish liver oil, butter	Control of transfer of phosphorus and calcium between the blood and bones	Rickets, failure of growing bones to calcify

Minerals

Minerals are not biomolecules. They are inorganic chemicals (simple atoms and ions) necessary in tiny amounts. They must be taken in the diet. Minerals have no energy value. Two examples of plant and animal minerals are provided below:

Plant Minerals	Source	Function	Deficiency
Phosphate (PO_4)	Soil	Part of nucleic acids	Poor root growth
Magnesium (Mg)	Soil	Part of chlorophyll	Lack of chlorophyll
Animal Minerals			
Iron (Fe)	Liver, meat	Part of haemoglobin and many enzymes	Low red blood cell count
Calcium (Ca)	Milk, cheese	Bones, nerve transmission	Weak bones

Water

Water has no energy value but is essential for life. Enzymes can only function in a solution of water. Over 70% of our body is water. Water loss occurs through excretion, breathing and sweating. The average person loses between two and three litres of water per day which must be replaced in the diet.

MANDATORY ACTIVITIES – FOOD TESTS

Test for Protein

1. Place a small volume of the sample in a test tube.
2. Add an equal volume of 10% Sodium Hydroxide.
3. Add a few drops of 1% Copper Sulphate and mix.

Positive result = purple OR violet colour

Negative result = light blue colour

Control: use an equal volume of water as the sample.

Test for Reducing Sugar (e.g. Glucose)
1. Place a small volume of the sample in a test tube.
2. Add an equal volume of Benedict's Reagent and mix.
3. Place in a boiling water bath for 10 minutes.

Positive result = brick red OR orange colour. A green colour indicates slight positive result.

Negative result = blue colour

Control: use an equal volume of water as the sample.

Test for Starch
1. Place a small volume of the sample in a test tube.
2. Add a few drops of dilute Iodine and mix.

Positive result = blue/black colour

Negative result = yellow colour

Control: use an equal volume of water as the sample.

Test for Lipids
1. Heat the sample gently to 40°C or body temperature.
2. Add the sample to brown paper.
3. Hold the paper up to the light.

Positive result = a translucent grease spot is formed.

1.4 GENERAL PRINCIPLES OF ECOLOGY

A number of important definitions are provided below:

> **Ecology** is the scientific study of how organisms interact with each other and their environment.
>
> An **Ecosystem** is a definable area containing a self-sustained community of organisms interacting with their non-living environment. Examples: Pond, Woodland or Seashore ecosystems.
>
> **Biosphere** is the part of the earth occupied by organisms. It extends from the bottom of the oceans to the upper atmosphere. It is a relatively thin band compared to the total size of the earth and the atmosphere.
>
> A **Habitat** is the part of an ecosystem where individual organisms live.
>
> A **Niche** describes the role of an organism in an ecosystem. It shows *how* as well as *where* an organism lives. Example: A caterpillar feeds and lives on the leaves of an oak tree in a woodland. The caterpillar is also a food source for Blue Tits in this habitat.

ENVIRONMENTAL FACTORS IN AN ECOSYSTEM

The **distribution** of organisms in any habitat will be affected by two groups of factors:

1. **Abiotic factors** are physical non-living factors that influence living organisms. Abiotic factors include the following:
   (a) Climatic factors such as light, temperature, water availability and wind.
   (b) Edaphic factors (usually associated with soil) such as soil texture, pH and organic content.
   (c) Topographic factors such as the angle or aspect of a slope.

On the **seashore** abiotic factors would include tides, water temperature and wave action.

In a **woodland** ecosystem abiotic factors would include light, temperature, air humidity, soil pH and wind.

2. **Biotic factors** are due to the effects of living organisms.

The effect of abundant seaweeds on a rocky seashore is to provide shelter and food for a large community of organisms.

In a terrestrial ecosystem biotic factors could include parasitism. Greenfly act as parasites on green plants. They feed on the sap in the phloem causing harm to the plant.

ENERGY FLOW IN AN ECOSYSTEM

The energy for all living organisms comes originally from the sun. A **Food Web** shows all the feeding (energy change) relationships in a habitat, (see fig. 1.3).

Fig. 1.3 Food Web (Pond)

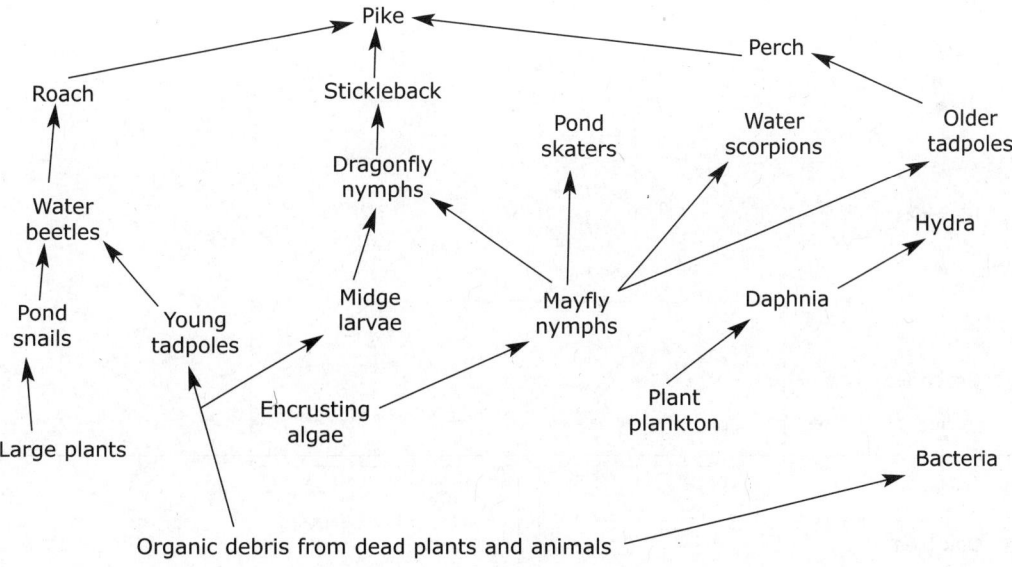

A **Food Chain** indicates the feeding relationships between a number of organisms in a community. A food chain from the pond food web is shown in fig. 1.4.

Fig. 1.4 Food Chain

Encrusting algae → Mayfly nymph → Pond skaters → Stickleback

A **Pyramid of Numbers** is produced when the number of organisms per unit area is counted at each trophic level in a food chain. Each organism is represented by a horizontal bar. The width of each bar represents the number of organisms at each trophic level.

Note: A food chain or pyramid rarely has more than five stages. This is due to the enormous amounts of energy lost (over 90%) when moving from one trophic level to the next. This loss is due to metabolism, excretion, movement or any other activities.

Limitations of a Pyramid of Numbers

(a) It is difficult to count the number of grasses or algae accurately in a trophic level.
(b) There is often more than one organism at any trophic level in a habitat.
(c) The shape of a pyramid will vary according to the time of year.
(d) It does not take into account the relative size of the organisms at each level. In a woodland habitat an example of a food chain and the associated pyramid of numbers is shown in fig. 1.5. This shape is called an inverted pyramid of numbers.

Fig. 1.5 Inverted Pyramid of Numbers

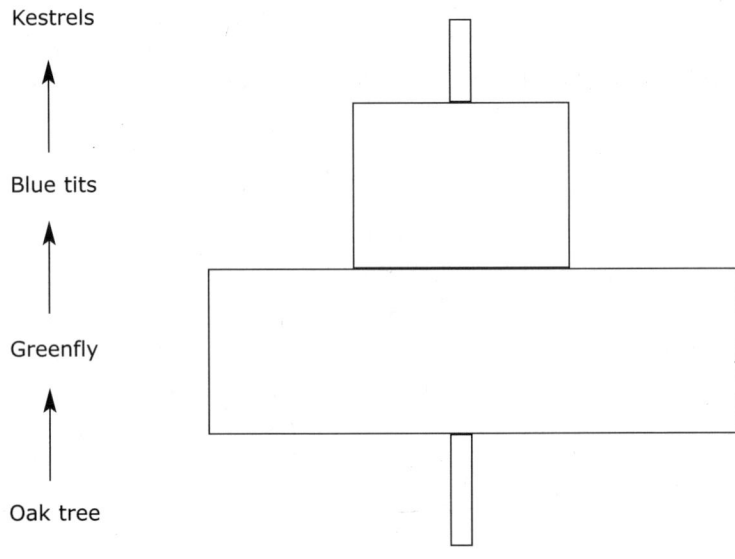

Pyramid of Biomass

An alternative approach to a pyramid of numbers is a pyramid of biomass. This is produced by estimating the dry mass of organisms per unit area at each level of a food chain (units = kg/m^2). This is regarded as a better procedure as:
(a) It usually produces the expected pyramid shape due to the inclusion of the factor of organism size into the calculations, (see fig. 1.6).
(b) It can allow for comparisons between ecosystems.

Fig. 1.6 Pyramid of Biomass

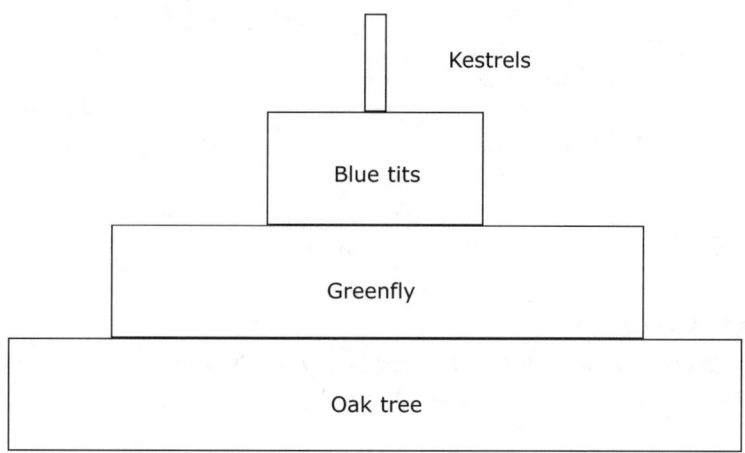

NUTRIENT RECYCLING

There is virtually a limitless supply of energy being supplied to the ecosystems by the sun. This is not the situation for nutrients, which must be constantly recycled in nature for the continuity of life. There are two main nutrient cycles:
(a) The Carbon Cycle
(b) The Nitrogen Cycle.

The Carbon Cycle

Carbon is a basic element of all living things. All organisms produce carbon dioxide gas as a waste product of respiration. Plants absorb Carbon Dioxide gas from the air for use in photosynthesis. This produces carbohydrate that can be converted to other foods required by the plant. The diagram shows a summary of the changes in the forms of carbon that occur in nature, (see fig 1.7).

Fig. 1.7 Carbon Cycle

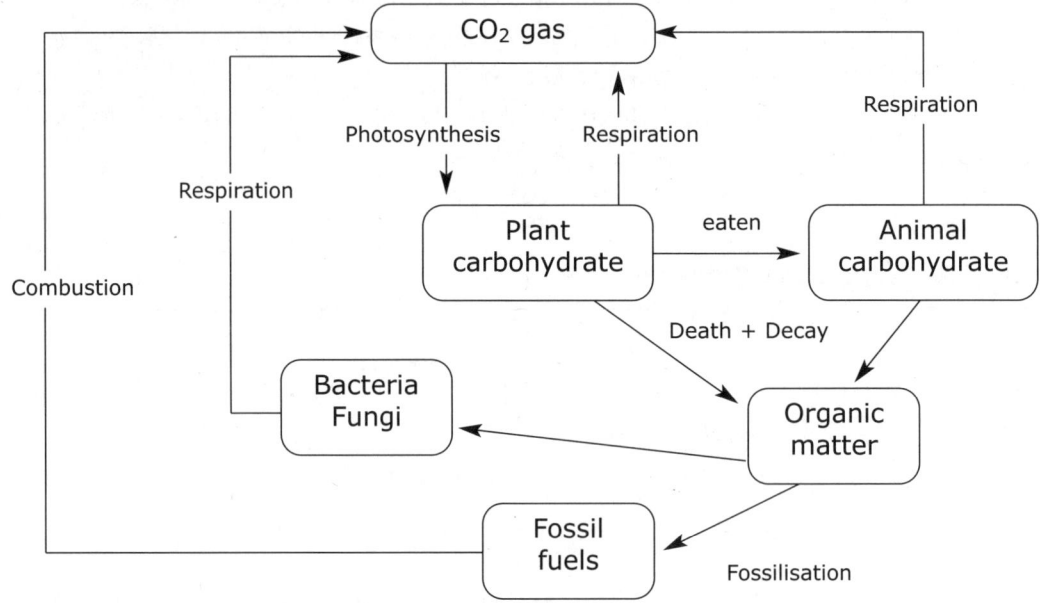

The Nitrogen Cycle

This describes the changes in the forms of nitrogen that occur in nature. The cycle is essential for the survival of organisms. Bacteria play a large role in the Nitrogen Cycle, (see fig. 1.8).

Fig. 1.8 Nitrogen Cycle

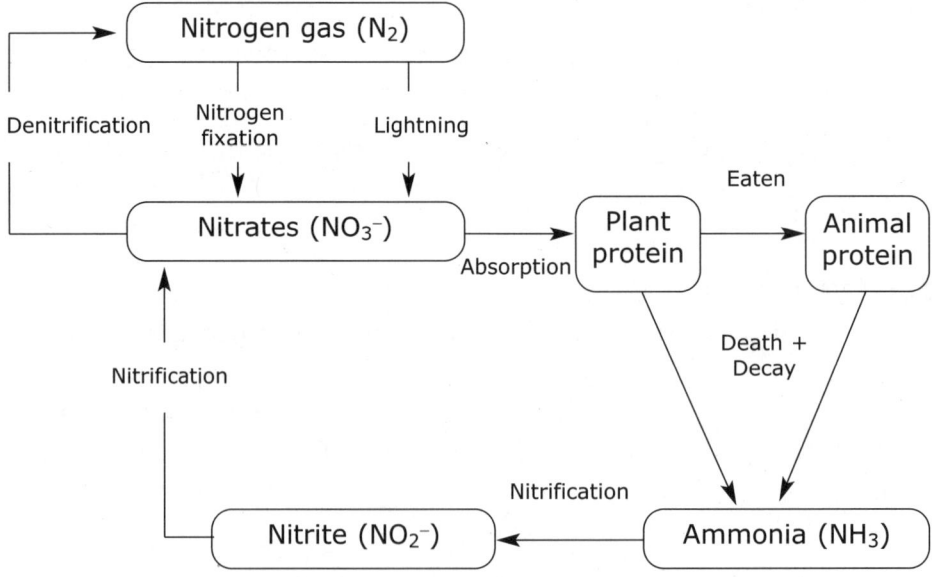

Nitrogen is a vital component of amino acids and proteins. Proteins (in the form of enzymes) control metabolism in all living things. Almost 80% of the atmosphere is made up of Nitrogen gas (N_2). In this form it cannot be used by plants or animals. Bacteria in the nitrogen cycle convert Nitrogen gas to Nitrates (NO_3^-). Nitrates can then be absorbed by the roots of plants and used to make plant protein. Animals consume the plants, converting them to animal protein.

Nitrogen Fixation is the term given to the conversion of Nitrogen to Nitrates. It is brought about by two different types of bacteria. One type is found on the **nodules** of the roots of **Legumes** (Clover, Pea and Bean plants). It fixes nitrogen for the plant while the plant in return supplies sugars to the bacteria. Such a relationship in nature where two different organisms live together is called **symbiosis**. When the association is beneficial to both the relationship is known as **mutualism**.

ECOLOGICAL RELATIONSHIPS

There are four main factors that can influence population numbers in a habitat:
(a) Competition,
(b) Predation,
(c) Parasitism,
(d) Symbiosis.

Competition

Most resources are in limited supply so organisms must compete for them. Plants compete for space, light and minerals. Animals compete for food, shelter and mates.

Example: In the pond food web we can see that Dragonfly nymphs, Pond skaters and Water scorpions all compete for Mayfly nymphs as a food source, (see fig. 1.3).

In the same habitat Plant plankton and Encrusting algae both compete for light.

Predation

A predator is an organism that feeds on another species, usually killing it first. The other species is called the prey. The abundance of prey is a factor limiting the numbers of the predator. In a food chain the predator-prey relationship causes both populations to oscillate, (see fig. 1.9). In this laboratory experiment the numbers of the predator (Paramecium) increase when there is a large population of prey (Yeast cells). The increase in predator numbers then causes a decrease in the prey population. At this point predator numbers begin to fall which allows for prey numbers to increase again.

Fig. 1.9 Predator-Prey Relationship

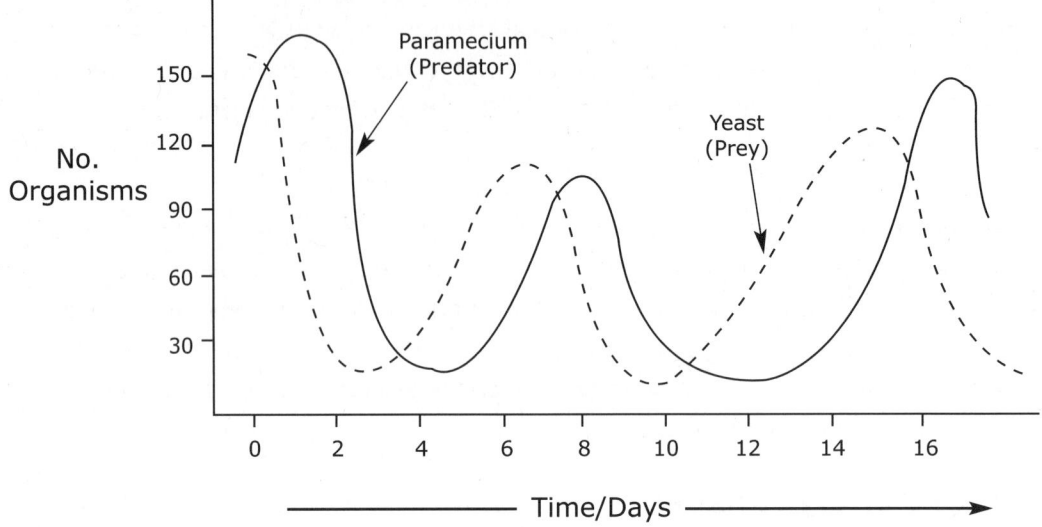

Parasitism

This is an association where one organism, the parasite, lives in or on another organism, the host. The parasite depends on the host for food and usually causes it harm. Parasitism can be a limiting factor for the population numbers of the host. This is particularly true when the parasite damages the tissues or causes the early death of the host.

Example: The myxoma virus is a parasite of the rabbit. Its effects cause the disease myxomatosis.

Symbiosis

This is a general term where two different organisms live in close association with one another. One form of symbiosis is Mutualism. This is where two different organisms live in close association which provides an advantage to both.

Example: Lichens consist of a fungus and an alga in a mutualistic relationship. The alga provides food while the fungus provides anchorage and minerals in exchange.

POPULATION DYNAMICS

In any predator-prey relationship it is likely that factors other than the direct feeding relationship causes variation in the population numbers.

Examples of such factors could include:
(a) Availability of food for the prey.
(b) Defence mechanisms developed by the prey.
(c) Improvement in techniques of capture by the predator.

(d) Competition from other animals in the food web.
(e) The possibility of migration by predator or prey.
(f) The introduction of disease into the predator or prey populations.

HUMAN POPULATION

Since 1700 there has been an exponential increase in human population. The main reason for this huge increase is the large reduction in child mortality and the improvement in life expectancy. Because of these factors more of the population reach the reproductive age and produce offspring.

The improved life expectancy is due to:

(a) **Reduction of disease**: Several important scientific advances have reduced disease. Immunisation, vaccination and antibiotics considerably improved the health of the population. The most important factor was probably the improvement in sanitation and public health. Water treatment and correct sewage disposal removed many sources of disease.

(b) **Increase in food supply**: Good agricultural practices improved the quality and quantity of produce. High yielding strains or breeds of plants and animals were developed. The development and use of artificial fertilisers and herbicides further improved yields.

It is thought that industrialisation, education and birth control in developed countries have largely stabilised populations. Many family planning programs have been introduced into developing countries in an attempt to reduce family size. Unfortunately there are often shortages of doctors and trained medical staff to explain family planning techniques. Many people still wish to have traditionally large families. Some people are suspicious of contraception. China and India are beginning to address their population explosion.

The world's population must begin to decline. Resources are limited. War, famine or disease may ultimately reduce human population. AIDS is seriously affecting some African populations. A lower level of population would ultimately allow for a better quality of life with sufficient resources for all.

HUMAN IMPACT ON AN ECOSYSTEM

Pollution

> Pollution is the release of substances or energy into the environment in large quantities that harm the natural inhabitants.

A pollutant may be physical (noise, heat, radiation) or chemical (industrial or biological wastes) that can cause harm to organisms in the environment.

Air Pollution

One form of air pollution is caused by the industrial release of greenhouse gases into the atmosphere. Greenhouse gases reduce the ability of the earth to reflect heat radiation back into space. The greenhouse effect is causing a steady increase in the temperature of the earth and the atmosphere.

Causes: The most important greenhouse gases are carbon dioxide, methane and chlorofluorocarbons (CFCs).

Carbon Dioxide gas is released when fossil fuels are burned. Since the Industrial Revolution the increasing use of fossil fuels for energy has produced a steady rise in the levels of carbon dioxide in the atmosphere. Many scientists link this increase to global warming. Methane is even more efficient than carbon dioxide at retaining heat in the atmosphere. Methane is released in large quantities from cattle and pigs. Landfill dumping is also a source of methane. CFCs were used as a liquid coolant in refrigerators. CFCs destroy the protective ozone layer in the upper atmosphere.

Effects: The effects of global warming are thought to cause:
(a) The rise of sea levels.
(b) The melting of polar ice.
(c) A change in weather patterns.

Control:
(a) Many countries have signed up to international agreements to limit the use of fossil fuels.
(b) New sources of renewable energy are being developed and refined. Wind and solar energy are two examples.
(c) New engines for transport are being developed. Hydrogen can be used to fuel car engines, water being the only waste product.
(d) Policies to increase public awareness of the importance and the means of energy conservation are being developed.

CONSERVATION

> Conservation is a series of measures designed to preserve a full range of habitats available to us. Human activities such as agriculture, urbanisation and industrialisation can contribute to habitat damage.

One example of conservation is seen in the fishing industry.

The scale of fishing around Britain and Ireland has seriously depleted stocks of many species. A ban of fishing for certain species has had some success in increasing population numbers. In 1976 a ban on herring fishing proved quite successful. Herring fishing was reintroduced in certain areas by 1984. New legislation by the European Union is now limiting the size of fishing fleets. The number of days at sea by trawlers is now also regulated to reduce catches. In addition, laws have been introduced to control the mesh size of nets. This ensures that younger (smaller) fish have a better chance of escaping.

WASTE MANAGEMENT

Urban communities produce huge quantities of household and commercial waste. The traditional method of waste disposal is by dumping the rubbish in landfill sites, such as disused quarries and gravel pits. This method leads to three main problems:
(a) There are insufficient sites to accommodate all the rubbish.
(b) Carbon-based waste when compacted and removed from air releases large amounts of the greenhouse gas methane.
(c) Toxic substances can leach into ground water presenting a threat to human supplies.

Many projects to minimise waste have been introduced. Waste minimisation can occur by:
(a) Separating household rubbish so that many materials can be recycled. Cardboard, paper, aluminium cans and glass can be recycled.
(b) Organic waste can be composted to produce natural organic fertilizer.
(c) Most old electrical items such as TVs, fridges, cookers etc. can all be stripped to recycle parts.
(d) The remaining rubbish that cannot be recycled can be incinerated to reduce volume.

SEWAGE

> Sewage is a liquid waste produced in large quantities in urban areas. The discharge of raw sewage into the environment could cause serious pollution. Sewage treatment is a process that uses micro-organisms to remove its harmful components. The main stages of sewage treatment are summarised in fig. 1.10.

Fig. 1.10 Stages in Sewage Treatment

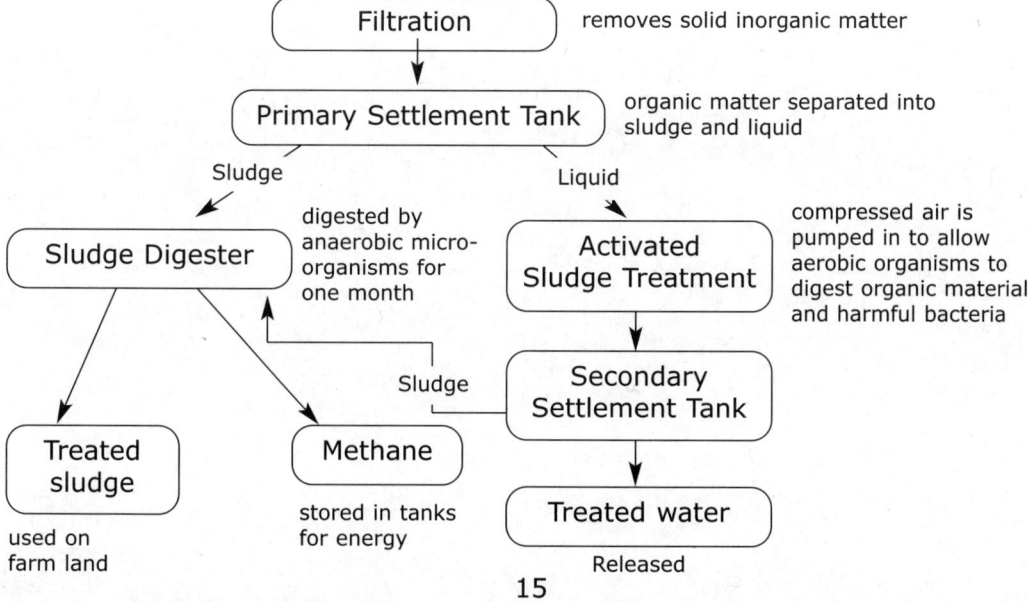

1.5 A STUDY OF AN ECOSYSTEM

The following points are to be used merely as a checklist for the procedures and exercises that are required to be carried out in the Study of any Ecosystem. Each student, under the supervision of their teacher, should:

1. Select and visit one Ecosystem.
2. Provide a broad overview of the ecosystem chosen.
3. Identify five plants and five animals in the ecosystem.
4. Locate and identify the different habitats present.
5. Describe the use of various apparatus used to collect plants and animals.
6. Conduct a quantitative study of plants using frequency and percentage cover techniques in a selected area of the ecosystem.
7. Conduct a quantitative study of animals in a selected area.
8. Present results in the forms of graphs, tables, diagrams etc.
9. Identify possible sources of error in the surveys carried out.
10. Investigate three abiotic factors in the habitat and relate the findings to the distribution of organisms.
11. Identify an adaptation of any organism to conditions in the habitat.
12. Construct a Food Chain, Food Web and a Pyramid of Numbers in the habitat.
13. Prepare a report of conclusions drawn from the results of the study.

UNIT 2 – THE CELL

2.1 THE CELL STRUCTURE

CELL ULTRASTRUCTURE

With the higher magnification possible using an electron microscope many different cell organelles can be identified. (fig. 2.1)

Fig. 2.1 Plant Cell

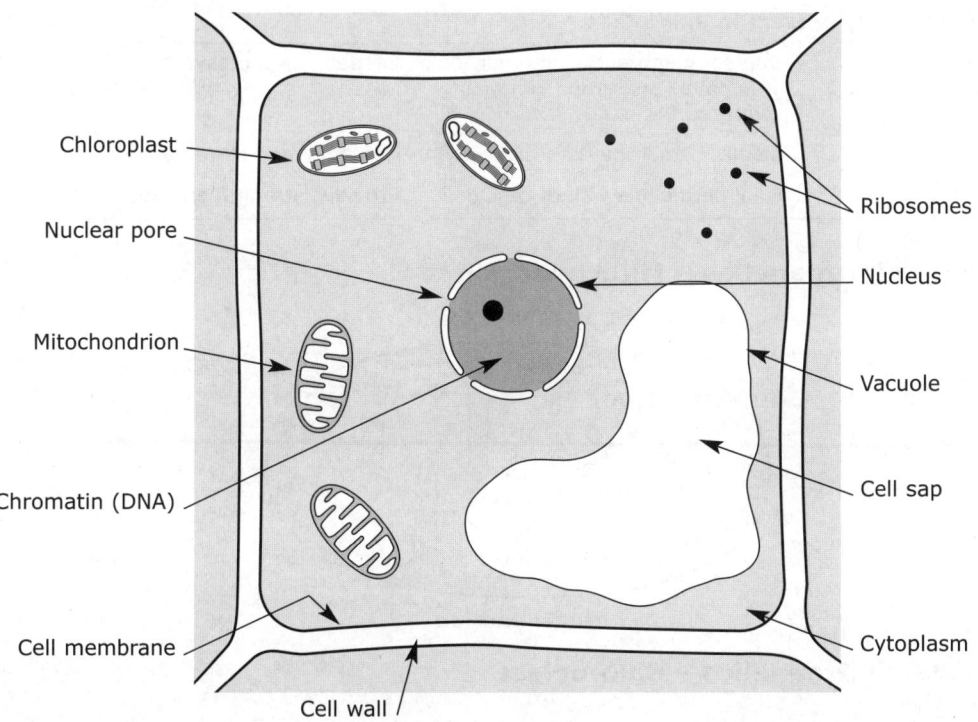

The structures and functions of the cell organelles are provided below:

Organelle	Structure	Function
Nucleus	Surrounded by a double membrane with many pores. Contains chromosomes (DNA) in the form of chromatin	Stores genetic information (DNA) and controls all activities in cell
Ribosome	Made of protein and RNA	Protein synthesis
Mitochondrion	Double membrane with inner foldings of cristae (see fig. 2.2)	Krebs' Cycle and Hydrogen Carrier Systems of aerobic respiration occur here
Cell Membrane	A phospholipid bilayer with protein (see fig. 2.4)	
Cytoplasm	Aqueous solution of salts with dissolved proteins and enzymes	Provides a liquid medium for enzymes and a suspension for cell organelles
Organelles only present in Plant Cells		
Chloroplast	Double membrane with inner folds of lamellae and grana containing chlorophyll (see fig. 2.3)	Carries out photosynthesis
Large Vacuole	Single membrane fluid-filled cavity	Contains food stored as cell sap
Cell Wall	Fully permeable wall of cellulose	Provides strength and support

Fig. 2.2 Cell Organelles – Mitochondrion

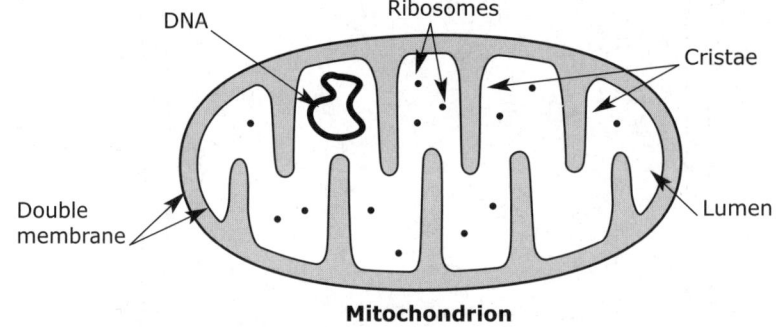

Mitochondrion

Fig. 2.3 Cell Organelles – Chloroplast

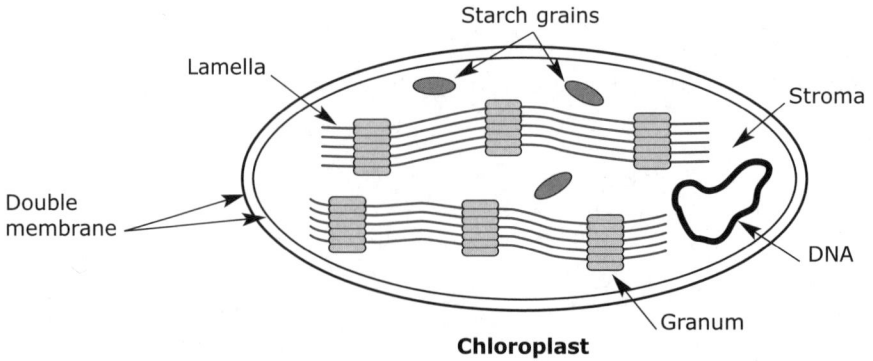

Chloroplast

Fig. 2.4 Cell Organelles – Cell Membrane

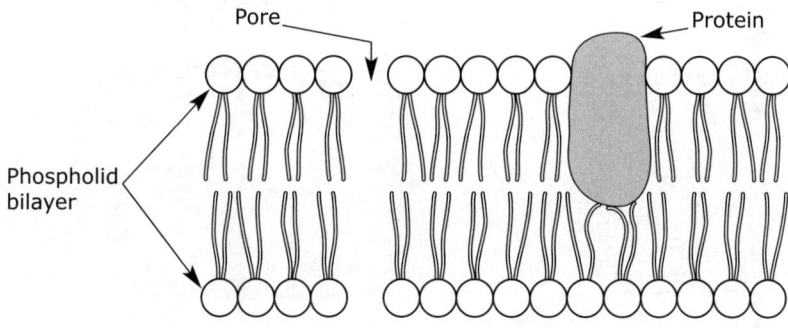

Movement through Cell Membranes

The cell membrane is a selectively permeable barrier. A number of different mechanisms are used to transport materials across membranes.

Osmosis is the movement of water from a hypotonic (high concentration of water) solution to a hypertonic (low concentration of water) solution across a cell membrane. No energy is required for the process. Plant root hairs absorb water from the soil by osmosis. The high sugar concentration in jams acts as a preservative as it prevents the growth of micro-organisms. The sugar draws water from the cells of the micro-organisms by osmosis. This prevents their growth and reproduction.

Diffusion is the movement of a substance from its region of high concentration to its region of low concentration along a diffusion gradient. No energy is required for this process. Oxygen gas in the lungs moves across the alveoli into the blood capillaries by diffusion.

Turgor

Many plants use lignified xylem cells (wood) to support their aerial parts. Non-woody green plants do not have this support. These plants pack their cells and vacuoles with water by osmosis. Cells in this condition are said to be fully **turgid**. If a green plant is not watered for a number of days the cells lose their water and the plants wilt due to the loss of turgidity and support, (see fig. 2.5).

Fig. 2.5 Turgor

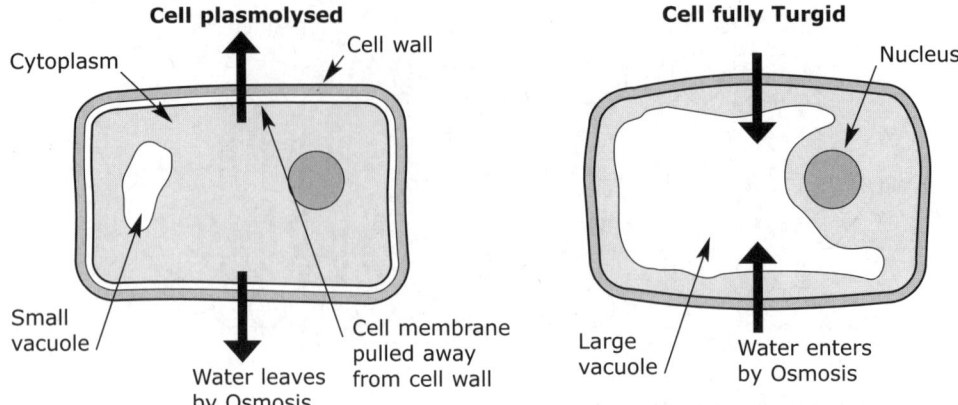

MANDATORY ACTIVITY

Experiment to Demonstrate Osmosis

1. Place a strong sugar solution into a thistle funnel.
2. Tightly attach a layer of Visking Tubing to the open end of the funnel.
3. Invert the thistle funnel in a beaker of distilled water, (see fig. 2.6).
4. Mark the height of sugar solution in the funnel.
5. Leave for 30 minutes.

Result: Water enters through the Visking Tubing by osmosis. This causes the sugar solution to rise up the thistle funnel.

Fig. 2.6 Experiment to Demonstrate Osmosis

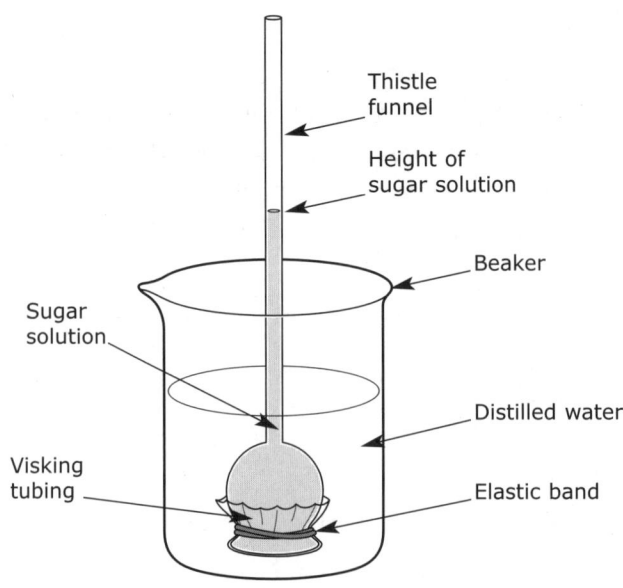

MICROSCOPY

The light microscope is used to observe and magnify prepared slides. The slide is placed on the stage and the fine and coarse adjusters are used to focus the image produced in the eyepiece.

MANDATORY ACTIVITY

Experiment to Make Slides and Observe under the Light Microscope

(a) **Preparation of the slide**: A very thin slice (thin enough for light to pass through) of the specimen is placed on a clean glass slide with a drop of water. A drop of glycerol can be used to reduce the rate of drying out of the slide. A cover slip is placed over the specimen (carefully, to prevent the entry of any air bubbles).

(b) **Staining**: is done to highlight different structures in the specimen. **Iodine** is added to onion cells to highlight the nucleus and starch grains. **Methylene blue** is used to highlight the nucleus and cytoplasm of cheek cells.

Precautions Using the Microscope

1. Never touch electric light sources as they can cause burns.
2. When focusing at low power (×100) use the coarse adjuster before finishing focusing with the fine adjuster.
3. At high power (×400) always bring the lens and stage to near contact while viewing from the side. Focusing is then done using the fine adjuster to move the slide and lens away from one another while observing through the eyepiece.
4. Treat all dyes as poisonous.

To Prepare a Slide of an Animal Cell

(a) Use the blunt end of a match to scrape cells off the inside of the cheek.
(b) Gently spread the cells (to avoid crushing) on a clean glass slide and allow drying in the air to fix the cells onto the slide.
(c) Add methylene blue for 1 minute and gently rinse off using dripping water. This stains the nucleus and the cytoplasm.

To Prepare a Slide of a Plant Cell

(a) Peel a single layer of cells from an onion.
(b) Place the sample onto a slide with a drop of water, carefully, to avoid air bubbles.
(c) Add some Iodine to stain the nucleus and the vacuole.

Drawings of each type of cell as seen under the light microscope are shown in fig. 2.7.

Fig. 2.7 Plant and Animal Cells using the Light Microscope

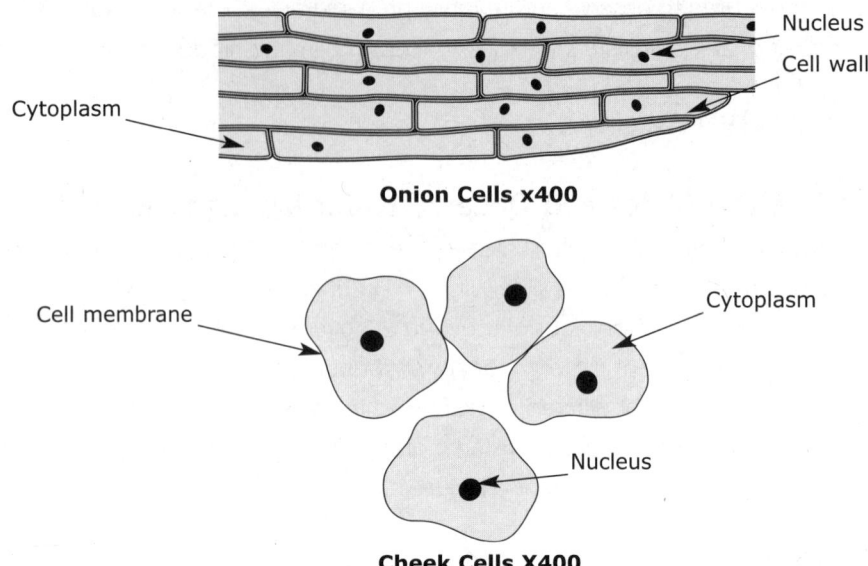

EUCARYOTIC AND PROCARYOTIC CELLS

Animal, plant and fungi cells all have their nuclear material (DNA) stored in a nuclear membrane sac. Such cells are known as **eucaryotic**.

Bacteria are described as **procaryotic** organisms. They are much smaller than eucaryots and their nuclear material is not bound by a membrane but spread around the cytoplasm.

Differences between Eucaryotic and Procaryotic organisms

Eucaryotic	Procaryotic
1. Membrane bound nucleus separating it from cytoplasm	1. Nuclear material spread around organism in ring shapes
2. Larger cell with many membrane bound organelles	2. Smaller with no membrane bound organelles
3. Cell wall, if present, made of cellulose or chitin	3. Cell wall made of protein

2.2 CELL METABOLISM

ENZYMES

Enzymes are biological catalysts, protein in nature, and control metabolic reactions. Each type of enzyme is made up of a long chain of amino acids with a secondary structure that provides it with a unique folded shape. This shape provides the enzyme with a specific active site.

Important Terms

Active Site: The point on an enzyme of temporary attachment to the substrate. It is specific.

Coenzyme: A non-protein part of some enzymes. It is essential for the enzyme to function. It is a vitamin or vitamin-derived, except Vitamin B.

Denatured Enzyme: Loss of activity due to an irreversible change in enzyme structure (active site). It is caused by heat, pH change etc.

Enzymes: Biological catalysts, protein in nature, and control metabolic reactions.

Enzyme Saturation: Enzyme functioning at a maximum rate under specific circumstances. The rate cannot increase, even if more substrate is added, unless enzyme concentration is increased.

Substrate: A substance that attaches to the enzyme, at the active site. It is converted to product(s) and released.

Factors That Affect Enzyme Activity

(a) **pH**

Most enzymes function in a near neutral pH (7), (see fig. 2.8). Outside this range most enzymes tend to **denature**, i.e. the active site changes shape and it can no longer function. An exception is the enzyme pepsin found in the stomach. It can function at a pH of 1·5.

Fig. 2.8 Rate of Enzyme Activity vs pH

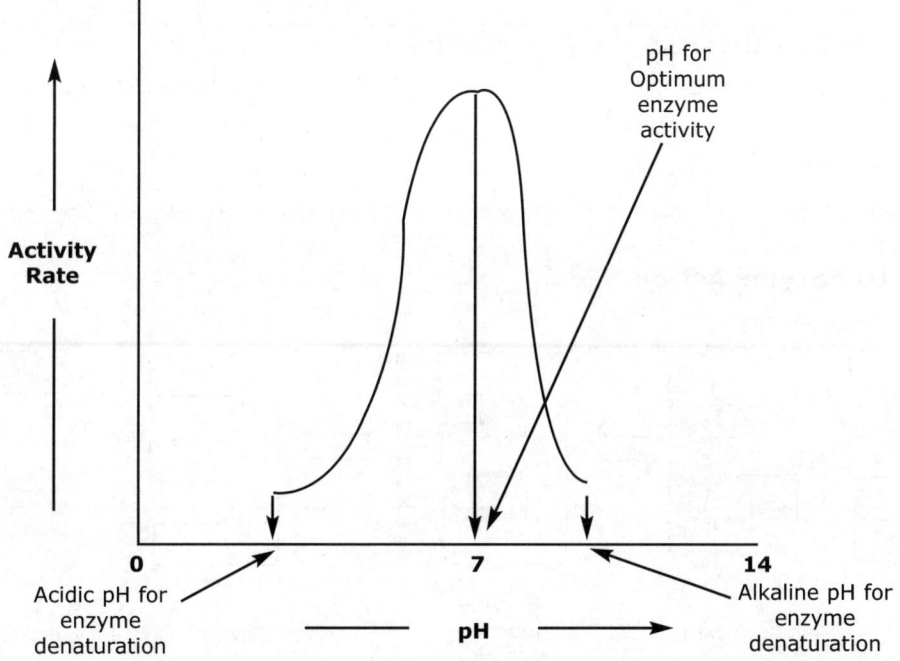

(b) Temperature

Enzymes can only function in a fluid environment. In ice an enzyme has an activity rate of zero. The rate of enzyme action increases as the temperature increases up to a limit of around 40°C (for warm blooded animals). Above that temperature the enzyme becomes **denatured**. Plant enzymes often have an optimum temperature of around 25°C, (see fig.2.9).

Fig. 2.9 Rate of Enzyme Activity vs Temperature

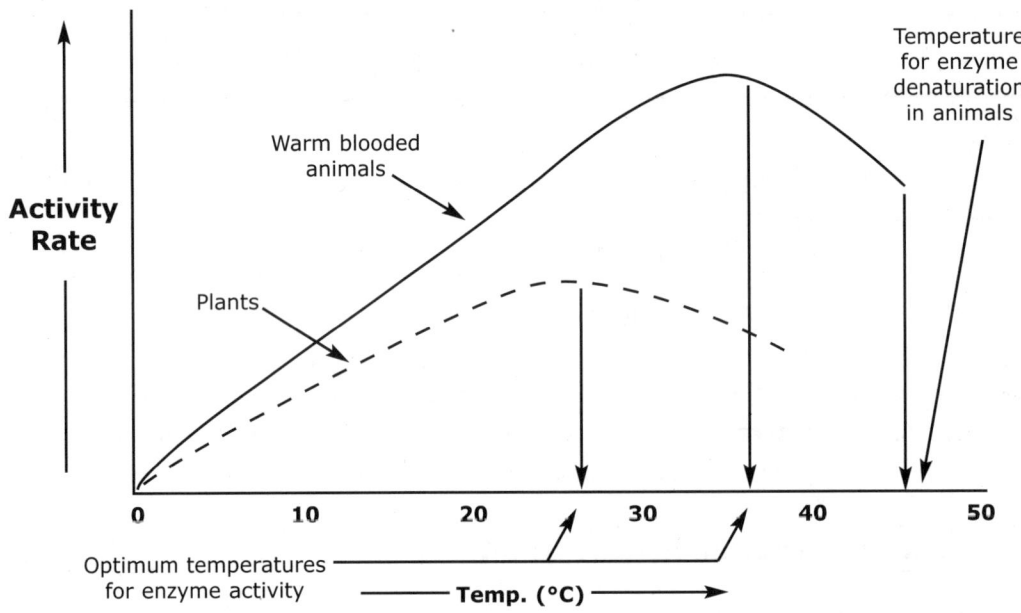

Enzyme Action (How an Enzyme Works)

Enzymes catalyse reactions by temporarily joining their Active Site to the Substrate to produce an Enzyme Substrate Complex. The Products are formed and released. The enzyme remains unchanged, (see fig. 2.10).

The specific shape of the active site means only a specific substrate can bind with the enzyme.

Fig. 2.10 Enzyme Action

Specific Active Site

Enzyme + Substrate ⇌ Enzyme Substrate Complex ⇌ Enzyme + Products

MANDATORY ACTIVITY

Experiment to Investigate the Effect of pH on the Rate of Amylase Activity

Enzyme = Amylase (in saliva)   **Substrate** = 2% Starch solution

Solutions
Five pairs of test tubes are set up in five water baths A, B, C, D and E.

Water Bath	A	B	C	D	E
Test Tube 1	1 ml saliva	1 ml saliva	1 ml saliva	1 ml saliva	1 ml saliva
Test Tube 2	10 ml Starch + 10 drops of Acetic Acid	10 ml Starch + 4 drops Acetic Acid + 6 drops Water	10 ml Starch + 10 drops Water	10 ml Starch + 4 drops Sodium Bicarbonate + 6 drops Water	10 ml Starch + 10 drops Sodium Bicarbonate

Apparatus
The apparatus used is shown in fig. 2.11.

Fig. 2.11 To Investigate Factors Affecting Enzyme Activity

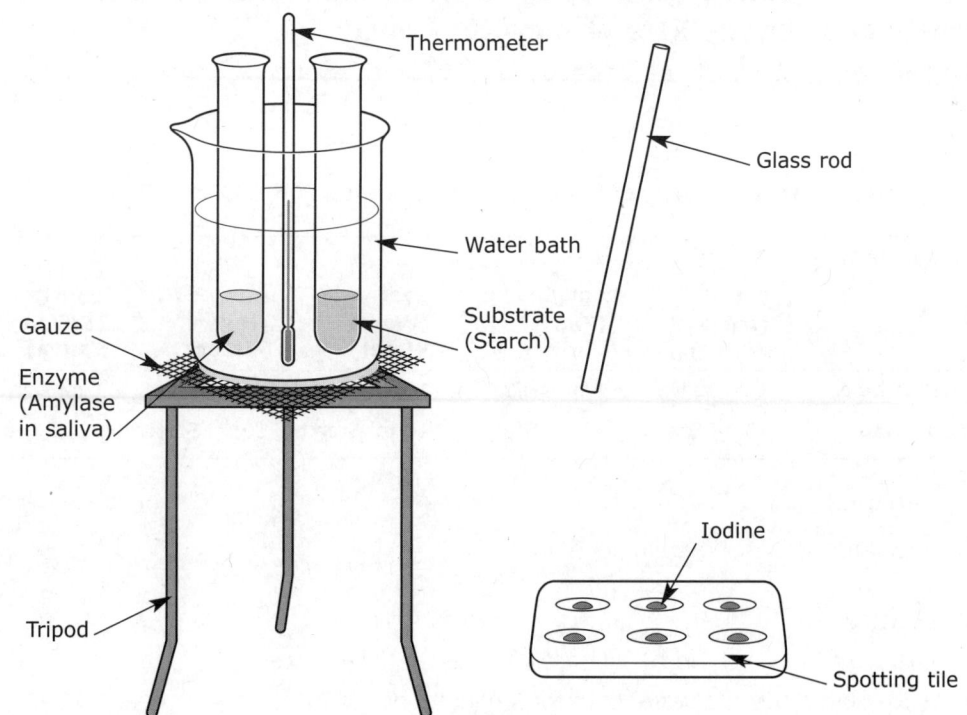

Procedure

1. Place 10 ml of starch and 1 ml of saliva in separate test tubes.
2. Leave both tubes in a water bath for 5 minutes at 30°C.
3. Pour the starch into the saliva, mix and start timing the experiment.
4. At 30-second intervals using a glass rod, test 1 drop of the mixture with Iodine.
5. Repeat until no more blue colour is produced on mixing with the Iodine.
6. Record the time taken for this to occur.

Note: The control is identical to the test experiment except that the saliva is boiled (denatured).

Only the factor we are testing is varied. All other relevant factors must be kept constant.

Enzyme concentration is kept constant by using equal volumes of the same enzyme (Amylase) solution in all test tubes.

Substrate concentration is kept constant by using equal volumes of the same substrate (Starch) solution in all test tubes.

Temperature is kept constant by using a thermometer with ice or hot water as necessary.

MANDATORY ACTIVITY

Experiment to Investigate the Effect of Temperature and Heat Denaturation on the Rate of Amylase Activity

Enzyme = Amylase (in saliva)   **Substrate** = 2% Starch solution

Solutions

Five pairs of test tubes are set up in five water baths A, B, C, D and E.

Water Bath	A 0°C (Ice + Water)	B 10°C (Tap Water)	C 37°C (Warm Water)	D 60°C (Hot Water)	E 100°C (Boiled Saliva)
Test Tube 1	1 ml saliva	1 ml saliva	1 ml saliva	1 ml saliva	1 ml saliva
Test Tube 2	10 ml Starch	10 ml Starch	10 ml Starch	10 ml Starch	10 ml Starch

Apparatus

The apparatus used is shown in fig. 2.11.

Procedure

1. Place 10 ml of starch and 1 ml of saliva in separate test tubes.
2. Leave both tubes in a water bath for 5 minutes at 30°C.

3. Pour the starch into saliva, mix and start timing the experiment.
4. At 30-second intervals using a glass rod, test 1 drop of the mixture with Iodine.
5. Repeat until no more blue colour is produced on mixing with the Iodine.
6. Record the time taken for this to occur.

Note: The control is identical to the test experiment except that the saliva is boiled (denatured).

Only the factor we are testing is varied. All other relevant factors must be kept constant.

Enzyme concentration is kept constant by using equal volumes of the same enzyme (Amylase) solution in all test tubes.

Substrate concentration is kept constant by using equal volumes of the same substrate (Starch) solution in all test tubes.

pH is kept constant by using buffers in the solutions to stabilise the pH.

ENZYME IMMOBILISATION

This describes a procedure to extract useful enzymes, usually from micro-organisms. The enzymes are then stabilised so that they can be repeatedly used to catalyse chemical reactions producing large quantities of useful products.

Industrial Procedure for Enzyme Production and Immobilisation

(a) Suitable strains of micro-organisms are selected for culture.
(b) The organisms are introduced to large sterile vessels (bioreactors) containing a liquid nutrient medium.
(c) Sterile air is pumped through the vessels, to provide oxygen. The temperature is kept between 18°C and 37°C depending on the needs of the organism.
(d) Separation of the new cells and the nutrient liquid is carried out by centrifuge.
(e) The cells are then liquidised and cellular fragments are removed leaving the enzymes in a liquid solution.
(f) Water is removed from the solution by low temperature vacuum evaporation.
(g) The enzymes are then attached to an inert medium that stabilises and fixes the enzymes in position.
(h) A solution of the substrate is then passed over the immobilised enzymes and the new products are collected.

Advantages of Enzyme Immobilisation

(a) Easy recovery of enzymes for reuse.
(b) Easy harvesting of products (no enzyme contamination).
(c) Greater enzyme stability.

(d) Prevents cells from metabolising some of the substrate.
(e) The optimum condition for individual enzymes is often different to that of the whole cell.

Applications of Enzyme Immobilisation

(a) **The production of fructose for use in canned drinks.** Fructose is sweeter than glucose or sucrose so it is preferred for sweetened drinks. Glucose Isomerase converts glucose to Fructose. This enzyme is difficult to produce so it is reused through enzyme immobilisation.

(b) **To make lactose-free milk.** Many people are lactose intolerant. They cannot produce the enzyme lactase that breaks lactose down. Immobilised lactase is used to remove lactose from milk.

(c) **Clarification of fruit juices.** Fruit juices contain binding carbohydrates called pectins. These can make the juices more viscous and cause cloudiness. Immobilised pectinase is used to remove pectins from fruit juices.

(d) **Production of vinegar.** Bacteria are immobilised to convert ethyl alcohol and oxygen to Acetic Acid or vinegar.

(e) **Diagnostic reagents.** Dipsticks with the immobilised enzyme glucose oxidase can be used to test for glucose concentrations in blood samples.

MANDATORY ACTIVITY

Experiment to Prepare an Enzyme Immobilisation and Examine its Application

1. Add 0·4 g of Sodium Alginate to 10 ml of water.
2. Mix 2 g of yeast in 10 ml of distilled water and leave for 5 minutes.
3. Prepare 1·4% calcium chloride solution and place in a tall beaker.
4. Mix the alginate solution and the yeast suspension and draw the mixture into a syringe.
5. From a height of about 10 cm release the mixture from the syringe, one drop at a time, into the calcium chloride solution. Each drop will form a bead, (see fig. 2.12).
6. Leave the beads to harden for 20 minutes.
7. Filter the beads and wash with distilled water. Place in a 100 ml beaker labelled A.
8. Mix 2 g of yeast with a little water to form a paste in a 100 ml beaker labelled B.
9. Prepare 100 ml of a 1% sucrose solution with water at 40°C.
10. Divide this solution into two 50 ml beakers and pour one into each of A and B beakers.
11. Immediately dip a Clinstix strip into each beaker A and B. Remove and after 10 seconds compare each strip colour to the container chart.
12. Note the time it takes to completely hydrolyse the sucrose in each beaker.

Fig. 2.12 Enzyme Immobilisation

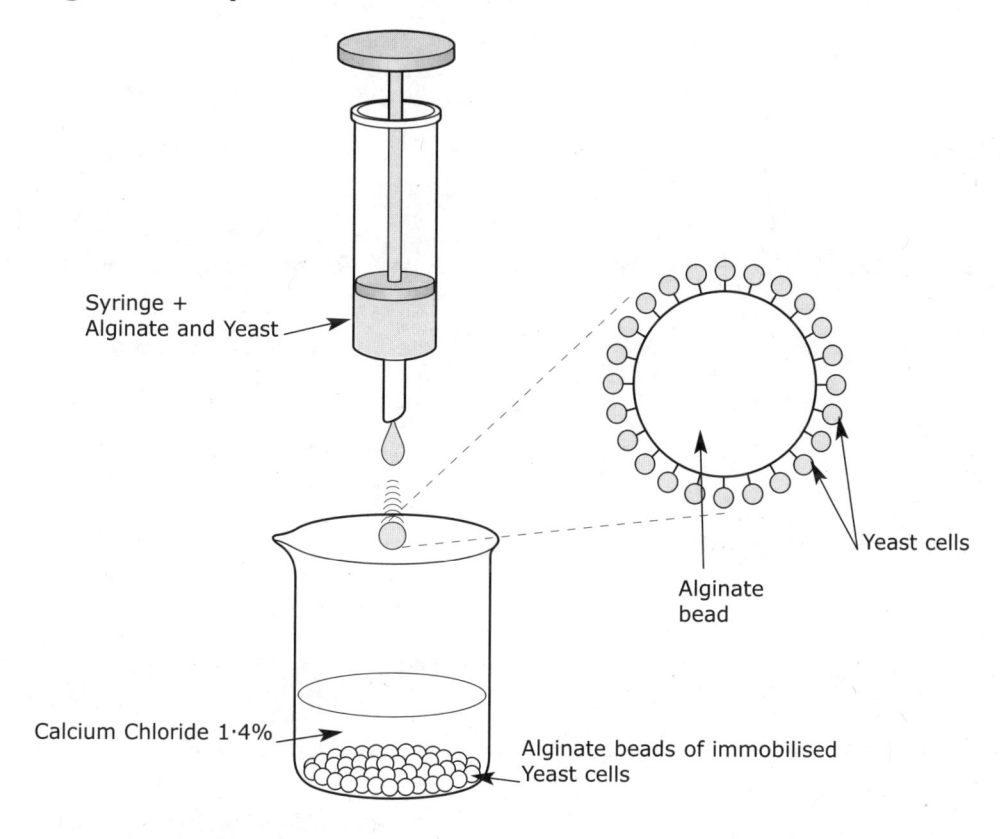

PHOTOSYNTHESIS

This process is an example of an Anabolic chemical reaction. Such a reaction requires energy to make complex biomolecules from simple inorganic molecules. Photosynthesis can be summarised by the equation:

$6CO_2 + 6H_2O + \text{Sunlight Energy} \rightarrow C_6H_{12}O_6 + 6O_2$

Energy in the Cell

Organisms must store energy so that it is available when required. The only means of storing energy in the cells is in chemical form, that is, in chemical bonds. Adenosine Triphosphate (ATP) is a molecule that stores energy in cells. It is made up of Adenine (Amino Acid), Ribose (Sugar) and three phosphate molecules. The energy is stored in the chemical bonds linking the phosphate molecules. When a cell requires energy ATP is converted to ADP + P, releasing energy. Energy from respiration is stored when ADP + P join to form ATP. This process is called phosphorylation, (see fig. 2.13).

NAD and NADP are two molecules also involved in the storage of energy in the cell. They store and transfer Hydrogen ions and electrons for metabolism.

Fig. 2.13 Energy in Cells

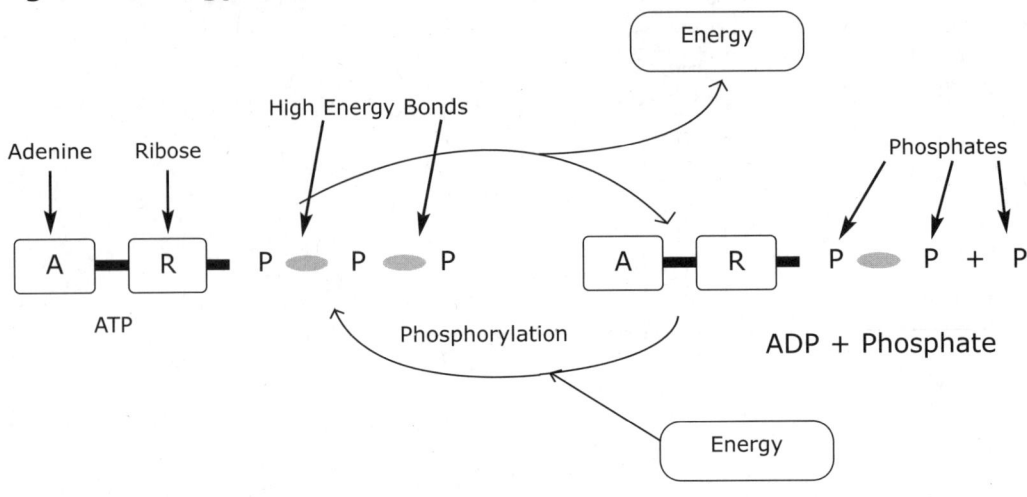

Biochemistry of Photosynthesis

The process of photosynthesis can be divided into two stages:

1. **Light Stage**, which is dependent on the presence of light and occurs in the **grana** of the chloroplast.
2. **Dark Stage**, which is light independent (goes on night and day) ... and occurs in the **stroma** of the choloroplast.

1. Light Stage

This occurs in two parts:
(a) Light Stage I (Cyclic)
(b) Light Stage II (non-Cyclic).

Light Stage I

Light energy trapped by chlorophyll is passed to an electron. The electron moves to an electron acceptor and is passed through a number of carriers. Energy is released at each step and used to form ATP. The electron finally returns to the chlorophyll.

See fig. 2.14.

Fig. 2.14 Light Stage I

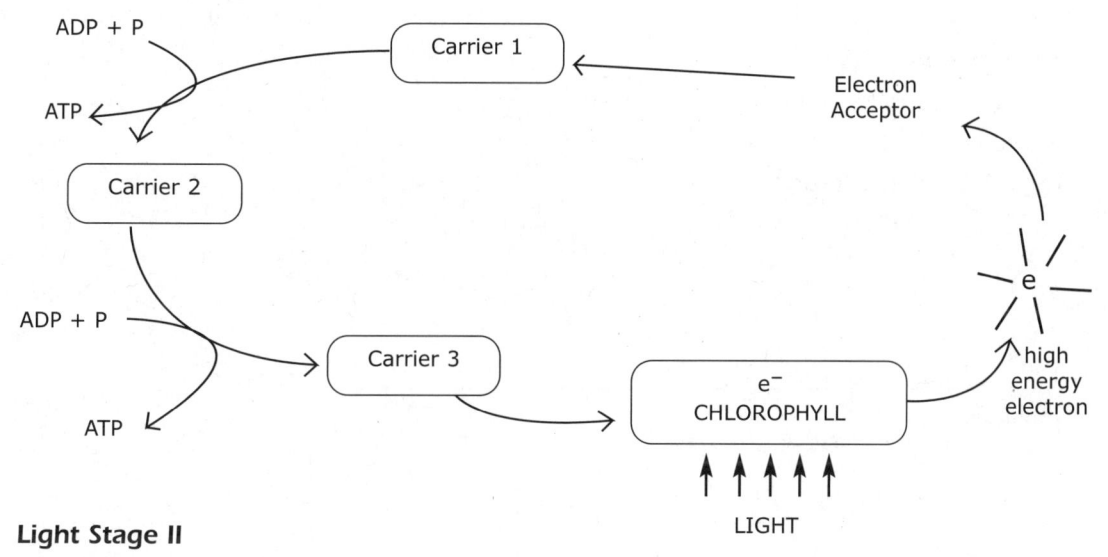

Light Stage II

Light energy trapped by chlorophyll is passed to two electrons. Both electrons join with NADP. The NADP^{--} then causes H_2O to split releasing oxygen, two electrons and two H^+ ions.

(a) The oxygen can be used for respiration or released as waste.
(b) The electrons are passed through carriers releasing energy to form ATP.
(c) The two Hydrogen atoms released when water is split **reduce** NADP to NADPH$_2$.

See fig. 2.15

Fig. 2.15 Light Stage II

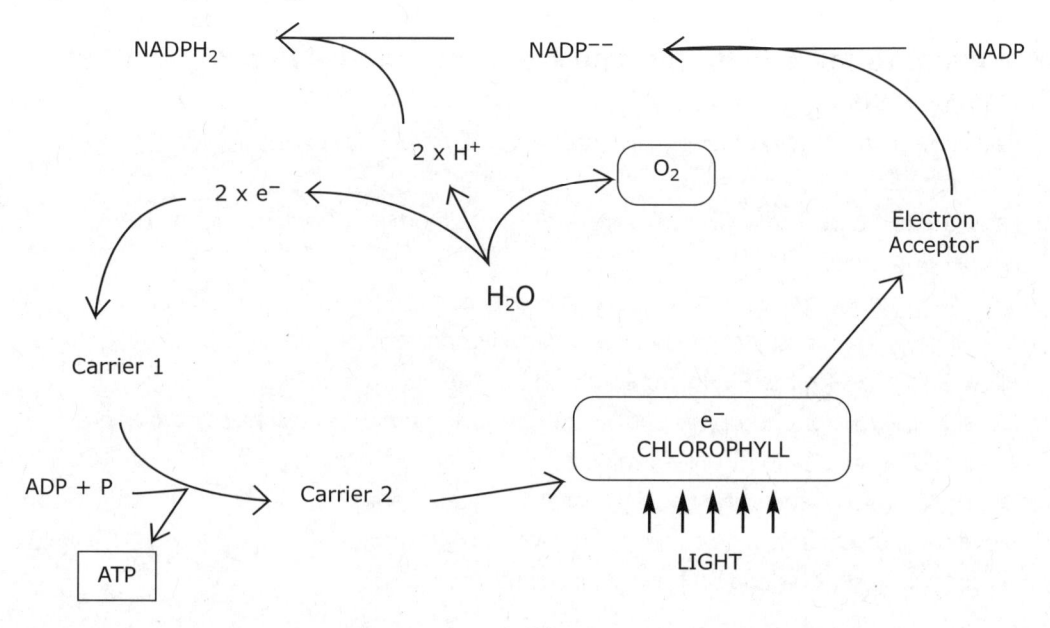

2. Dark Stage

ATP and NADPH$_2$ produced in the light stage are used to reduce CO$_2$ from the air to glucose and starch, (see fig. 2.16).

The ADP and NADP produced are reused in the light stage.

Fig. 2.16 Dark Stage

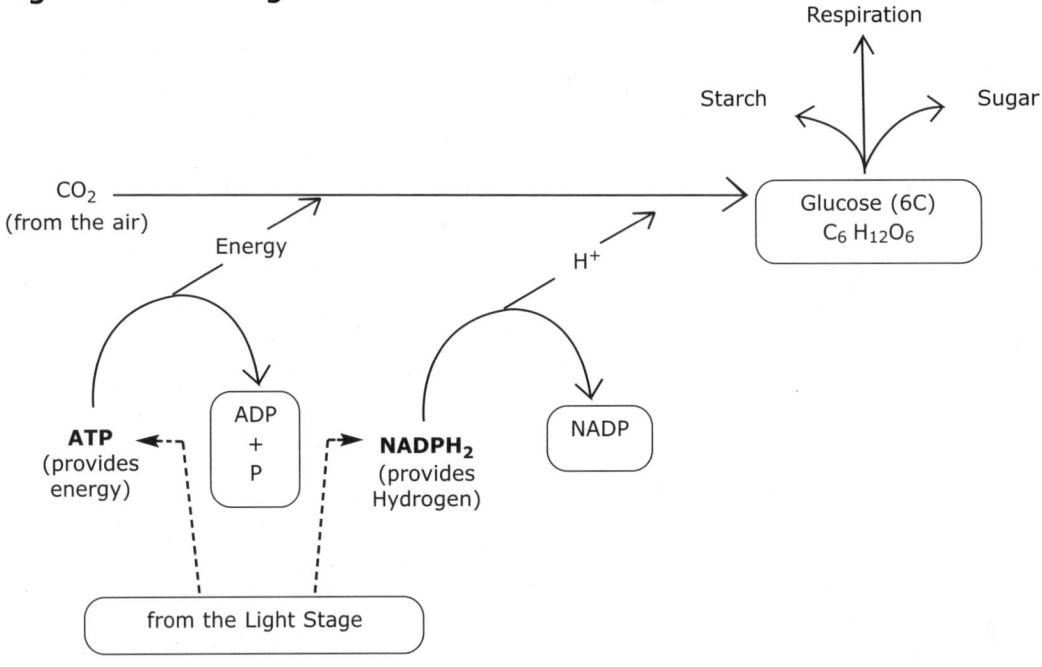

MANDATORY ACTIVITY

Experiment to Investigate the Effect of Light Intensity on the Rate of Photosynthesis

1. Place a freshly cut stem of Elodea in a test tube of water with excess Sodium bicarbonate.
2. Place the test tube in a beaker of water with a thermometer. This is to check the temperature does not vary.
3. Set a lamp beside the beaker. Measure the distance from the lamp to the beaker and record the light intensity at the beaker using a light meter, (see fig. 2.17).
4. Allow 5 minutes for the Elodea to equilibrate to the new conditions.
5. Measure the rate of photosynthesis by counting the number of bubbles of oxygen gas produced per unit time (usually 5 minutes).
6. Record the result, repeat the count and calculate an average.
7. Move the lamp to a new position and repeat steps 3 to 6.
8. Graph your results when you have your full set of readings.

Fig. 2.17 To Investigate the Effect of Light Intensity on the Rate of Photosynthesis

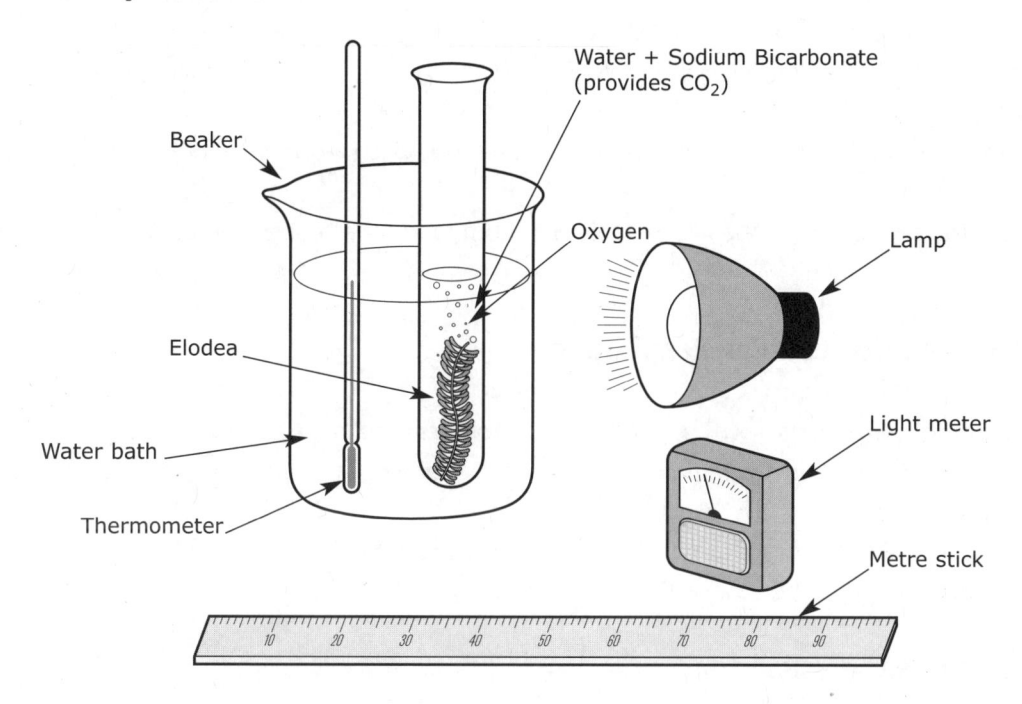

Greenhouse Cultivation

The knowledge we have, of the requirements and optimal conditions for photosynthesis, gave rise to the development of greenhouses for certain types of crop. In a greenhouse light type and intensity, temperature, carbon dioxide concentrations and mineral levels can all be controlled artificially. This helps protect the crop and ensures maximum productivity.

Light: Light is probably the most important factor affecting photosynthesis. Small increases in light intensity can sharply increase the rate of photosynthesis. In the greenhouse light can be provided for longer periods artificially. It is important to provide light of the correct wavelengths in greenhouses to maximise photosynthesis.

Temperature: All metabolic reactions in plants are controlled by enzymes. Plant enzymes generally function best at a temperature of between 20° to 25°C. Controlled heating can ensure an optimum temperature for plant growth.

Carbon Dioxide: The levels of CO_2 in the air can also be controlled. Tomato plant yields can be increased if the CO_2 levels are raised from the normal 0·03%, in air, to 1% in the atmosphere inside the greenhouse.

RESPIRATION

Respiration is the chemical breakdown of food to release energy. It is a **catabolic** chemical reaction. Respiration occurs in every cell in the body. In the process complex biomolecules are broken down to simple inorganic molecules releasing energy. There are two types of respiration:

(a) Aerobic respiration is the release of energy from food which requires the presence of oxygen.
(b) Anaerobic respiration is the release of energy from food, which does not require the presence of oxygen.

Biochemistry of Cellular Respiration

Aerobic Cellular Respiration occurs in three stages:
1. **Anaerobic Glycolysis** – which occurs in the **cytoplasm** and does **not** involve Oxygen.
2. **Krebs'** or **Citric Acid Cycle** – which occurs in the **lumen** of the mitochondrion and Oxygen is necessary.
3. **Oxidative Phosphorylation** or **Electron Transport Chain** – which occurs on the **cristae** of the mitochondrion and Oxygen is necessary.

Anaerobic Glycolysis

This is the breakdown of Glucose to Pyruvic Acid with ATP being produced. In plants, if no oxygen is present the pyruvic acid is converted to Ethyl Alcohol and Carbon Dioxide. This process is called fermentation. Animal cells, in the absence of oxygen, convert the pyruvic acid to Lactic Acid.

Krebs' Cycle

If Oxygen is present the pyruvic acid is converted to Acetyl Co-enzyme A (Acetyl Co A), releasing a molecule of Carbon Dioxide. The Acetyl Co A then enters Krebs' Cycle.

Electron Transport Chain

The products of Krebs' Cycle enter the electron transport chain, which produces ATP and the waste H_2O.

Aerobic Respiration is summarised in fig. 2.18.

Fig. 2.18 Aerobic Respiration

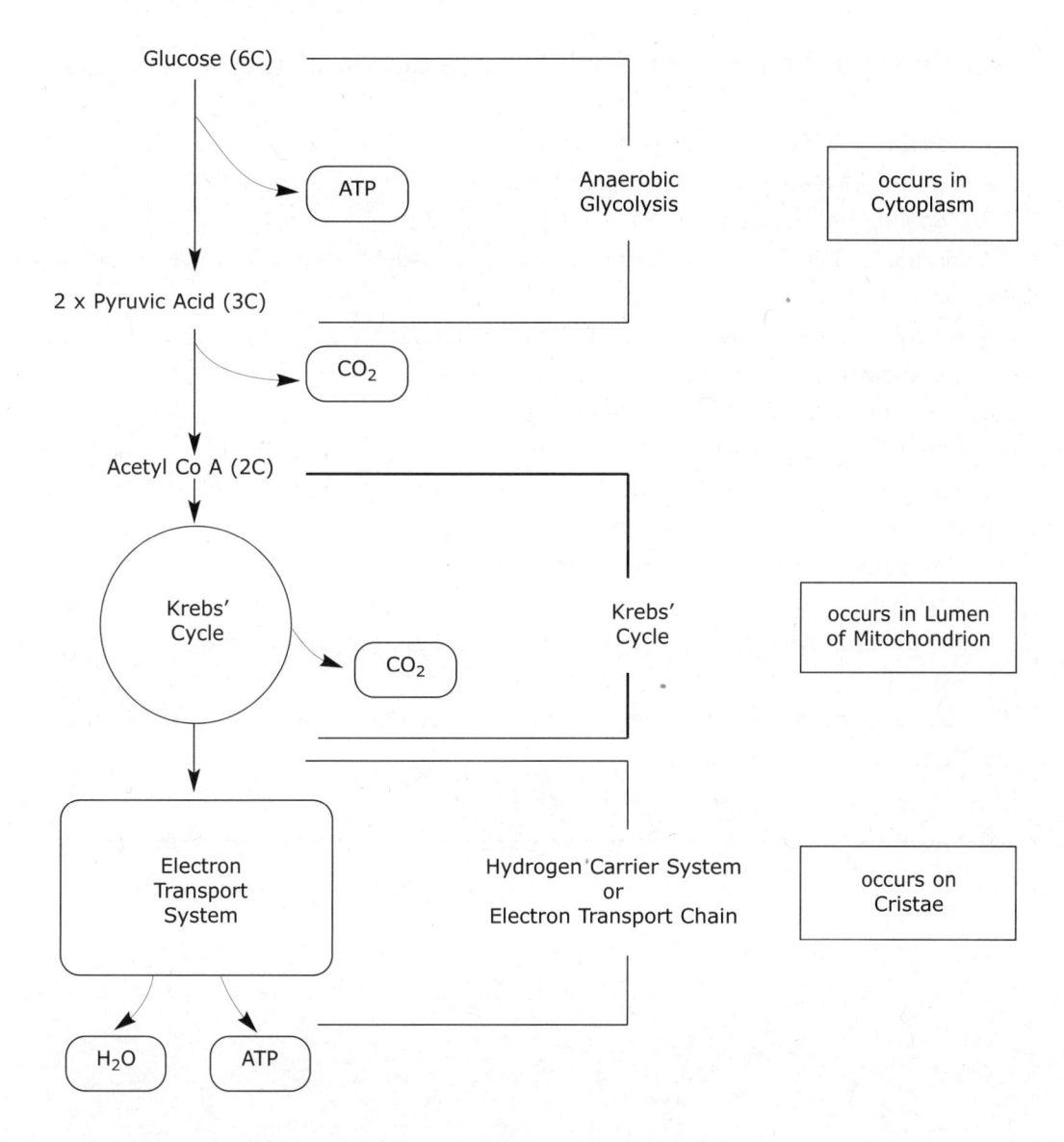

```
Glucose (6C) ──────────────┐
    │                      │
    ├──→ ATP               │  Anaerobic         occurs in
    │                      │  Glycolysis        Cytoplasm
    ▼                      │
2 × Pyruvic Acid (3C)      │
    │                      │
    ├──→ CO₂               │
    ▼                      │
Acetyl Co A (2C) ──────────┤
    │                      │
    ▼                      │
 ╭───────╮                 │
 │ Krebs'│                 │  Krebs'            occurs in Lumen
 │ Cycle ├──→ CO₂          │  Cycle             of Mitochondrion
 ╰───────╯                 │
    │                      │
    ▼                      │
┌──────────┐               │
│ Electron │               │  Hydrogen Carrier System
│ Transport│               │  or                occurs on
│ System   │               │  Electron Transport Chain   Cristae
└──────────┘               │
   │    │                  │
   ▼    ▼                  │
  H₂O  ATP ────────────────┘
```

Differences between Aerobic and Anaerobic Respiration

Aerobic Respiration	Anaerobic Respiration
Oxygen necessary	Oxygen not necessary
Occurs in mitochondria	Occurs in cytoplasm
Large amount of energy produced	Small amount of energy produced
End products are CO_2 + H_2O	End products are lactic acid or ethyl alcohol and CO_2

MANDATORY ACTIVITY

Experiment to Prepare and Show the Production of Alcohol by Yeast

1. Add 4 g of Sodium Alginate to 100 ml of water.
2. Mix 20 g of yeast in 100 ml of distilled water and leave for 5 minutes.
3. Prepare a 1·4% calcium chloride solution in a beaker.
4. Mix the Sodium Alginate solution with the yeast suspension and draw the mixture into a syringe.
5. From a height of about 10 cm release the mixture from the syringe, one drop at a time, into the calcium chloride solution, (see fig. 2.19).
6. Leave the beads to harden for 20 minutes.
7. Filter the beads and wash with distilled water.
8. Place the beads into a plastic bottle as shown in the diagram fig. 2.20.
9. Rinse the beads with distilled water.
10. Slowly pour a glucose solution over the beads.
11. Collect the liquid at the other end.
12. Test for alcohol by measuring the density of the liquid with a hydrometer.

Fig. 2.19 Experiment to Prepare and Show the Production of Alcohol by Yeast

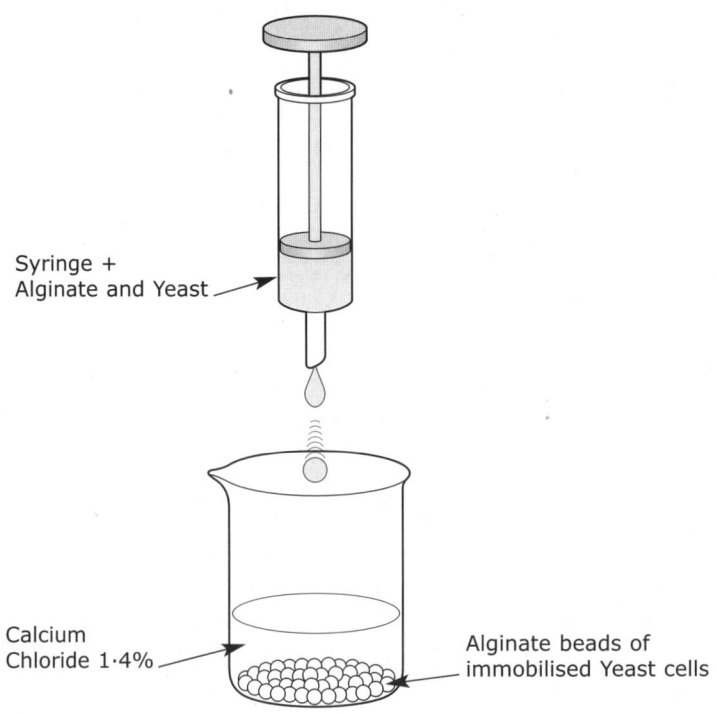

Fig. 2.20 Experiment to Prepare and Show the Production of Alcohol by Yeast

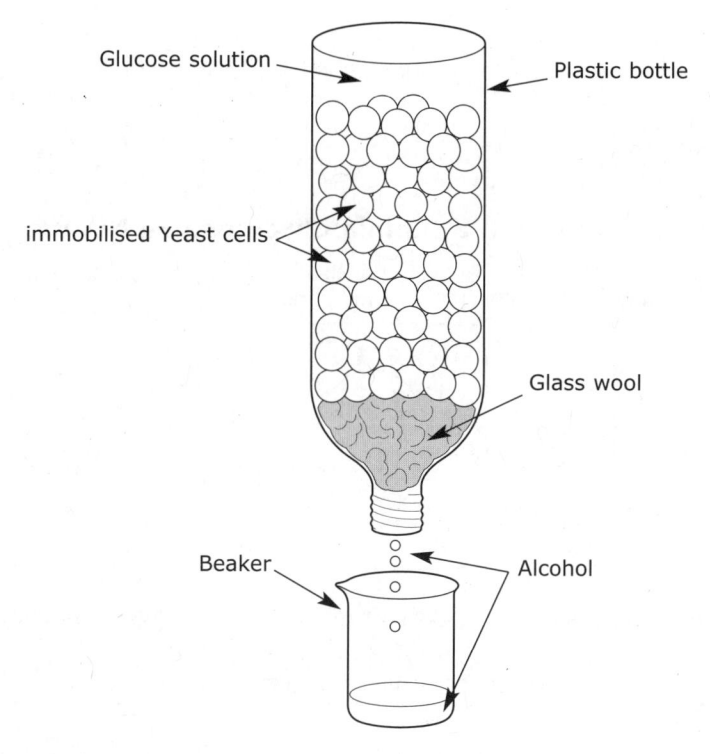

2.3 CELL CONTINUITY

Cell division is essential to all living things. It allows a Multicellular organism to replace worn or damaged cells. It is also the basis of reproduction in every organism. Chromosomes, made up of DNA and protein, carry the genetic code in the nucleus from one generation to the next. In any one individual it is vital that this code is copied faithfully from one cell generation to the next. This is what is known as cell continuity.

HAPLOID AND DIPLOID CELLS

A haploid cell has half the full complement of chromosomes (n). They are usually either spores or gametes produced during sexual reproduction.

A diploid cell has the full complement of chromosomes (2n). All somatic cells (cells not involved in reproduction) are diploid.

MITOSIS

Mitosis is a form of cell division where one cell divides to form two cells each identical to the parent. Mitosis occurs in somatic cells (cells not involved in reproduction).

Significance of Mitosis

(a) In multicellular organisms genes are faithfully transmitted from one cell generation to the next.
(b) Unicellular organisms use mitosis to produce genetically identical offspring.

Stages of Mitosis (See fig. 2.21.)

Fig. 2.21 Mitosis in a Cell with a Diploid Chromosome Number = 4

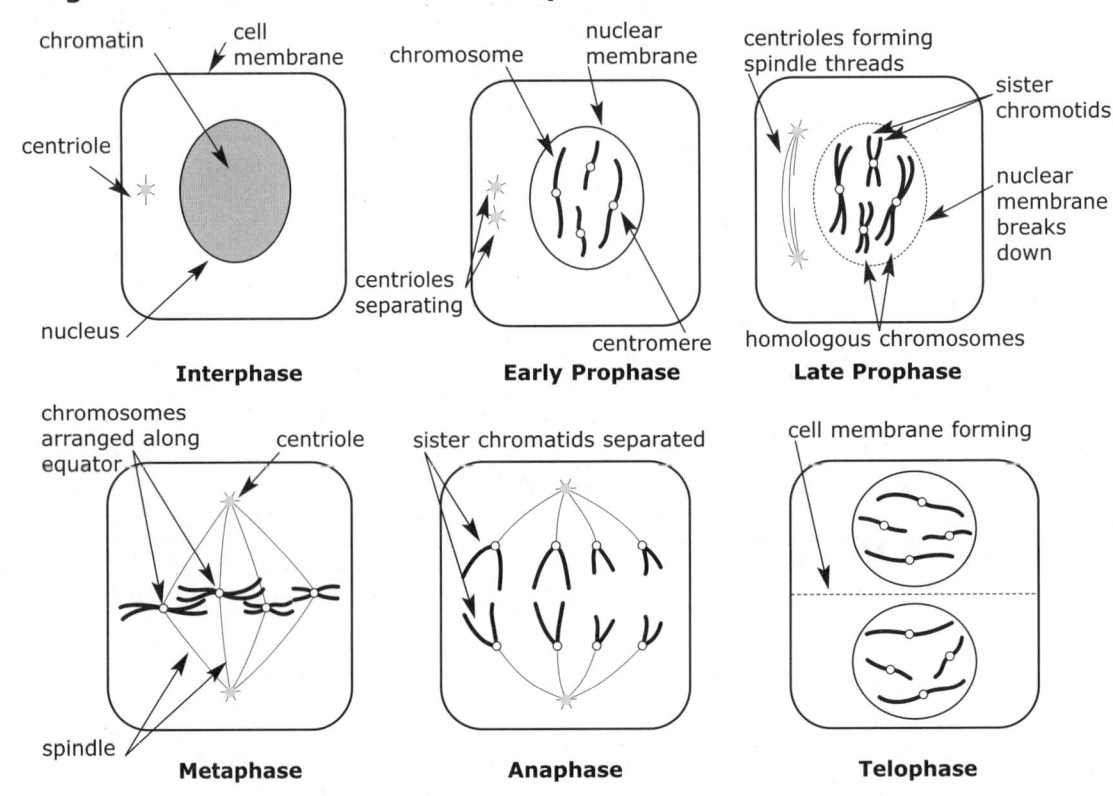

[Diagram showing six stages of mitosis: Interphase, Early Prophase, Late Prophase, Metaphase, Anaphase, Telophase, with labels including chromatin, cell membrane, chromosome, nuclear membrane, centrioles forming spindle threads, sister chromatids, centriole, nucleus, centrioles separating, centromere, nuclear membrane breaks down, homologous chromosomes, chromosomes arranged along equator, sister chromatids separated, cell membrane forming, spindle.]

Interphase

This is a stage between cell divisions. During interphase the cell builds up a store of energy, while nuclear material (to build new chromosomes) and cell organelles replicate in preparation for cell division. The chromosomes are not individually visible and form a mass of chromatin.

Prophase

Chromosomes thicken and become visible. Homologous chromosomes lie together in pairs. Each chromosome forms an identical copy of itself and is joined to the original at the centromere. The pair are called sister chromatids. The centriole replicates and they move to opposite sides of the cell. The centrioles leave a trail of spindle threads. Finally the nuclear membrane breaks down.

Metaphase
The chromosomes (sister chromatids) lie in a straight line across the middle of the cell attached to the spindle threads by the centromere.

Anaphase
The spindle threads contract, separating the sister chromatids.

Telophase
A nuclear membrane forms around each set of chromosomes and a cell membrane forms to create two new cells each with a diploid chromosome number of four, identical to the parent cell.

Cell Cycle: This is the sequence of events that occurs between one cell division and the next in mitosis. It can be divided into three main stages:
(a) In Interphase the cell grows and carries out its functions. At the end of Interphase the chromosomes replicate forming sister chromatids. Interphase takes up 90% of the cell cycle.
(b) Nuclear division takes place forming two new nuclei.
(c) The cytoplasm finally divides forming two new daughter cells.

MEIOSIS
A second form of cell division can occur. It is known as meiosis or reduction division.

Meiosis is cell division where one cell divides to form four cells, each with half the number of chromosomes of the parent cell.

Significance of Meiosis
(a) It is a mechanism of producing gametes (**spores** in higher plants) with half the number of chromosomes of the parent cell, so at fertilisation the full complement is restored.
(b) It is a means of producing changes in genotype leading to variation in the offspring.

CANCER
Cancer is a general term to describe a disorder in the body's growth. Cancer cells fail to respond to normal controls on their multiplication and enlargement. The growth of cancer cells results in a tumour which crowds out healthy cells. There are two types of tumour. A **benign** tumour grows slowly and the adverse effects are usually to simply apply physical pressure to surrounding tissues. A **malignant** tumour consists of rapidly growing cells that invade and can destroy other tissues. When malignant tumours invade the blood or lymphatic systems it can spread to other parts of the body.

Lung Cancer

Cigarette smoking has been directly linked to lung cancer. Cigarette smoke contains carcinogens which change or mutate genes that control cell division and development in cells. The most common form of death from cancer in males is lung cancer.

Skin Cancer

Skin cancer can be caused by ultraviolet (UV) radiation from sunlight. The UV rays penetrate skin cells causing mutations in the DNA. With the deterioration of the protective ozone layer, a significant increase in the incidences of skin cancer can be expected.

2.4 CELL DIVERSITY

When organisms evolved to a multicellular state their cells became specialised. Cells no longer needed to be capable of carrying out all activities to maintain life. Division of labour meant that different cells or groups of cells could carry out specialised functions. Multicellular organisms could organise similar cells into tissues. A **tissue** is a group of similar cells working together. Cells in tissues are more efficient than cells working individually.

Examples of animal tissues are:
(a) Connective tissue, the skin for protection.
(b) Muscle tissue to move body parts.
(c) Nerve tissue for coordination.

Examples of plant tissues are:
(a) Xylem tissue, which transports water and provides support.
(b) Phloem tissue, which transports dissolved foods.

Organs consist of a group of tissues working together. The heart, in animals, is an organ made up of muscle, nerve and connective tissues functioning together. The root, in plants, is an example of a plant organ, containing xylem, phloem and epidermal tissues.

ORGAN SYSTEMS

The kidney is an organ that works with other organs such as the bladder, renal arteries and veins, and the ureters and urethra. Together, these form the excretory system. This system's function is to rid the body of the wastes of metabolism.

The digestive system is made up of the gut with accessory organs such as the pancreas and the liver. The digestive system carries out the physical and chemical digestion of food in the body.

TISSUE CULTURE

Whole plants can be cultured asexually from very small pieces of tissue extracted from a parent plant. The process can be called micropropagation, tissue culture or cloning. By this process a single plant can produce thousands of genetically identical offspring.

Advantages of Tissue Culture in Plants Include:
(a) Advantageous genetic characteristics can be faithfully passed to all the offspring.
(b) Enormous numbers of offspring can be produced.
(c) The timing of development can be controlled.
(d) Rare plants can be reproduced easily.

Disadvantages Include:
(a) All offspring are susceptible to the same diseases and pests which increases the rates of transmission.
(b) Long-term micropropagation can lead to plants becoming sterile.

2.5 GENETICS
Genetics is the study of heredity, that is, the transmission of characteristics or traits from one generation to the next. Modern genetics is concerned with the study of genes.

Important Definitions
Alleles: Different genes that control the same trait and have the same locus on homologous chromosomes, **e.g.** T and t.

Dihybrid Cross: Genetic cross where two characteristics (pairs of genes) are studied, **e.g.** TtYy × TTYY.

Dominant: The gene that is expressed in the phenotype of the heterozygous condition, **e.g.** Tt has a tall stem, T is dominant.

Gamete: A haploid sex cell capable of fusion (fertilisation).

Genes: These are units of heredity, made of DNA, that control characteristics in an organism.

Genotype: The genetic make-up of an organism, **e.g.** Rr.

Heterozygous: An organism that has two different genes controlling the same trait. **e.g.** Tt.

Homozygous: An organism that has two identical genes controlling the same trait, **e.g.** TT or tt.

Incomplete Dominance: When neither allele is completely expressed in the phenotype of the heterozygous condition, **e.g.** in cattle the C^R gene codes for red coat, the C^W gene codes for white coat. In the heterozygous condition $C^R C^W$ codes for Roan coat colour.

Monohybrid Cross: A genetic cross where only one characteristic or trait (pair of genes) is studied, **e.g.** Tt × Tt.

Phenotype: The physical appearance of an organism, **e.g.** Tall stem.

Recessive: The gene that is not expressed in the phenotype of the heterozygous condition, **e.g.** Tt has a tall stem, t is recessive.

GREGOR MENDEL

Mendel was a very careful worker who planned his experiments on a large scale. He recognised that by taking a large number of separate measurements he could eliminate chance effects. He chose the Pea plant to study because it had several very sharply contrasting characteristics that did not have intermediate forms (no incomplete dominance).

Mendel's first experiment was to cross a tall stem (pure breeding – homozygous) pea plant (TT) with a short stem plant (tt). He gathered the seeds produced and planted them. He then crossed two of the F_1 generation, (see fig. 2.22).

From these results Mendel formulated his first law – the Law of Segregation.

Fig. 2.22 Mendel's Law of Segregation

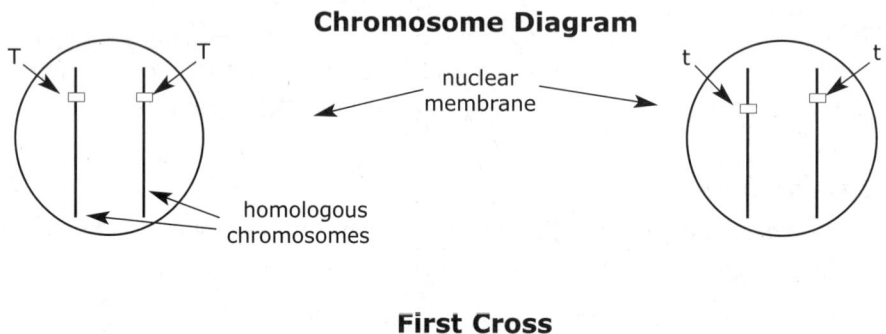

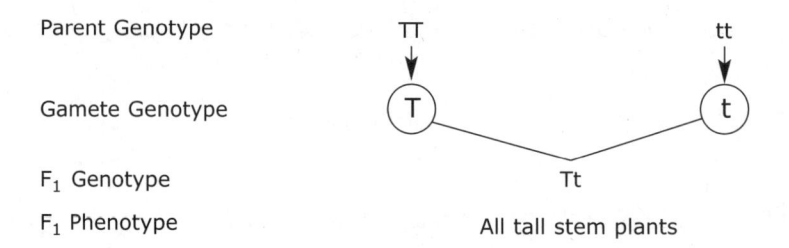

Chromosome Diagram

homologous chromosomes
nuclear membrane

First Cross

Parent Genotype	TT	tt
Gamete Genotype	T	t
F_1 Genotype	Tt	
F_1 Phenotype	All tall stem plants	

Second Cross

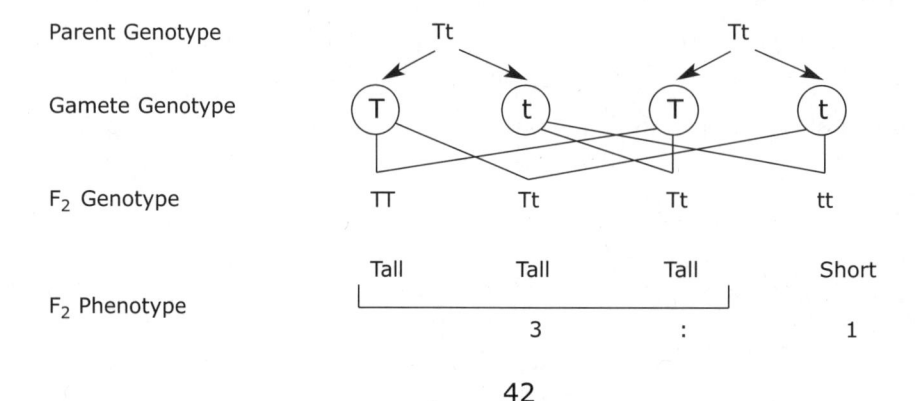

Parent Genotype	Tt		Tt	
Gamete Genotype	T	t	T	t
F_2 Genotype	TT	Tt	Tt	tt
F_2 Phenotype	Tall	Tall	Tall	Short
	3	:		1

> **Mendel's Law of Segregation:** Traits are controlled by pairs of factors (genes). Only one of any pair can enter a gamete.

Mendel then studied the inheritance of two characteristics at a time. He crossed a plant homozygously dominant for two characteristics, tall stem and yellow seeds (TTYY) and a plant doubly recessive for the same characteristics (ttyy). He planted the seeds produced and then crossed two of the new offspring, (see fig. 2.23).

From these results Mendel formulated his second law – the Law of Independent Assortment.

Fig. 2.23 Mendel's Law of Independent Assortment

A dihybrid cross between two plants with genotypes of **TTYY** and **ttyy** is carried out below:

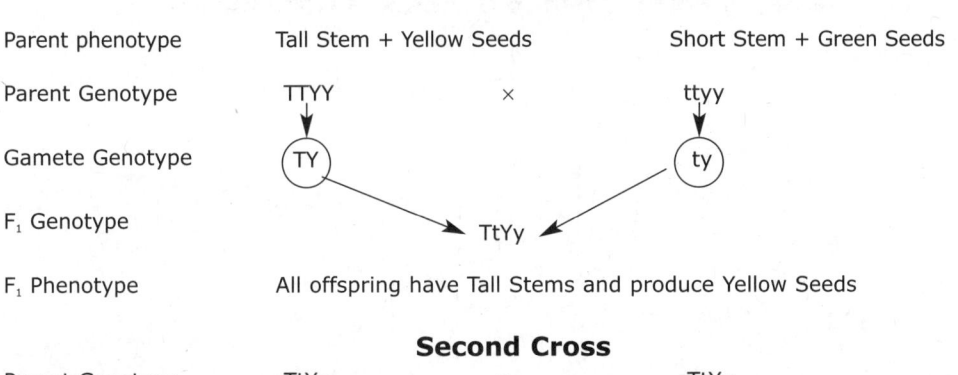

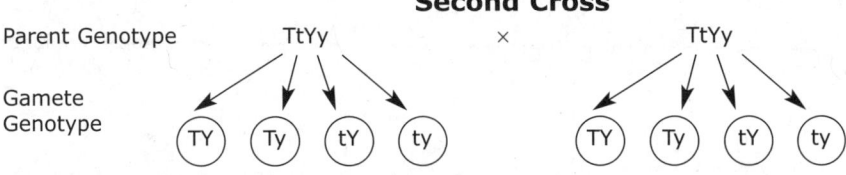

Parent phenotype	Tall Stem + Yellow Seeds		Short Stem + Green Seeds
Parent Genotype	TTYY	×	ttyy
Gamete Genotype	TY		ty
F_1 Genotype		TtYy	
F_1 Phenotype	All offspring have Tall Stems and produce Yellow Seeds		

Second Cross

Parent Genotype	TtYy	×	TtYy
Gamete Genotype	TY Ty tY ty		TY Ty tY ty

This cross will produce 16 possible options in the F_2 Genotype. The easiest way to carry out the cross accurately is to use a Punnet Square:

F_2 Genotypes

Gametes	TY	Ty	tY	ty
TY	TTYY	TTYy	TtYY	TtYy
Ty	TTYy	TTyy	TtYy	Ttyy
tY	TtYY	TtYy	ttYY	ttYy
ty	TtYy	Ttyy	ttYy	ttyy

F_2 Phenotype		
	9	Tall + Yellow
	3	Tall + Green
	3	Short + Yellow
	1	Short + Green

Mendel's Law of Independent Assortment: When gametes are formed either of a pair of alleles can enter a gamete with either of another pair.

LINKAGE

Non-allelic genes (genes that control different traits) that are found on the same chromosome are said to be linked.

When Mendel formulated the Law of Independent Assortment he had studied two traits that were controlled by pairs of genes that were on different homologous pairs of chromosomes. If the genes were linked his results would have been different. Linked genes do not follow Mendel's Law of Independent Assortment. The gametes formed are very different, (see fig. 2.24).

Fig. 2.24

Gametes Formed When Genes Are Not Linked

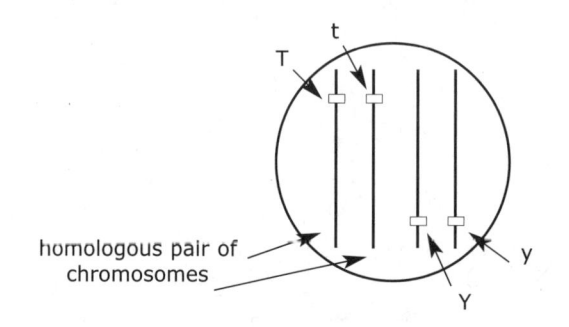

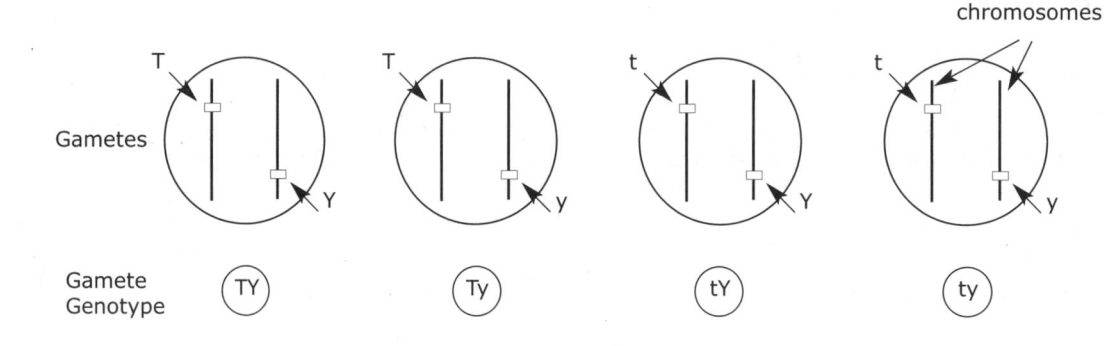

Gametes				
Gamete Genotype	TY	Ty	tY	ty

Gametes Formed When Genes Are Linked

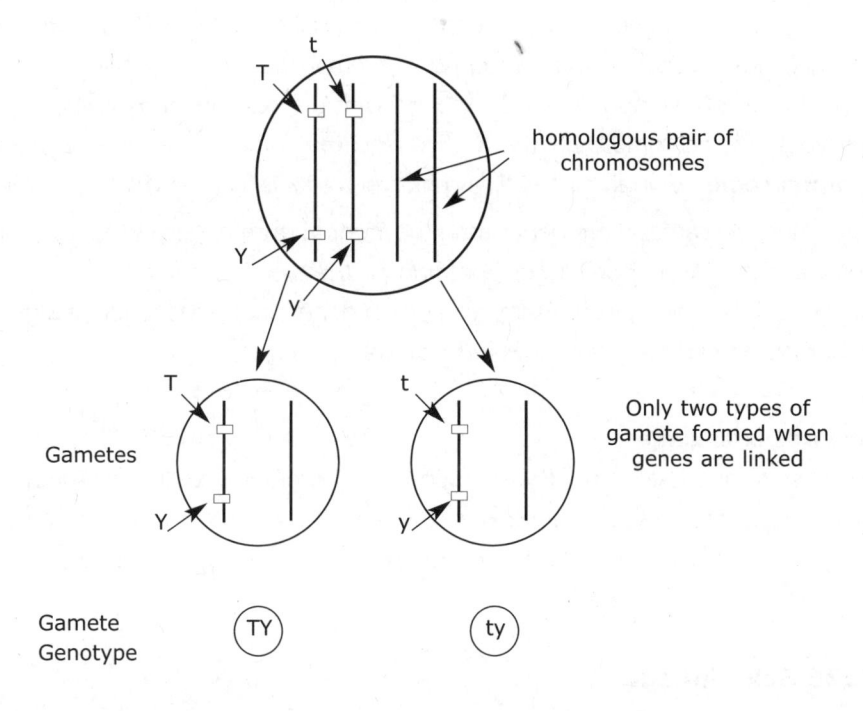

homologous pair of chromosomes

Gametes

Only two types of gamete formed when genes are linked

Gamete Genotype: TY   ty

Consider the situation if an individual with a genotype TtYy is crossed with an individual with a genotype ttyy and **the genes are linked**. The chromosome diagrams and the cross are shown in fig. 2.25.

Fig. 2.25 Genes Are Linked

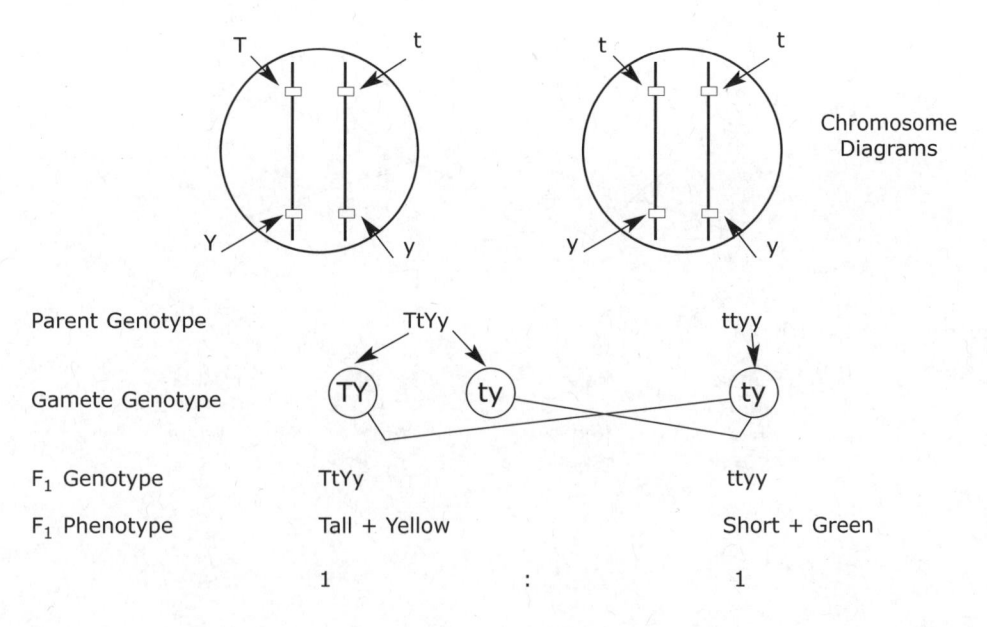

Chromosome Diagrams

Parent Genotype	TtYy	ttyy
Gamete Genotype	TY ty	ty
F_1 Genotype	TtYy	ttyy
F_1 Phenotype	Tall + Yellow	Short + Green
	1 :	1

SEX LINKAGE

In humans the diploid number of chromosomes is 23 pairs. Of these, 22 are **autosomes** that control almost all characteristics except sex determination. The last pair of chromosomes determine the sex of the individual and are known as the **sex chromosomes**. There are two different types of sex chromosome, the **X chromosome** (which is the larger of the two) and the **Y chromosome**. An individual with a genotype of XX is female while XY is male.

The X chromosome carries more genes than the Y chromosome. Genes that exist on the X chromosome but have no homologous position on the Y chromosome are said to be completely sex-linked or X-linked. Examples of such genes are the gene for **red/green colour blindness** and the gene for **Haemophilia**.

Example of Sex Linkage

In Drosophila melanogaster (Fruit Fly) the gene for eye colour is sex-linked. The gene for red eye, R, is dominant to the gene for white, r. A white-eyed male X_rY is crossed with a heterozygous red-eyed female X_RX_r. The genotypes and phenotypes of the offspring produced are shown in fig. 2.26.

Fig. 2.26 Sex Linkage

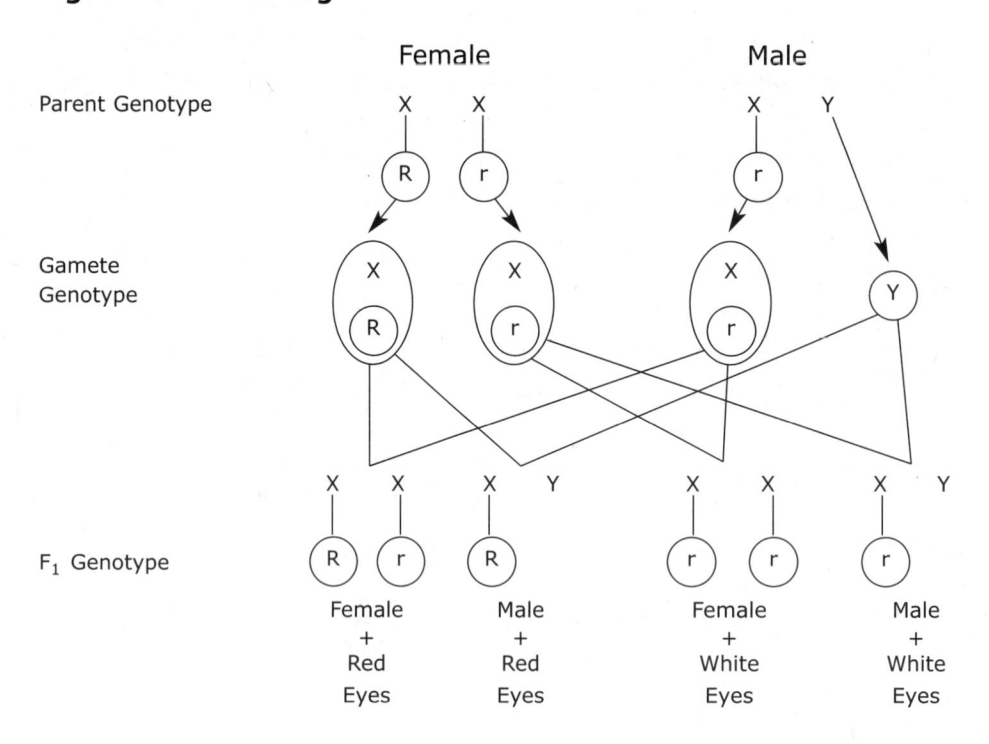

	Female	Male
Parent Genotype	$X_R X_r$	$X_r Y$
Gamete Genotype	X_R X_r	X_r Y
F_1 Genotype	$X_R X_r$ $X_R Y$	$X_r X_r$ $X_r Y$
	Female + Red Eyes Male + Red Eyes	Female + White Eyes Male + White Eyes

DNA

Chromosomes are made up of Deoxyribonucleic acid (DNA). DNA is the substance that carries the genetic code. It is made up of chains of single units called nucleotides. A **nucleotide** consists of a sugar (Deoxyribose), a phosphate molecule and a nitrogen-containing base. There are four different types of base, **adenine**, **thymine**, **cytosine** and **guanine**. Adenine and Guanine are Purine bases while Thymine and Cytosine are Pyrimidine bases.

Fig. 2.27 DNA Double Helix

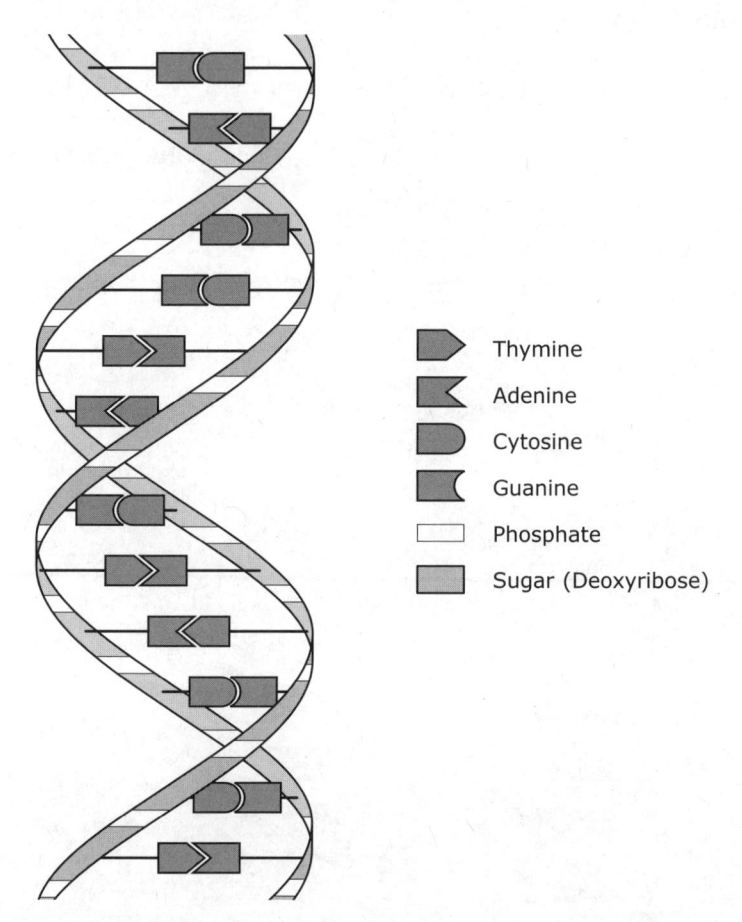

DNA has a **double helix** shape, (see fig 2.27). As you can see from the diagram it is a ladder-like structure that has been twisted in opposite directions at either end. The deoxyribose and the phosphate form the uprights of the ladder and the rungs are pairs of the nitrogen-containing bases. The deoxyribose and phosphate strands are anti-parallel (run in opposite directions). A purine base can only link to a pyrimidine base due to size restrictions. **Adenine** and **thymine** can only be paired together, similarly only **guanine** and **cytosine** can be paired. The base pairs in DNA are held together by Hydrogen Bonds, which are bonds of electrical attraction.

DNA Replication

This is the means by which chromosomes (DNA) can form identical copies of themselves. DNA replication begins when the base pairs of the parent DNA separate. This causes the double helix to unwind. Each strand of the DNA now acts as a template. Nucleotides, with specific bases from the cytoplasm, match the free bases on each of the parent strands of DNA. This process produces two DNA helices identical to the first. One half of each double helix contains the original parent strand, (see fig. 2.28).

Fig. 2.28 DNA Replication

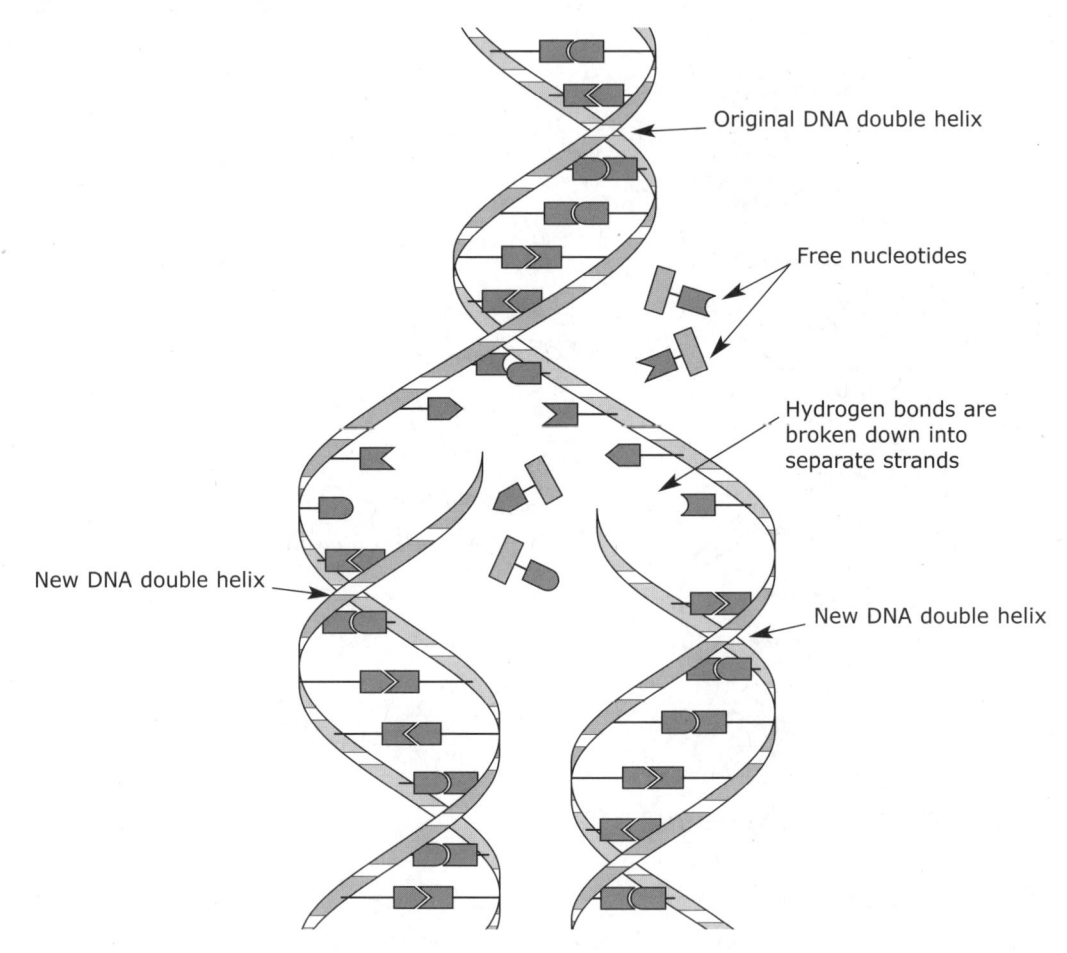

DNA and Protein Synthesis

Specific enzymes control all chemical reactions in the body. Enzymes are proteins made up of a defined sequence of amino acids. DNA codes for these amino acids, and their correct sequence, through a **triplet code**. The nitrogen-containing bases in DNA are arranged in threes along the double helix. Each triplet forms a **codon** that codes for one specific amino acid.

Enzymes are not synthesised in the nucleus. Ribosomes, in the cytoplasm, make the enzymes. Ribosomes are made of **rRNA**. DNA sends its code for an enzyme to the ribosome by messenger RNA or **mRNA**.

The whole process of **Protein Synthesis** occurs in the following steps:

(a) When a particular enzyme is needed by a cell the portion of DNA in the nucleus that codes for it, unwinds, exposing its bases.
(b) A strand of mRNA is produced, from RNA nucleotides, mirroring the DNA code.
(c) When complete, the strand of mRNA separates from the DNA and moves to a ribosome (rRNA) in the cytoplasm.
(d) At the ribosome the mRNA code is matched by nucleotides of transfer RNA (tRNA). Each nucleotide of tRNA carries a specific amino acid.
(e) The tRNA carries the specific amino acids in the correct sequence to the ribosome.
(f) The amino acids are then linked together in strict order producing the enzyme, which then assumes its unique folded shape.

Differences between DNA and RNA

	Structure	Function	Location
DNA	Deoxyribose is the sugar Double Helix Shape Base Pairing Has the base Thymine instead of Uracil	Codes for Genotype	Nucleus
RNA	Ribose is the sugar Single Helix No Base Pairing Has the base Uracil instead of Thymine	mRNA carries code from nucleus to rRNA (Ribosomes). tRNA transports Amino Acids	Cytoplasm

Non-nuclear Inheritance of DNA

Cell organelles such as mitochondria and chloroplasts contain their own DNA. These organelles can replicate themselves in the cell. Many scientists believe that these organelles evolved from forms of bacteria. Through evolution they became assimilated into larger-celled organisms. The two organisms then formed a mutualistic relationship giving rise to plant and animal cells. Non-nuclear DNA does not undergo meiosis or fertilisation during sexual reproduction.

MANDATORY ACTIVITY

To Isolate DNA from a Plant Tissue

1. Place about 100 ml of peas into a blender and switch on to high for 15 seconds. This will fragment the cells.
2. Strain the mixture into a second container.

3. Add some liquid detergent and swirl to mix. This will separate cell and nuclear membranes (protein and phospholipids) from the DNA. Leave to rest for ten minutes.
4. Enzymes are added (meat tenderiser enzymes) and the mixture is stirred gently. This will separate DNA from the protein it is naturally combined with.
5. Add an equal volume of 95% Ethyl Alcohol to the mixture, gently down the side of the test tube. The DNA will slowly rise to the top into the layer of alcohol.
6. Use a spatula to remove the DNA.

DNA Profiling

Humans have 23 pairs of chromosomes in the nucleus of every cell in the body (with the exception of gametes). A single chromosome can have up to 4,000 genes, which code for different traits. It is known that 50 to 60% of DNA does not code for any gene or protein in the body. These sections of DNA often have repeating nucleotide sequences called **core nucleotide sequences**. The number and length of the repeats vary between individuals but are similar in related individuals. DNA Profiling or DNA Fingerprinting uses these sections of DNA to identify an individual. Forensic scientists use DNA Profiling to compare DNA from hair, saliva, blood or semen found at the scene of a crime.

The procedure for DNA Profiling is outlined in fig. 2.29.

Fig. 2.29 DNA Profiling

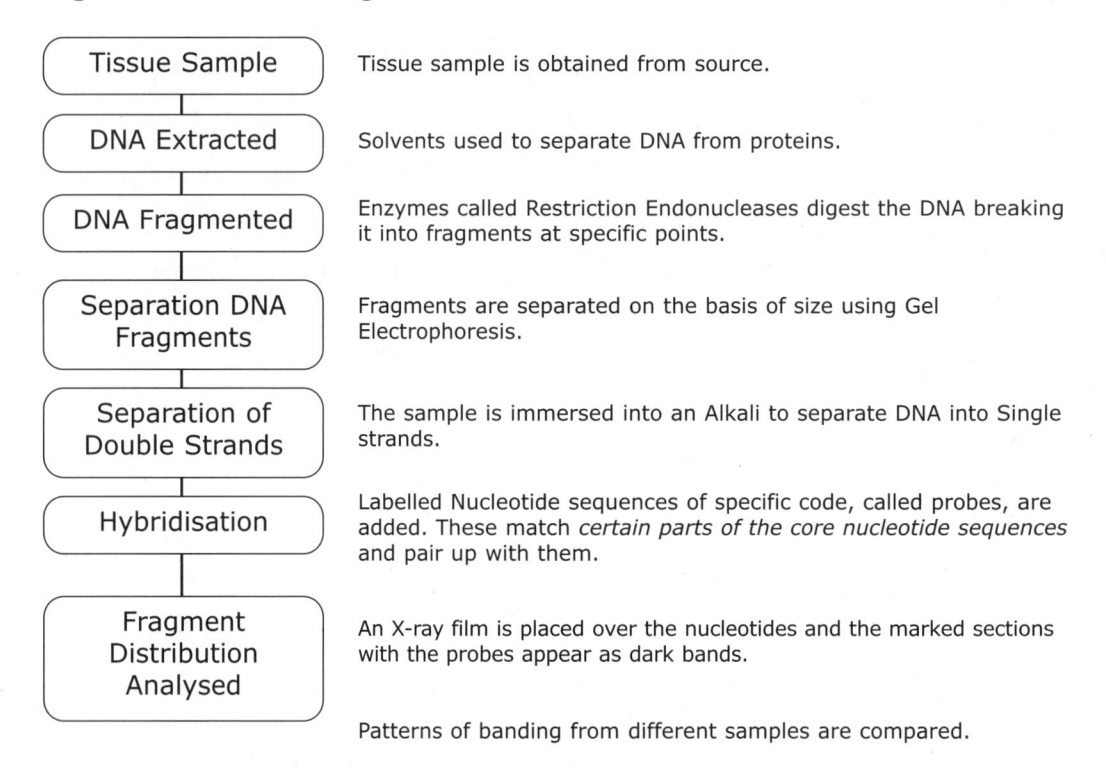

Tissue Sample	Tissue sample is obtained from source.
DNA Extracted	Solvents used to separate DNA from proteins.
DNA Fragmented	Enzymes called Restriction Endonucleases digest the DNA breaking it into fragments at specific points.
Separation DNA Fragments	Fragments are separated on the basis of size using Gel Electrophoresis.
Separation of Double Strands	The sample is immersed into an Alkali to separate DNA into Single strands.
Hybridisation	Labelled Nucleotide sequences of specific code, called probes, are added. These match *certain parts of the core nucleotide sequences* and pair up with them.
Fragment Distribution Analysed	An X-ray film is placed over the nucleotides and the marked sections with the probes appear as dark bands.

Patterns of banding from different samples are compared.

Applications of DNA Profiling

(a) It can be used to prove the parentage of a child.
(b) It can be used to detect criminals guilty of violent crimes.
(c) It can be used to confirm pedigree in animals.

GENETIC SCREENING AND TESTING

This process is used to identify the presence of a disease-causing gene in an individual. Amniocentesis is a procedure of withdrawing a sample of amniotic fluid surrounding a foetus in the womb. Cells in the sample can be tested to detect any defective genes such as those that cause Down's syndrome, Cystic Fibrosis or Haemophilia.

Individuals could be tested to see if they possessed disease-causing genes that their relatives or parents may have had. Parents can also be genetically screened to determine the probability of a disease occurring in their offspring.

GENETIC ENGINEERING

Genetic engineering is a process where genes from one organism are introduced into the genome (DNA) of an unrelated organism, usually micro-organisms. The micro-organisms with the new genes are replicated and used to create large quantities of useful chemicals. The process is often referred to as **recombinant DNA technology**.

The process involves the following steps:
(a) Locating a specific gene in a donor cell.
(b) Isolation of the gene.
(c) Insertion of the gene into the DNA that has been removed from a micro-organism.
(d) Transferring of the DNA and new gene back into the micro-organism.
(e) Replicating the micro-organism and harvesting the chemicals produced due to the new gene.

The process is summarised in fig. 2.30.

Fig. 2.30 Genetic Engineering

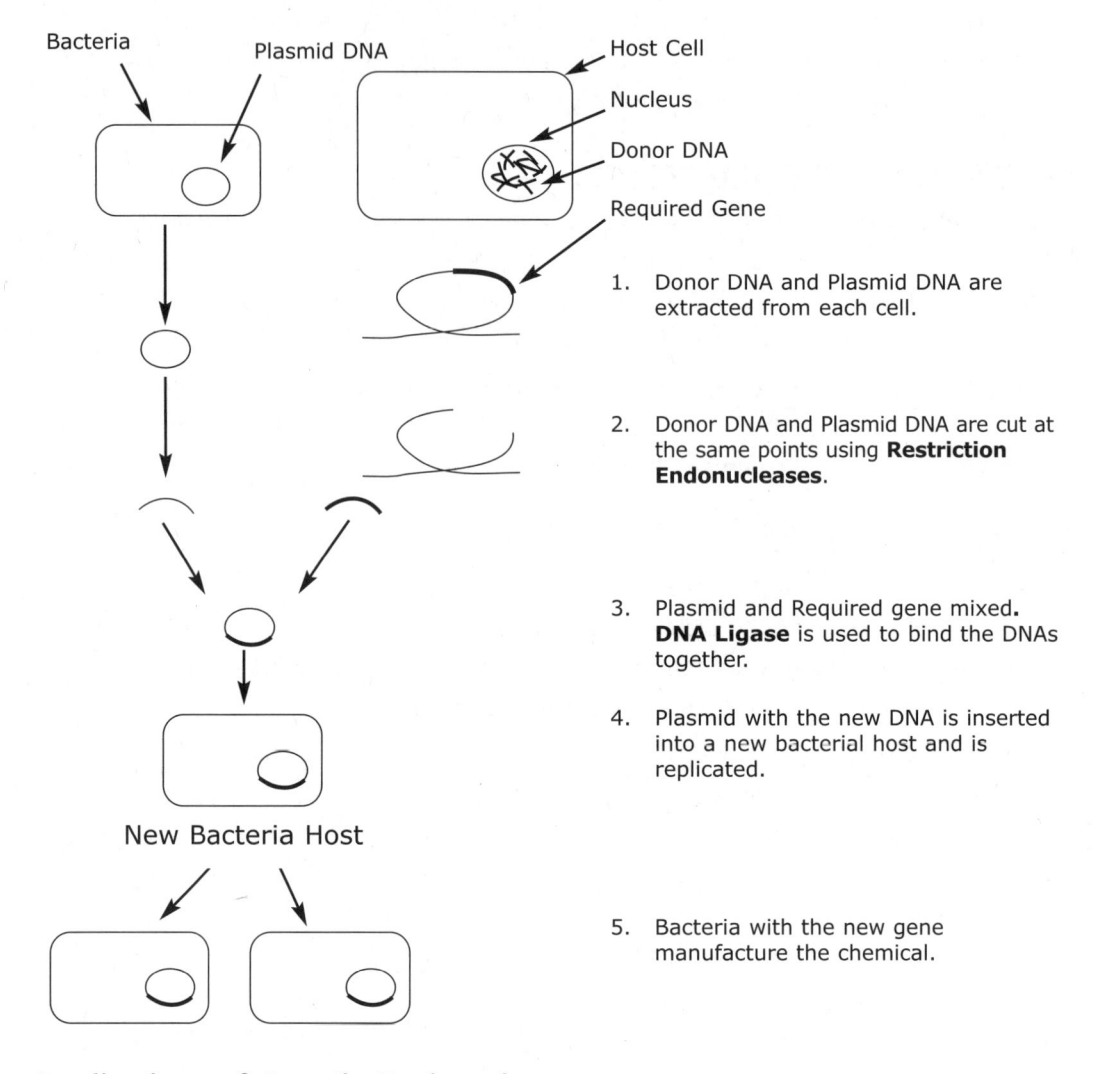

1. Donor DNA and Plasmid DNA are extracted from each cell.

2. Donor DNA and Plasmid DNA are cut at the same points using **Restriction Endonucleases**.

3. Plasmid and Required gene mixed. **DNA Ligase** is used to bind the DNAs together.

4. Plasmid with the new DNA is inserted into a new bacterial host and is replicated.

5. Bacteria with the new gene manufacture the chemical.

Applications of Genetic Engineering

(a) There is enormous demand for the hormone insulin to treat insulin-dependent diabetes. This disease used to be treated by using insulin obtained from the pancreas of cattle and pigs. Subtle differences in the forms of insulin stimulated antibody responses in some humans. Genetic engineering is now used to isolate the human gene for insulin production. The gene is inserted into a host bacterium to produce large quantities of human insulin.

(b) Genetically modified plants have an advantageous gene inserted into their DNA which is passed on to future generations. Characteristics such as disease and insect resistance have been introduced into food crops. The improved plant has greater yields.

(c) In animals, genetic engineering has been used to increase meat and milk yields in cattle.
(d) A defective gene causes Cystic Fibrosis. Viruses may be used to transfer the normal gene into cells in the lungs of the patient. The gene can then be absorbed into the DNA of the lung cells.

EVOLUTION

Evolution is the means by which modern animals and plants developed from their ancestors over millions of years. Charles Darwin developed the theory of Natural Selection to explain the process of evolution.

Natural Selection

This is the way in which organisms become better adapted to their environment due to a mutation. The genes for the improved characteristics can then be passed on to their offspring. Natural selection is thought to play a large role in the process of evolution.

Evidence for Evolution

There are different sources of evidence that support the theory of evolution. One source is the study of comparative anatomy.

Comparative Anatomy

This is a comparison of bone structure in the forelimb of very diverse animals such as the whale, mole, bat and human. They all have a **pentadactyl limb** arrangement of bones, (see fig. 2.31).

Fig. 2.31 Comparative Anatomy

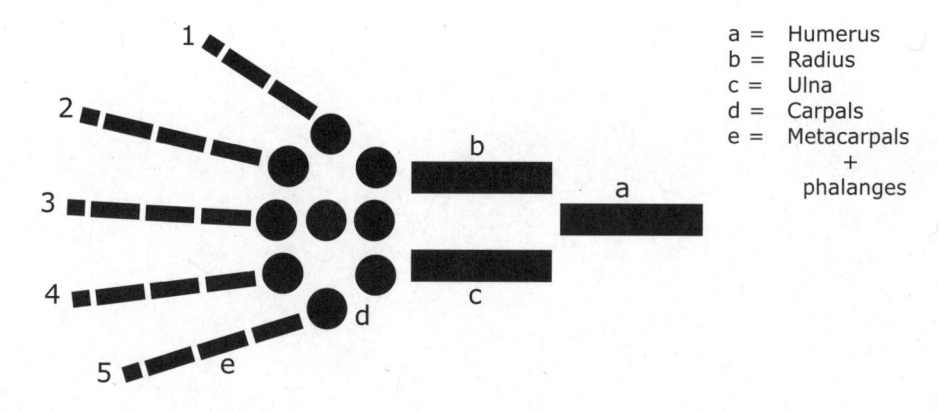

a = Humerus
b = Radius
c = Ulna
d = Carpals
e = Metacarpals
    +
    phalanges

Limbs of various animals that have the same basic structure but different functions are known as **homologous** structures. Different functions for limbs with similar structures are examples of **adaptative radiation**.

VARIATION OF SPECIES

A **species** is defined as a group of similar individuals of common ancestry that can interbreed to produce fertile offspring.

Different characteristics found in the individuals of a species are described as **variations**.

Variations can occur due to:

(a) The shuffling of genes that occurs during meiosis to produce gametes.
(b) Mutations.

A **mutation** is a change in the sequence of bases in a chromosome (DNA) that alters the genotype. Mutations are inherited if they are present in a gamete.

Causes: Mutations can occur with exposure to X-rays, radioactivity and chemicals called carcinogens.

UNIT 3 – THE ORGANISM

3.1 DIVERSITY OF ORGANISMS

There is an enormous variety of living things in the biosphere. To simplify the study of these different organisms we try to classify them into groups. The groupings are based on internal and external features. Most classification systems reflect the evolutionary relationships between organisms. Marguilis and Schwartz produced the most recent **Five Kingdom Classification**. The kingdoms are:

Kingdom	Characteristics	Examples
1. Procaryotes	1. No membrane bound organelles	Bacteria, Cyanobacteria
2. Fungi	1. Eucaryotic 2. Non-cellulose cell wall 3. Non-photosynthetic, absorbs food through hyphae 4. Produces spores	Moulds, Mushrooms, Yeasts
3. Protoctists	1. Eucaryotic 2. Most are unicellular	Protozoa (Amoeba), Algae (Fucus)
4. Plants	1. Eucaryotic 2. Cell wall of cellulose 3. Photosynthetic 4. Multicellular	Liverworts, Mosses, Ferns, Conifers, Angiosperms
5. Animals	1. Eucaryotic 2. Non-photosynthetic 3. Nervous system 4. Multicellular	Platyhelminthes, Nematodes, Annelids, Molluscs, Arthropods, Echinoderms, Chordates

BACTERIA

Bacteria are micro-organisms found everywhere (ubiquitous). They are neither plants or animals, as they do not have a membrane-bound nucleus. They are much smaller in size than either plant or animal cells.

Bacteria are classified according to their shape:

(a) **Coccus**: are round,

(b) **Rods**: are cylindrical, and

(c) **Spirals**: have random shapes.

A generalised bacterium is shown in fig. 3.1.

Fig. 3.1 Bacteria

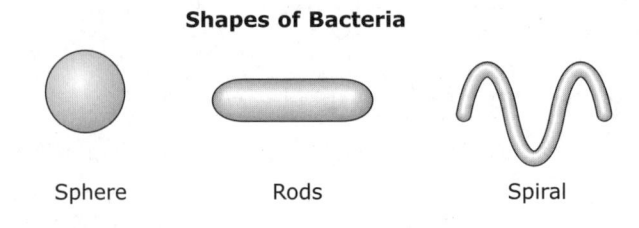

Shapes of Bacteria

Sphere   Rods   Spiral

Generalised Structure of a Bacterium

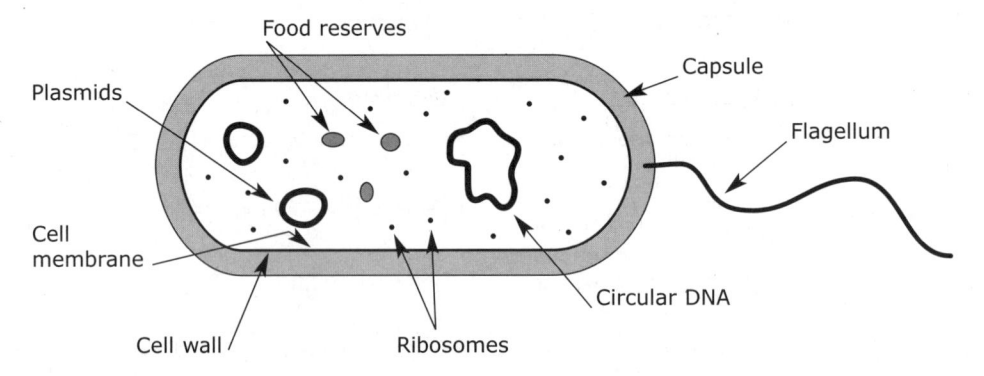

(Labels: Food reserves, Capsule, Flagellum, Circular DNA, Ribosomes, Cell wall, Cell membrane, Plasmids)

Bacteria can also be classified as:
(a) **Aerobic**: which require oxygen to live.
(b) **Anaerobic**: which do not require oxygen.

Reproduction

Bacteria reproduce asexually by **binary fission**. One mature cell divides to form two identical daughter cells. Reproduction can occur as often as once every twenty minutes under suitable conditions. The growth rate of a colony of bacteria can be represented by a Growth Curve. Different rates of growth in numbers are observed over time, (see fig 3.2).

Fig. 3.2 Growth Curve of Micro-organisms

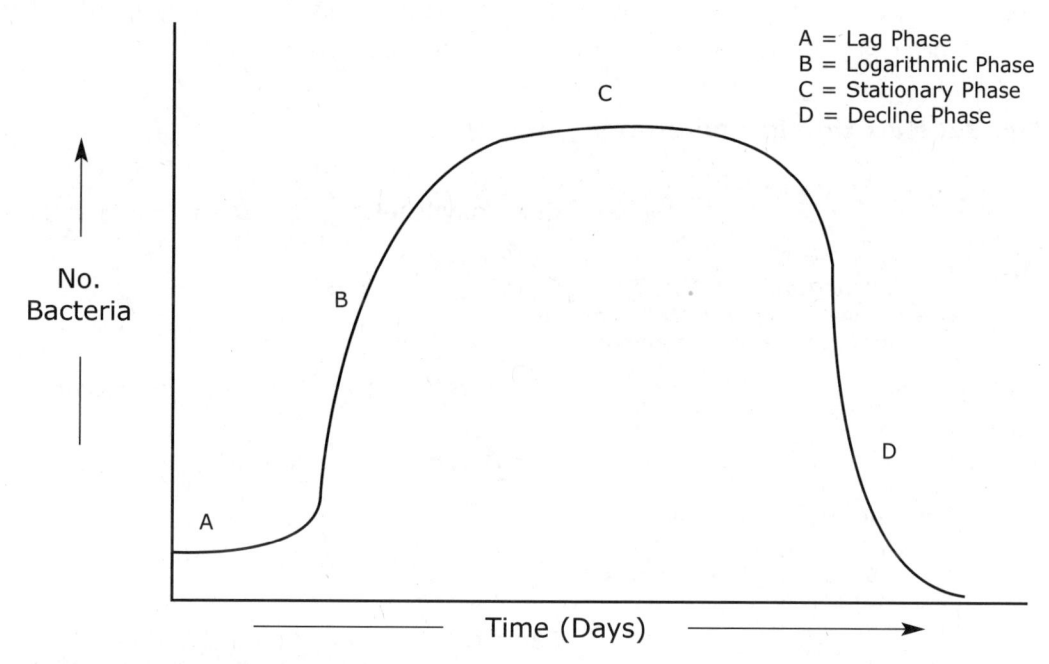

A = Lag Phase
B = Logarithmic Phase
C = Stationary Phase
D = Decline Phase

No. Bacteria

Time (Days)

Stages of a Growth Curve

(a) The Lag Phase: A slow growth rate as the bacteria have only started to grow and a period of time is necessary for adaptation to the new environment.
(b) The Logarithmic Phase: A rapid growth stage due to an abundance of resources such as food, oxygen, space, etc.
(c) The Stationary Phase: A period where bacterial numbers neither increase or decrease. This is due to competition for food, space and the build-up of toxic wastes.
(d) The Decline Phase: The final period where bacterial numbers decline due to the increased competition for space and food and the build-up of toxic wastes.

Factors Affecting the Growth of Bacteria

(a) Temperature: Metabolism is controlled by enzymes which are sensitive to temperature. In general, a temperature of 30° to 40°C is optimal.
(b) Food: An abundant source of nutrition is vital for rapid growth.
(c) Oxygen (if the bacteria is aerobic).
(d) pH: Most bacterial enzymes work optimally at a pH range close to 7.
(e) An absence of competition and toxins or wastes.

Nutrition in Bacteria

Since bacteria can be found anywhere in the biosphere they must be able to gain nutrition in many different ways. Fig. 3.3 summarises the types of nutrition in bacteria.

Fig. 3.3 Nutrition in Bacteria

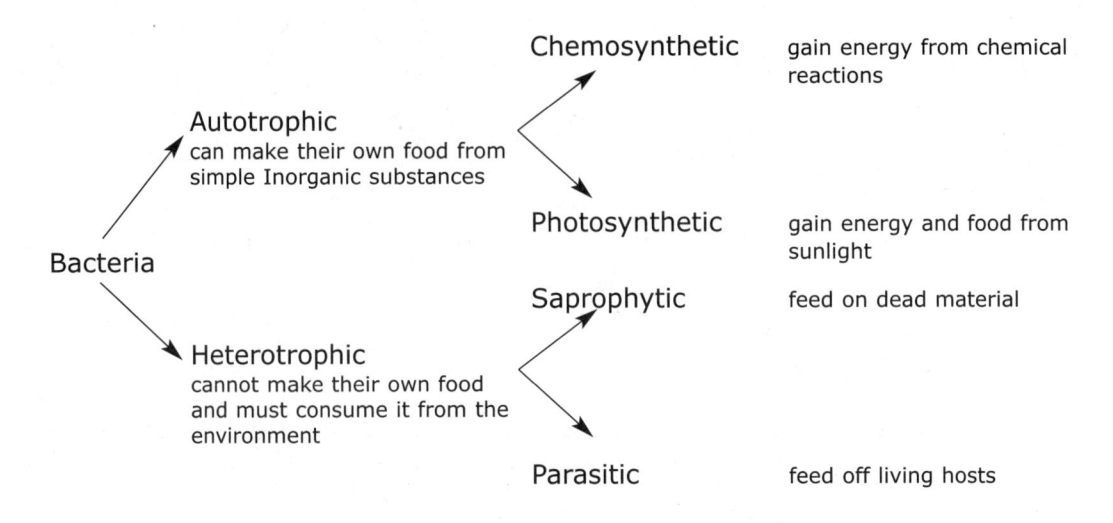

Bacteria
- Autotrophic — can make their own food from simple Inorganic substances
  - Chemosynthetic — gain energy from chemical reactions
  - Photosynthetic — gain energy and food from sunlight
- Heterotrophic — cannot make their own food and must consume it from the environment
  - Saprophytic — feed on dead material
  - Parasitic — feed off living hosts

Chemosynthetic bacteria are involved in many parts of the Nitrogen Cycle. These and other bacteria are very important in the recycling process of minerals which is vital for all living things.

Photosynthetic bacteria such as Cyanophytes use sunlight to make food. These are vital in nature as they often form the first stages of freshwater and marine food chains.

Saprophytic bacteria include Pseudomonas which break down the remains of dead plants and animals to Ammonia. Saprophytic bacteria play an essential role in recycling the materials of dead organisms. **Humus** in soil is formed by such bacterial activity. It is the remains of organic matter undergoing further decomposition. Humus is a vital component of fertile soil. It improves drainage, aeration, mineral and water retention.

Parasitic bacteria cause diseases such as Tuberculosis and Cholera. Parasitic bacteria play an important role in nature causing disease and death which acts as a form of population control.

Economic Effects of Bacteria

(a) The bacteria Streptococcus is used in yoghurt-making.
(b) Streptomyces is cultured to make antibiotics.
(c) The disease Tuberculosis in cattle is caused by Mycobacterium.
(d) Cholera is caused by the bacteria Vibrio.

Antibiotics

> Antibiotics are chemicals which, in low concentrations, slow the growth of bacteria. They are usually produced by other micro-organisms.

Antibiotics are powerful weapons against infectious diseases caused by pathogenic bacteria. Penicillin was the first antibiotic to be produced in large quantities. Its use saved many injured casualties in the Normandy battles of 1944. Today there are over fifty different antibiotics used in medicine.

Antibiotic Resistance in Bacteria

Sometimes a few members of a population of bacteria are able to resist the effects of an antibiotic. This resistance is usually due to a mutation. Excessive use of the antibiotic removes non-resistant strains leaving the resistant bacteria to flourish. New, more powerful antibiotics must then be developed.

Intensive farming of chickens and pigs often involves the addition of small quantities of antibiotics to the animal feed. This has produced healthier animals that grow more quickly. Unfortunately, widespread use facilitates the development of resistant strains of bacteria. The residues of the antibiotics are then consumed by humans, assisting the development of more antibiotic resistant bacteria.

FUNGI

Fungi are eucaryotic, heterotrophic micro-organisms. Their cell walls are made of chitin. Many fungi have their cells arranged in a network of threads called hyphae.

Saprophytic fungi break down the remains of dead plants and animals. In the soil they play an essential role in recycling the materials of dead organisms. **Humus** in soil is formed by such activity. It is the remains of organic matter undergoing further decomposition. Humus is a vital component of fertile soil. It improves drainage, aeration, mineral and water retention. **Parasitic** fungi can cause disease in animals and plants.

There are two types of saprophytic fungi studied:

(a) **Rhizopus** (Bread Mould): a multicellular, saprophytic fungus with aseptate hyphae.

(b) **Saccharomyces** (Yeast): a unicellular saprophytic fungus.

Rhizopus

Rhizopus is a saprophytic multicellular fungus. It is aseptate, i.e. it does not have cross walls separating its cytoplasm into separate cells, (see fig. 3.4).

Fig. 3.4 Rhizopus

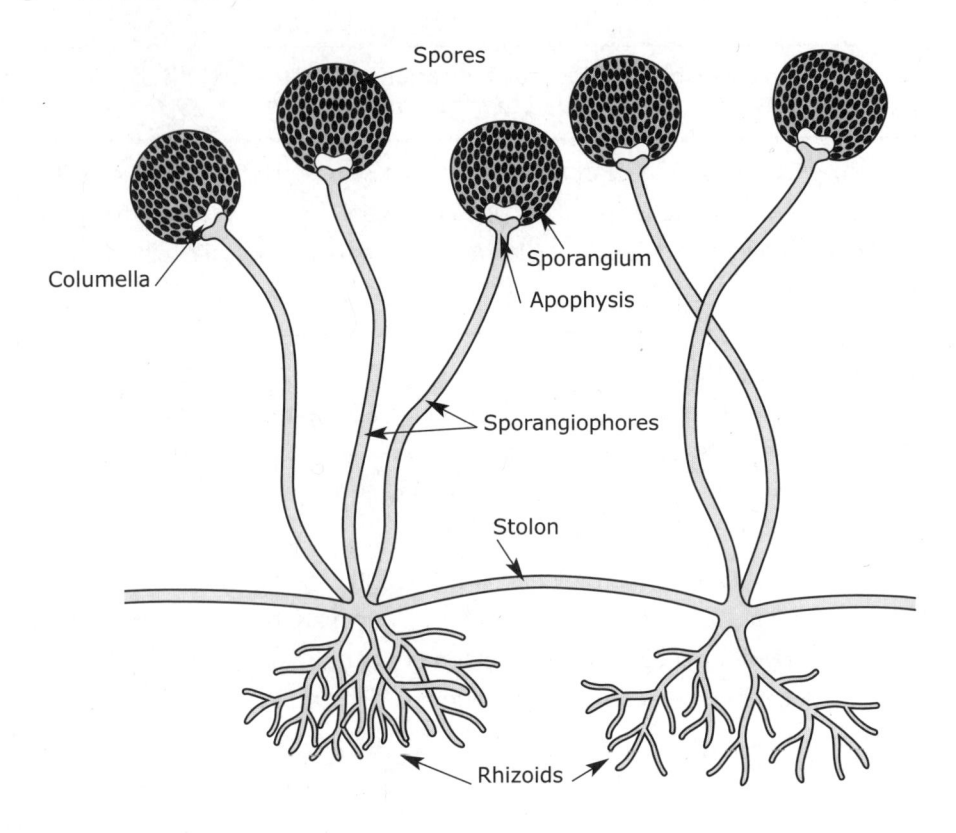

Life Cycle

There are two forms of reproduction: Asexual and Sexual.

Asexual Reproduction: Rhizopus reproduces asexually by producing spores in sporangia. Under dry conditions the spores are released and spread by the air. Spores can then germinate to produce new hyphae.

Sexual Reproduction: occurs when the hyphae of two different strains of Rhizopus come in contact with one another. Outgrowths occur on the hyphae forming gametangia. These fuse, forming a thick-walled, diploid zygospore. Under suitable conditions the zygospore germinates to produce a sporangium. Finally the sporangium bursts when mature, releasing spores, (see fig. 3.5).

Fig. 3.5 Sexual Reproduction in Rhizopus

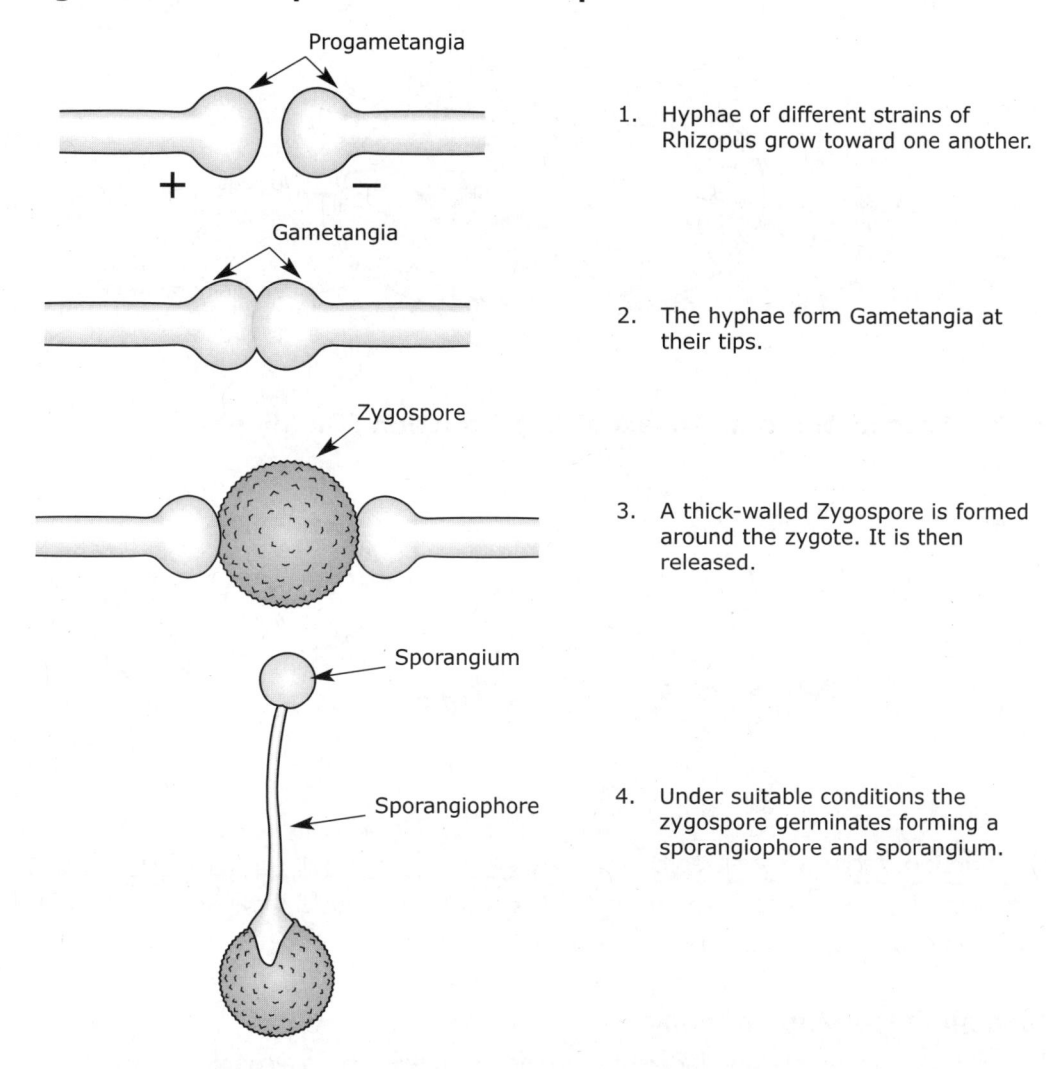

1. Hyphae of different strains of Rhizopus grow toward one another.
2. The hyphae form Gametangia at their tips.
3. A thick-walled Zygospore is formed around the zygote. It is then released.
4. Under suitable conditions the zygospore germinates forming a sporangiophore and sporangium.

Nutrition

The hyphae secrete digestive enzymes onto the substrate on which they grow. These externally digest any carbohydrates, lipids or proteins present. The products of digestion are then absorbed into the hyphae.

Saccharomyces (Yeast)

Saccharomyces is a saprophytic, unicellular fungus, (see fig. 3.6).

Fig. 3.6 Saccharomyces – Adult Yeast Cell

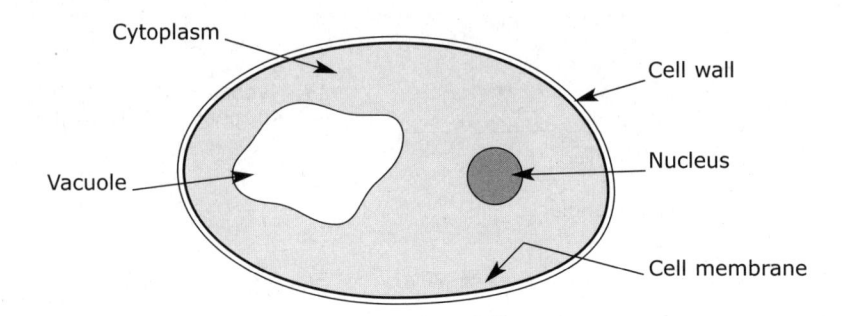

Fig. 3.7 Saccharomyces – Asexual Reproduction (Budding)

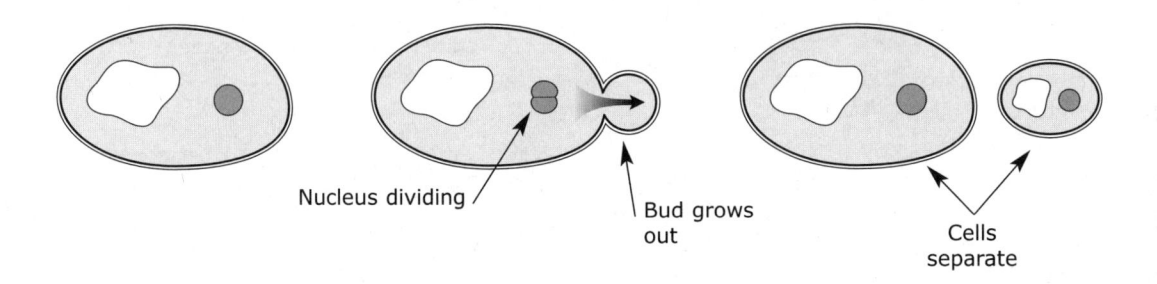

Reproduction: Saccharomyces reproduces asexually in a process called budding. A mature cell nucleus divides by mitosis to produce two new nuclei. The nuclei separate as a new cell is formed, budding out of the parent, (see fig. 3.7).

Economic Importance of Fungi

(a) Yeast is used in the brewing industry converting carbohydrate to alcohol.
(b) The carbon dioxide produced during the respiration of yeast causes dough to rise in the baking industry.
(c) Potato blight is caused by the fungus Phytophera. Heavy infection destroys crop yields.
(d) The fungus Merulius causes dry rot in wood.

LABORATORY PROCEDURES WHEN HANDLING AND CULTURING MICRO-ORGANISMS

The culturing of bacteria and fungi is essential for the study of micro-organisms. The Aseptic technique, described below, is used to ensure that the culturing medium remains free from contamination.

A. Preparation of the Medium
1. Boil some agar, peptone and water in a beaker.
2. Pour the mixture into boiling tubes.
3. Sterilise the tubes and agar in a pressure cooker.
4. Tighten the lids on the boiling tubes when cool and store in a fridge.

B. Pouring Agar Plates
1. Loosen the caps on the boiling tubes and place in boiling water to melt the nutrient agar.
2. Remove the cap of the boiling tube and flame its mouth in a bunsen burner (to prevent contamination).
3. Remove the lid of a sterile petri dish holding it just above the base.
4. Quickly pouring the agar, replace the lid and swirl gently to spread evenly.
5. Leave to set for 5 minutes, (see fig. 3.8).

Fig. 3.8 Pouring Agar Plates

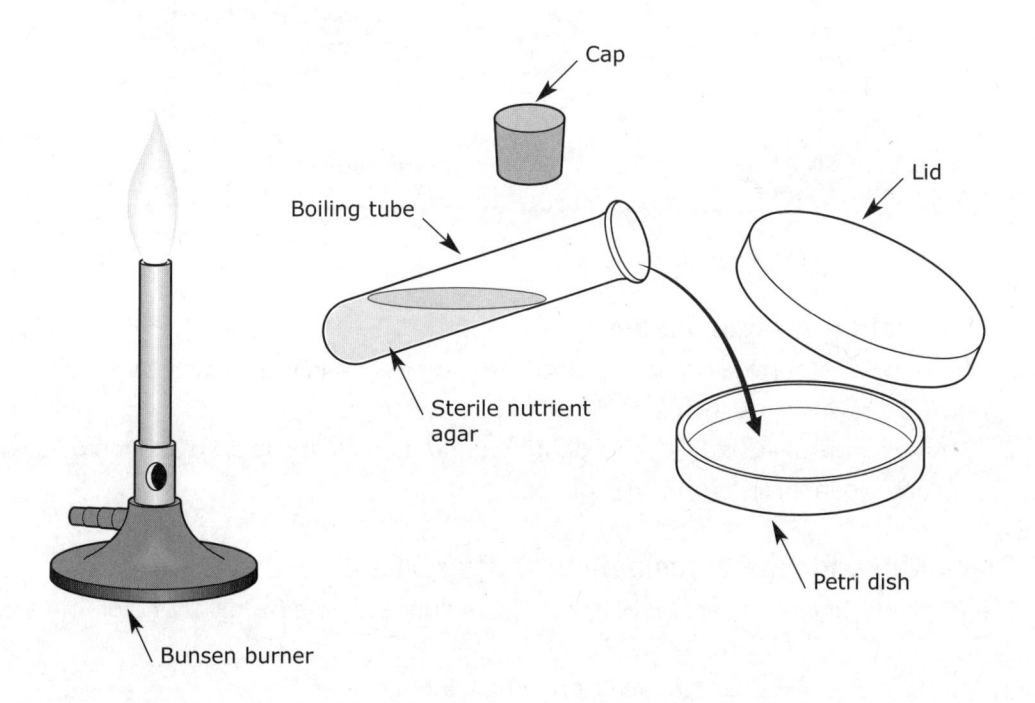

C. Inoculation of Agar Plates
1. Heat an Inoculating loop in a bunsen flame to sterilise it.
2. Touch it away from the source of micro-organisms to cool it and then pick up some living cells.
3. Remove the lid of a sterile petri dish holding it just above the base.
4. Streak the agar with the inoculating loop to inoculate the petri dish.
5. Replace the lid, seal and label, (see fig. 3.9).

Fig. 3.9 Inoculation of Agar Plates

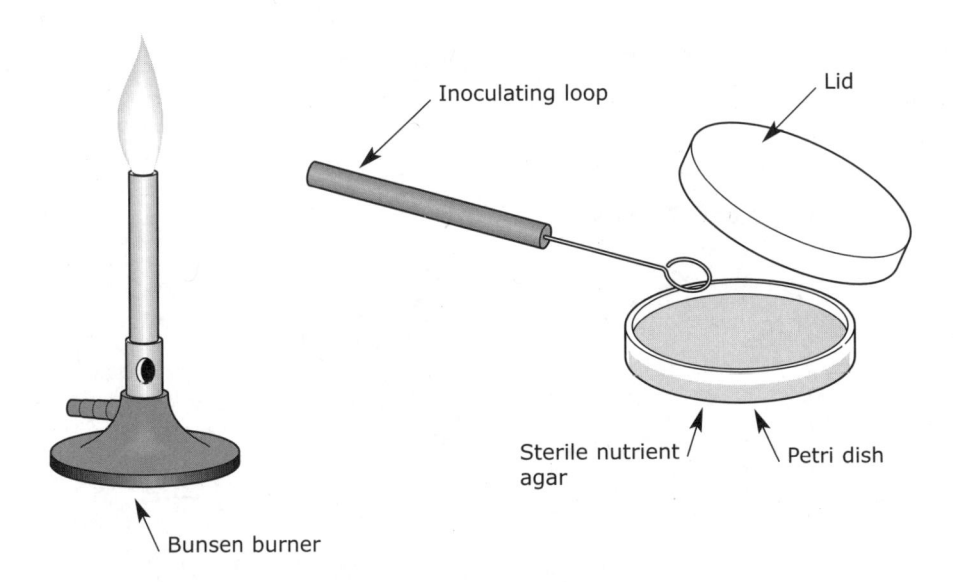

D. Incubation of Agar Plates
1. Store the plates upside down in an incubator to prevent an evaporation condensation cycle as this increases the possibility of contamination.
2. Set the temperature at 37°C for 3 days. This is to promote the growth and reproduction of each organism to form visible colonies.

Precautions for the Examination of Agar Plates
The following precautions are necessary in case pathogens have been cultured on the agar plates:
1. All micro-organisms must be treated as if harmful to humans.
2. The plates should be sterilised with a few drops of formaldehyde 24 hours before inspection.
3. The plates should never be opened for inspection.

Identification of Micro-organisms
Fungi are seen as black or white, thread-like or furry growths. Bacteria are seen in colonies as small, shiny pinheads.

Use of a Control
In all experiments a control is used as a test of the validity of the results. A petri dish of sterile nutrient agar is always poured and incubated with the other petri dishes. This is called the control and is not inoculated with any micro-organisms. If the culturing technique is good there will be no colonies of micro-organisms on the control.

Disposal
All petri dishes and reusable equipment must be sterilised in a pressure cooker at high pressure before disposal or storage.

MANDATORY ACTIVITY
To Investigate the Growth of Leaf Yeast
1. Select trees such as Ash or Lilac in the sample area.
2. Remove four sample leaves from different sides of each tree and place in sterile plastic bags, labelling each sample.
3. Remove prepared Malt Agar plates from their sterile wrapping. Do not remove their lids.
4. Using a cork borer remove a 2 cm disc from each leaf in a sample.
5. Using petroleum jelly, quickly attach each disc by its underside to the inside of the lid of the Malt Agar plate.
6. Label each dish carefully.
7. Leave some Malt Agar plates unopened to act as a control.
8. Leave each dish for 24 hours in an upright position to allow the yeast spores to fall onto the Malt Agar.
9. Turn the dishes upside down for three days and leave at room temperature.

Result: The number of yeast colonies (pink in colour) on each dish is recorded. The greater the number of colonies the better the quality of air.

PROTOCTISTA (PROTISTA)
All the organisms in this group are eucaryotic and most are unicellular. Amoeba is an example of a unicellular animal in this group. Amoeba has heterotrophic nutrition as seen in fig. 3.10.

Fig. 3.10 Protista e.g. Amoeba

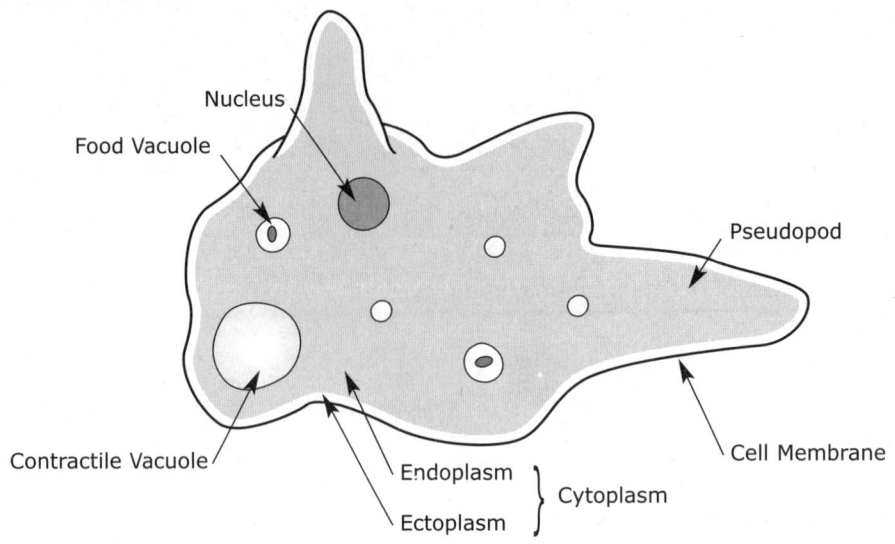

Diagram labels: Nucleus, Food Vacuole, Pseudopod, Contractile Vacuole, Endoplasm, Ectoplasm, Cytoplasm, Cell Membrane

Movement
Movement occurs by the alternation of the outer ectoplasm (clear) and inner endoplasm (granular) between plasmagel (solid) and plasmasol (liquid) states. These changes cause streaming in the cytoplasm and the formation of **pseudopods**, (see fig. 3.10).

Reproduction
Reproduction is asexual. A single cell divides by mitosis, to produce two new identical daughter cells. This is referred to as **binary fission**.

Contractile Vacuole
Water constantly enters the cell by osmosis. Energy (ATP) is necessary to pump it out against the diffusion gradient. The water is gathered in the contractile vacuole and it is pumped outside the cell using Active Transport. Marine (sea-living) amoebae do not have the need for a contractile vacuole as their cytoplasm is isotonic with the sea water and excess water does not diffuse into the cell.

3.2 ORGANISATION AND VASCULAR STRUCTURES

ORGANISATIONAL COMPLEXITY OF THE FLOWERING PLANT
There are two main types of flowering plants:
(a) Monocotyledons, and
(b) Dicotyledons.

Differences between Monocotyledons and Dicotyledons

Monocots.	Dicots.
1. Seeds contain a single cotyledon.	1. Seeds contain two cotyledons.
2. Fibrous root system.	2. Tap root system.
3. Herbaceous (non-woody) plant.	3. Woody plant.
4. Flower parts in threes.	4. Floral parts in fours or fives.
5. Leaves narrow with parallel veins.	5. Netted pattern of leaf veins.
6. Vascular bundles are scattered in stem.	6. Vascular bundles in rings in stem.

Flowering plants can be divided into two main regions:

(a) Root system.

(b) Shoot system (stem, leaves and flowers).

System	Functions
Root System	1. Absorb water and minerals from soil.
	2. Anchor the plant.
	3. Sometimes to store food.
Shoot System	1. Stem supports leaves and flowers.
	2. Stem transports food, water and minerals.
	3. Leaves make food (photosynthesis).
	4. Leaves carry out gaseous exchange.
	5. Flowers carry out reproduction.

Plant Tissues

Plant tissues can be divided into four main types:

(a) Dermal Tissue which covers and protects the plant from water loss and the entry of disease. Example: Epidermis, (see fig. 3.11).

Fig. 3.11 Plant Tissues

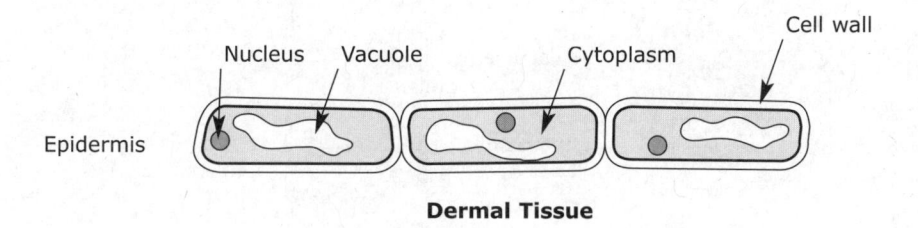

Dermal Tissue

Fig. 3.12 Plant Tissues

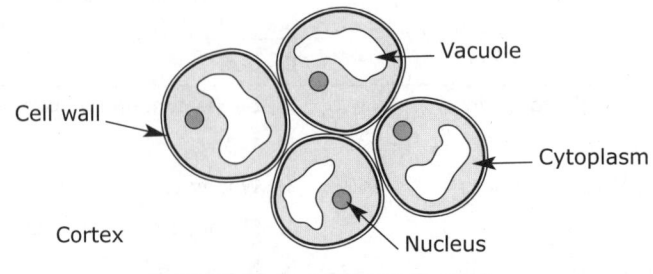

Ground Tissue (Parenchyma)

(b) Ground Tissue which has a packing and storage function. Example: Parenchyma in Cortex, (see fig. 3.12).
(c) Meristematic Tissue responsible for new growth and cell division.
(d) Vascular Tissue, involved in the transport of food, water and minerals around the plant. Example: Xylem and Phloem, (see fig. 3.13).

Fig. 3.13 Vascular Tissue

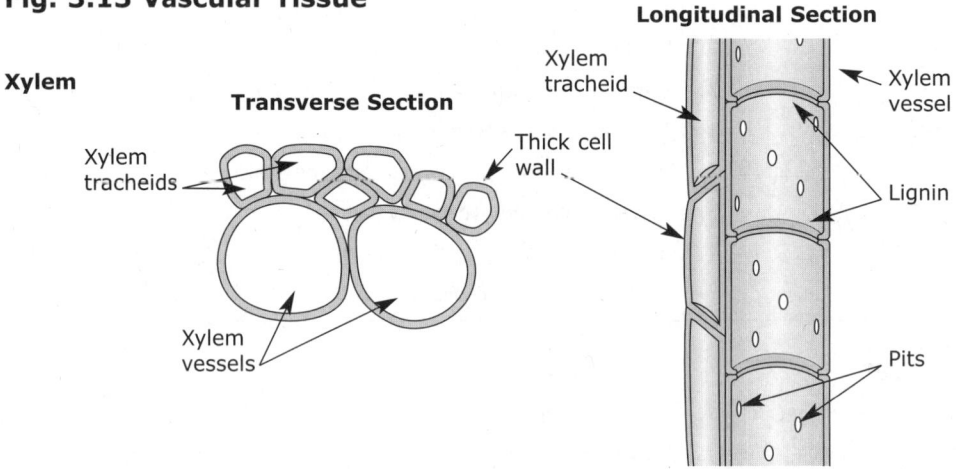

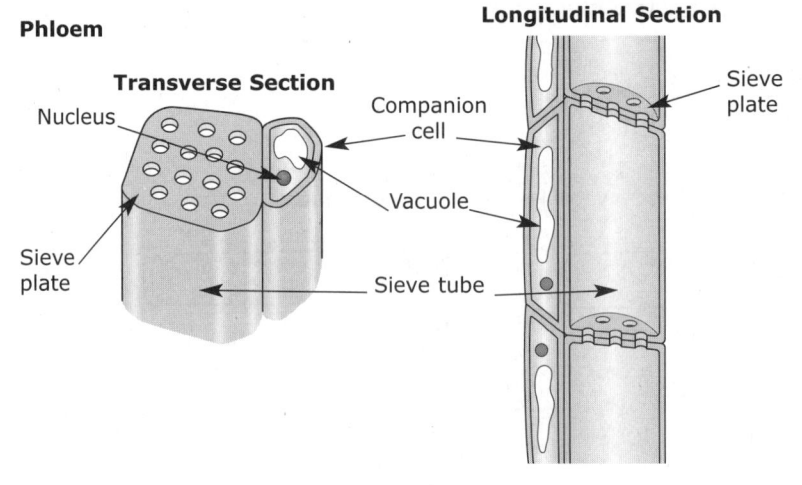

Xylem

Transverse Section

Longitudinal Section

Phloem

Transverse Section

Longitudinal Section

Xylem Tissue

Structure: Dead, lignified with thick cell wall.

Function: Transport of water and minerals.

Location: Vascular bundles and any vascular tissue.

Phloem Tissue

Structure: Living, thin-walled cells.

Function: Transport of food and hormones.

Location: Vascular Bundles.

Meristematic Tissue (Meristems)

Structure: Living, thin-walled cells.

Function: Cell division and Growth.

Location: Shoot and root tips and Cambium.

In general, there are two types of growth in plants:

(a) **Primary thickening**: which is the elongation of shoot and root tips by primary meristematic tissue dividing by mitosis.

(b) **Secondary thickening**: which is the widening of the shoots and roots by secondary meristematic tissue dividing by mitosis. It occurs when the meristematic **cambium cells** in the vascular bundles divide by mitosis to produce new phloem to the outside and new xylem to the inside. This process is repeated every year causing the widening and strengthening of the stem.

Diagrams of Monocot. and Dicot. Stems and Roots are seen in fig. 3.14.

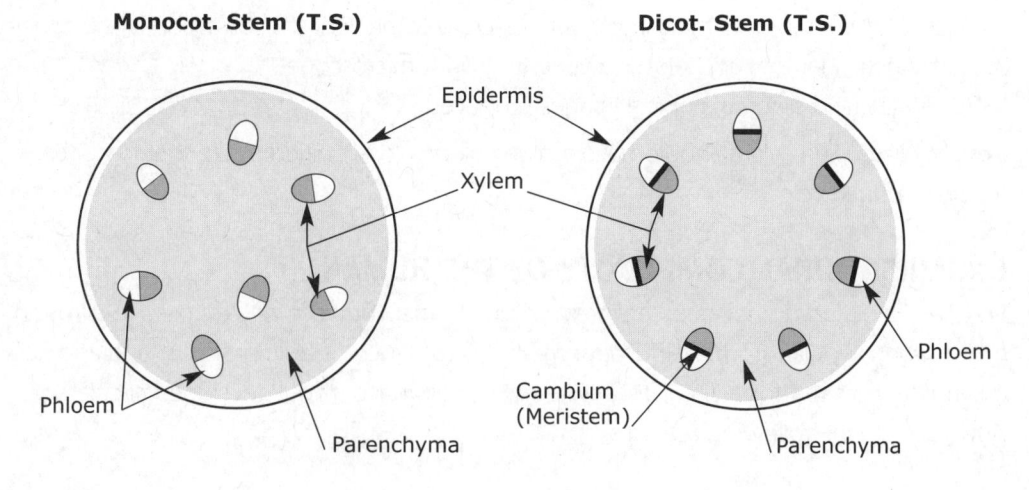

Fig. 3.14 Monocot. and Dicot. Stems

Monocot. Stem (T.S.) — labels: Epidermis, Xylem, Phloem, Parenchyma

Dicot. Stem (T.S.) — labels: Epidermis, Xylem, Phloem, Cambium (Meristem), Parenchyma

Fig. 3.14 Monocot. and Dicot. Roots

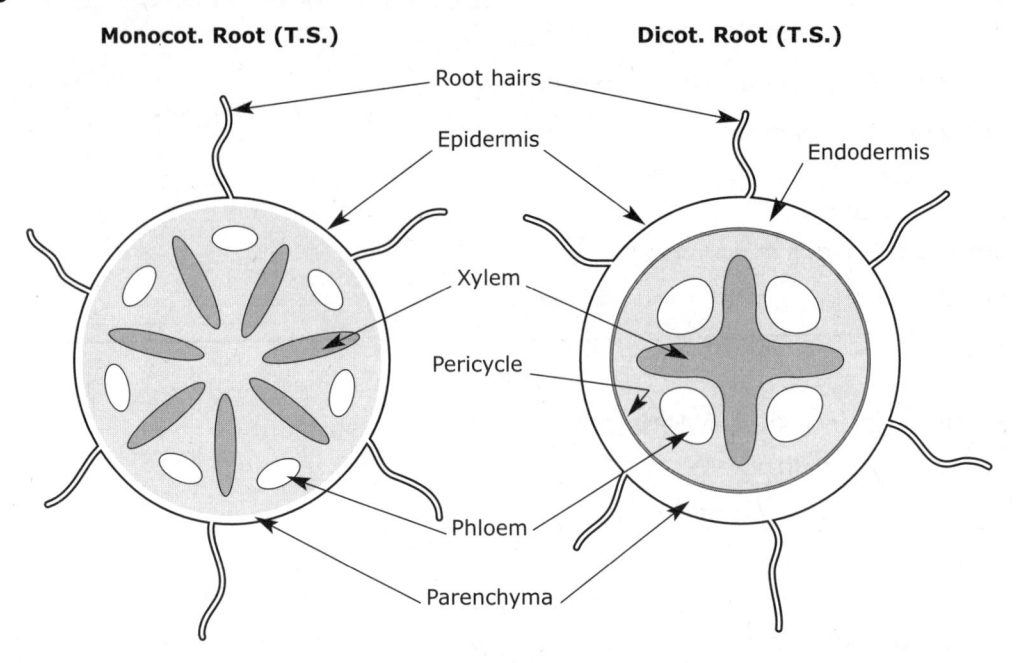

Monocot. Root (T.S.) — Dicot. Root (T.S.)

Labels: Root hairs, Epidermis, Endodermis, Xylem, Pericycle, Phloem, Parenchyma

MANDATORY ACTIVITY

To Examine Microscopically the Transverse Section of a Dicot. Stem

1. Place a buttercup stem in a cut-out potato to provide support.
2. Use a wet, backed blade to cut very thin sections from an internode section of the stem.
3. Place a drop of water on a glass slide and gently place a cutting onto the drop preventing the formation of any air bubbles.
4. Add a few drops of toluidine blue stain and leave for one minute.
5. Rinse off excess stain gently using dripping water from a tap.
6. Place a cover slip over the sample very carefully to prevent the formation of air bubbles.
7. Examine under low and high power with a light microscope.
8. Draw labelled diagrams of the images produced.

Result: All lignified xylem should have a blue colour. Non-lignified tissue should appear with a pink or purple colour.

ORGANISATIONAL COMPLEXITY OF THE HUMAN

Very small animals do not need a system of circulation. They can rely on passive diffusion for their oxygen supplies from their environment. Factors such as animal size, shape and activity determine the need for a circulatory system. Humans have a well-developed circulatory system. It has the following features:

(a) It is a **closed system** which means the blood is contained in a continuous system of blood vessels.
(b) There is a **muscular heart** pumping the blood under high pressure.
(c) It is a **double circulation** consisting of two separate circulations (shown in fig. 3.15):
    1. A pulmonary circulation, from the heart to the lungs and back again.
    2. A systemic circulation from the heart to the body and back again.

Fig. 3.15 Double Circulation

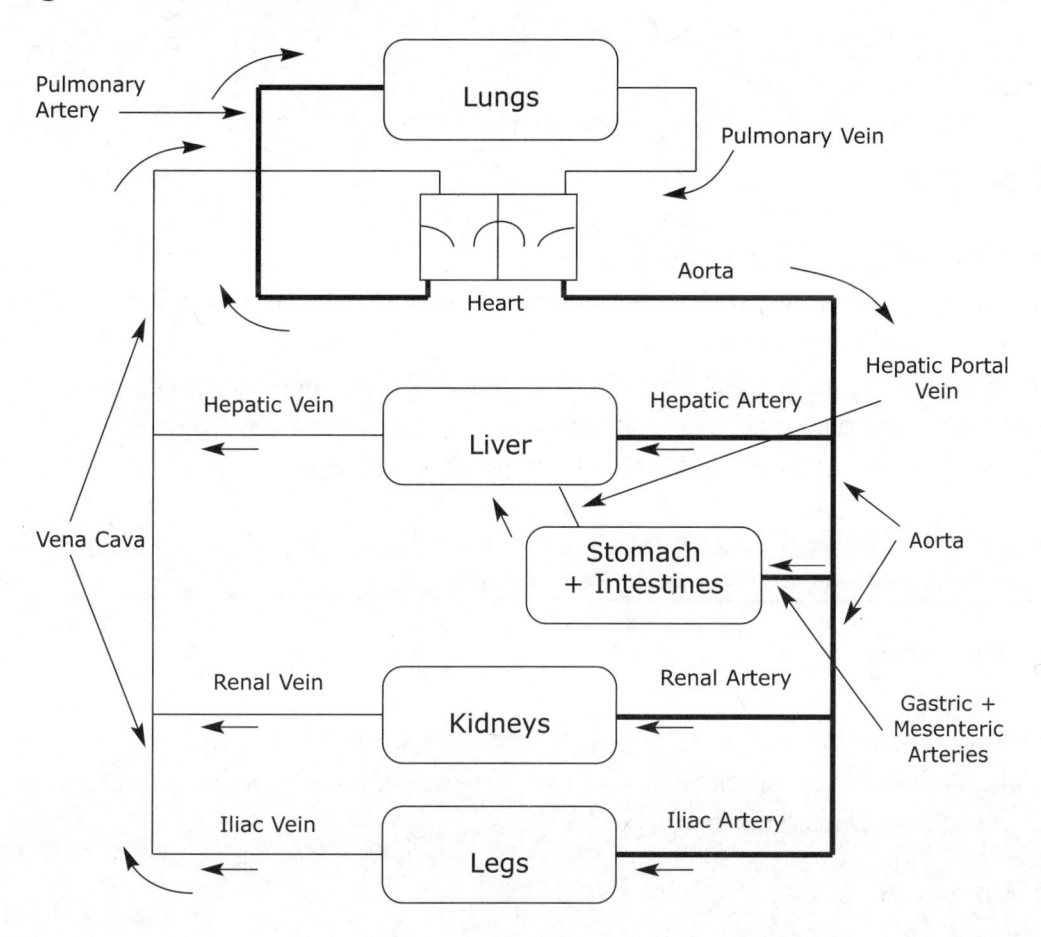

In humans the blood consists of two main components, cells and plasma. Plasma is 90% water which contains dissolved food, wastes and blood proteins. The different constituents of blood can be seen in fig. 3.16.

Fig. 3.16 Constituents of Blood

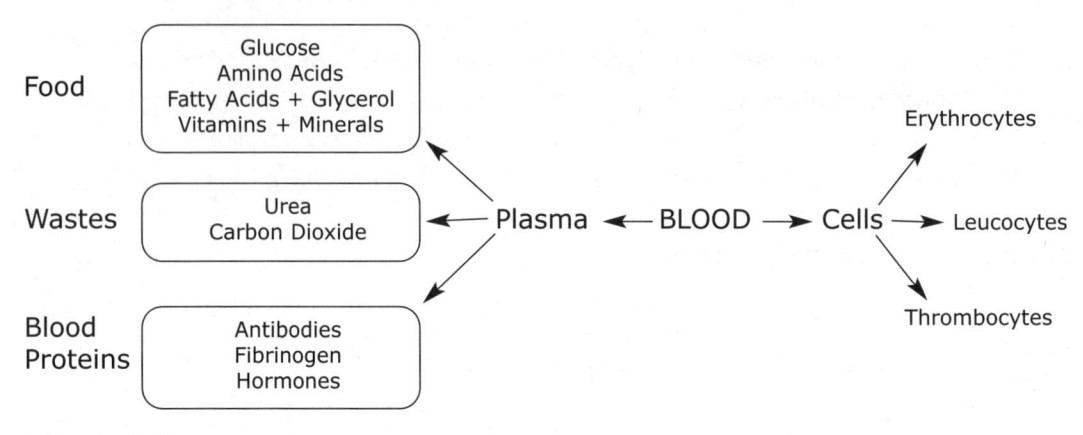

```
Food ──────► [ Glucose
              Amino Acids
              Fatty Acids + Glycerol
              Vitamins + Minerals ]
                                          ┌──► Erythrocytes
Wastes ────► [ Urea                       │
              Carbon Dioxide ] ◄── Plasma ◄── BLOOD ──► Cells ──► Leucocytes
                                          │
Blood                                     └──► Thrombocytes
Proteins ──► [ Antibodies
              Fibrinogen
              Hormones ]
```

Blood Cells

Erythrocytes (Red Blood Cells)

Structure: They have a biconcave shape and have neither a nucleus or mitochondria. They contain the protein haemoglobin.

Function: They transport oxygen gas in the blood. They can also transport carbon dioxide in the form of carbonic acid.

Source: They are produced in the red bone marrow of large bones.

Leucocytes (White Blood Cells)

There are two main types: (a) Lymphocytes and (b) Monocytes.

(a) Lymphocytes

Structure: Have a nucleus.

Function: Produce antibodies that help body cells to destroy foreign objects.

Source: Produced in the red bone marrow from stem cells or in the thymus. All lymphocytes operate from the lymphatic system.

(b) Monocytes

Structure: Large white blood cells with a nucleus.

Function: Leave the blood circulation by amoeboid movement to engulf foreign matter.

Source: Produced from stem cells in the red bone marrow.

Thrombocytes

Structure: No nucleus, very small.

Function: Blood clotting.

Source: Produced in the red bone marrow.

Blood Vessels
There are three main types:

(a) Arteries
Carry blood away from the heart. They have a thick muscle layer to help pump blood around the body. They usually carry oxygenated blood. They have a small lumen but no valves. **Arterioles** are small arteries carrying blood from larger arteries to capillaries.

(b) Veins
Carry blood to the heart. They have a thin muscle layer. They usually carry deoxygenated blood. They have a large lumen and have valves. Valves prevent the backflow of blood. **Venules** are small veins carrying blood away from capillaries to veins.

(c) Capillaries
Very small vessels the walls being only one cell thick. They allow dissolved substances to enter and leave the blood by diffusion, and through intercellular spaces. They are in close contact with tissue cells.

The Heart
The heart consists of four chambers, a left and right Atrium as well as a left and right Ventricle. The Tricuspid Valve on the right, and the Bicuspid Valve on the left side, separate the atria from the ventricles. The septum separates the left side of heart from the right side. Semilunar Valves prevent the backflow of blood once pumped out of the ventricles. (See fig. 3.17.)

Fig. 3.17 Heart

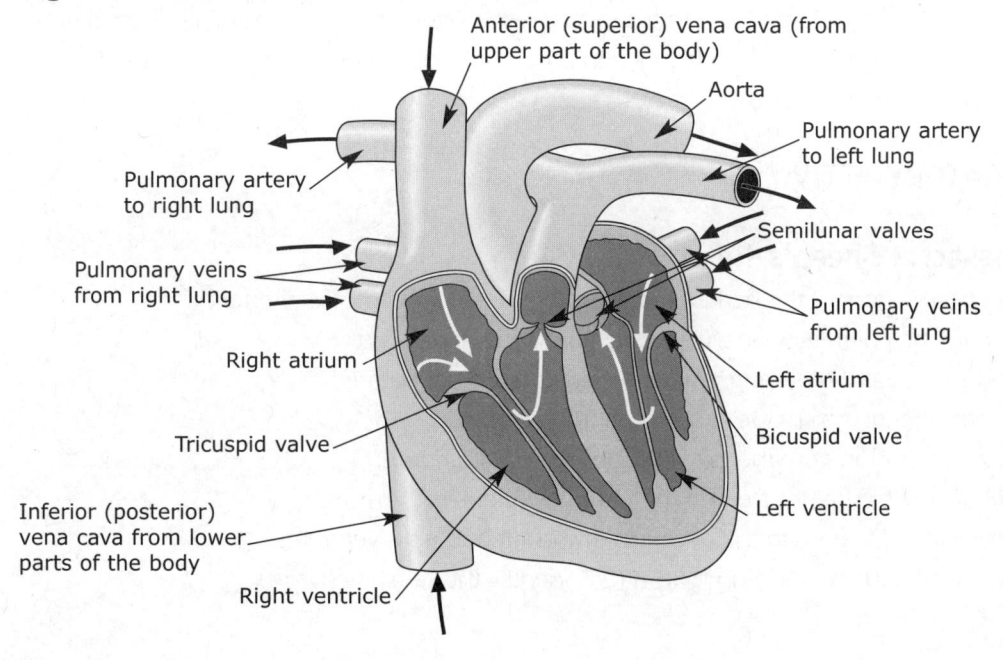

Cardiac Cycle or Heartbeat
The cycle begins with the atria in relaxed mode (Diastole). Blood fills both atria from veins and the AV Valves remain closed. As the pressure rises the AV valves open allowing blood to fill both ventricles. Both atria then contract (Systole). Both ventricles then contract when full closing the AV valves. Blood is pushed out through arteries and the cycle begins again.

Pulse
The pulse is caused by the wave of blood being forced through the arteries when the ventricles contract. It can be felt in the body where arteries are near the skin. Pulse rate is a measure of heartbeat rate. It is often measured at the wrist where the arteries are close to the skin.

Blood Supply to the Heart
Some of the blood leaving the left ventricle is passed to the three **coronary arteries**. These supply the thick heart muscle with blood rich in oxygen and nutrients. Deoxygenated blood is collected by the **coronary veins** which drain into the right atrium.

Control of Heartbeat
The pacemaker or Sino-atrial Node triggers heartbeat. It stimulates both atria to contract simultaneously. This contraction stimulates a second knot of muscle, the AV Node. The impulse is spread along the Bundle of His causing the ventricles to contract.

Factors Affecting the Rate of Heartbeat
Exercise, emotional disturbance and age all affect the rate of heartbeat. Stimulants increase the rate of heartbeat. Example: alcohol and adrenaline. Depressants reduce the rate of heartbeat. Example: sleeping pills.

MANDATORY ACTIVITY

To Dissect a Sheep's Heart
1. Identify the front of the heart by looking for the diagonal coronary arteries.
2. Identify the pulmonary artery and the aorta. The aorta has the thicker wall.
3. Using a scalpel, cut from the right ventricle to the right atrium.
4. Identify the tricuspid valve and the chordae tendinae.
5. Make an incision from the left ventricle to the left atrium.
6. Identify the bicuspid valve and the chordae tendinae.
7. Notice the difference in the thickness of the left and right ventricles.
8. Following each ventricle up to its artery, identify the semilunar valves.

9. Make an outline diagram of the dissected heart showing the location of each part.

MANDATORY ACTIVITY

To Investigate the Effect of Exercise on the Pulse Rate of Humans

1. Measure and record the pulse rate of an individual at rest.
2. Repeat Step 1 twice. Calculate and record the average rate.
3. Get the individual to jog on the spot for one minute.
4. Immediately measure and record the new rate of pulse.
5. Repeat Step 4 twice, recording the rate each time.
6. Compare the results.

Blood Pressure

Blood pressure is a measure of the pressure that the blood is under as it is pumped through the closed system of blood vessels in the body. The higher the pressure the more strain that is experienced by the heart. Blood pressure is controlled by:

(a) the regulation of the rate of heartbeat.
(b) the control of the diameter of arterioles supplying blood to capillaries.

Heart Disease

Three major factors in heart disease are smoking, poor diet and lack of exercise.

Smoking

Smoking can cause heartbeat and blood pressure to increase, straining the heart. Nicotine and Carbon monoxide in cigarette smoke can interfere with heartbeat and may cause the heart to stop beating. Heavy cigarette smoking causes **atherosclerosis**. This is a disease where the arterial walls thicken. Fatty deposits build up forming raised patches on the inside of the arteries. These restrict blood flow and increase the risk of internal blood clotting.

Poor Diet

Large amounts of animal fats in the diet raises the cholesterol levels in the blood. High cholesterol levels cause atherosclerosis. This increases the strain on the heart.

Lack of Exercise

Regular exercise leads to a healthy circulation. It reduces blood pressure by improving blood flow through arterioles. Exercise increases the capacity of the heart to pump blood, which reduces the rate of heartbeat.

Lymphatic System

Blood in capillaries is under pressure and leakage of plasma and its dissolved substances occurs forming extracellular fluid (ECF). All tissue cells are bathed in this fluid and it facilitates the diffusion of materials between the blood and the cells. Excess ECF must be returned to the blood. This occurs by:

(a) draining back into the bloodstream at the venous end of the capillary (lowest pressure).

(b) entering the lymphatic system through small tubes called **lymph capillaries**, (see fig. 3.18).

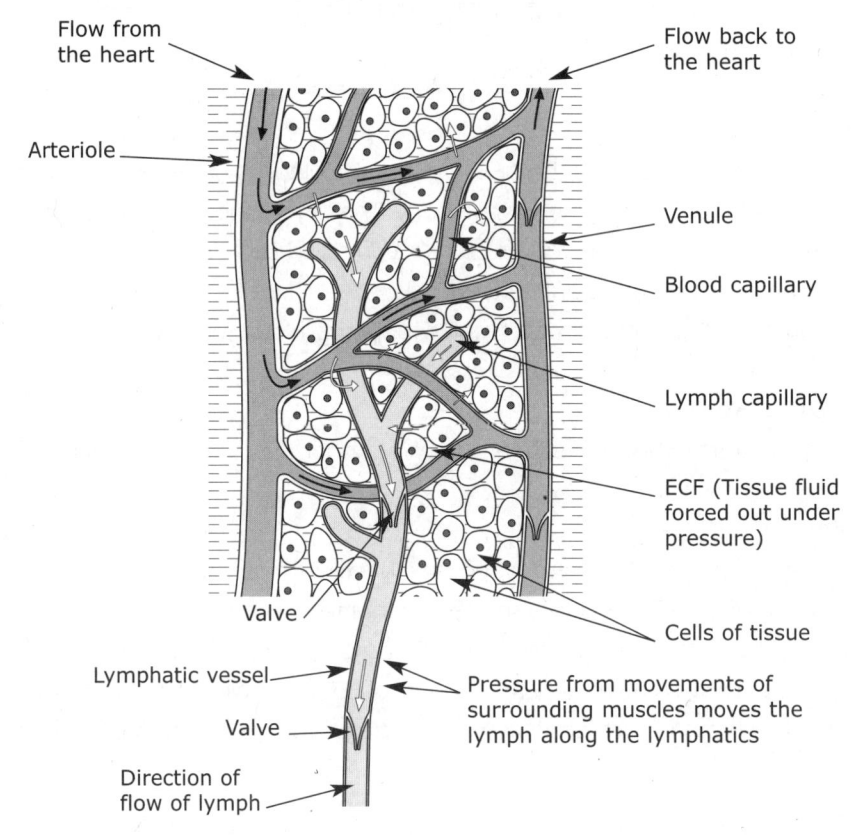

Fig. 3.18 Tissue, Blood and Lymphatic Systems

The fluid that enters these capillaries is called **lymph**. Lymph capillaries drain into larger vessels called **lymphatics**. The lymphatics have valves to prevent the backflow of lymph. Skeletal muscles involved in movement in the body provide the pressure to push lymph along the lymphatics.

The functions of the lymphatic system are to:

(a) Return lost fluids from the blood vessels to the blood.
(b) Detect and fight disease.
(c) Transport digested lipids and fat-soluble vitamins around the body.

Lymph Nodes are swellings along the lymph vessels where the lymph is filtered. They are a source of **lymphocytes** which in turn produce **antibodies** against disease.

3.3 TRANSPORT AND NUTRITION

NUTRITION IN THE FLOWERING PLANT

Nutrition in flowering plants can be considered under three headings:
(a) The uptake and transport of water and minerals.
(b) The absorption and use of carbon dioxide.
(c) The formation and transport of carbohydrates.

The Uptake and Transport of Water and Minerals

Dixon and Joly proposed that the main influence in the transport of water and minerals up the stem is a suction force developed by the transpiration of water vapour through the stomata in the leaves. Their **Cohesion-Tension Model of Xylem Transport** proposed that transpiration draws water up the xylem vessels in the stem. The cohesion forces of water molecules in the narrow xylem vessels are so strong that they can support a column of water up to 80 metres in height. The constant pull from the leaves allows for a constant flow of water from the root hairs across the root to the xylem vessels.

Water enters the roots through **root hairs**. These are tiny extensions of root epidermal cells. The root hairs are adapted to their function by the absence of a cuticle which would prevent the entry of water. The mechanisms by which water is transported across the root to the xylem vessels are:
(a) Osmosis from cell to cell through the cytoplasm and vacuoles of cortex cells. This force, due to osmosis, exerts a push from the root upwards and is known as **root pressure**.
(b) Diffusion through the spaces between cell walls. This pathway is thought to account for up to 90% of water transport across the root.

Minerals

Minerals dissolved in the soil water are transported into the plant along the same pathway as water. Minerals are essential to the manufacture of all the proteins, lipids and carbohydrates necessary for a healthy plant. The **endodermal cells** (endodermis) in the root are surrounded by an impermeable layer called the Casparian strip. All water and minerals must pass through the cytoplasm of the cells at this point. It is thought that the endodermal cells act as a selective barrier that controls the quantity and type of minerals that pass through to the xylem and up to the leaves, (see fig. 3.19).

Fig. 3.19 Transpiration Stream from the Root to the Leaf

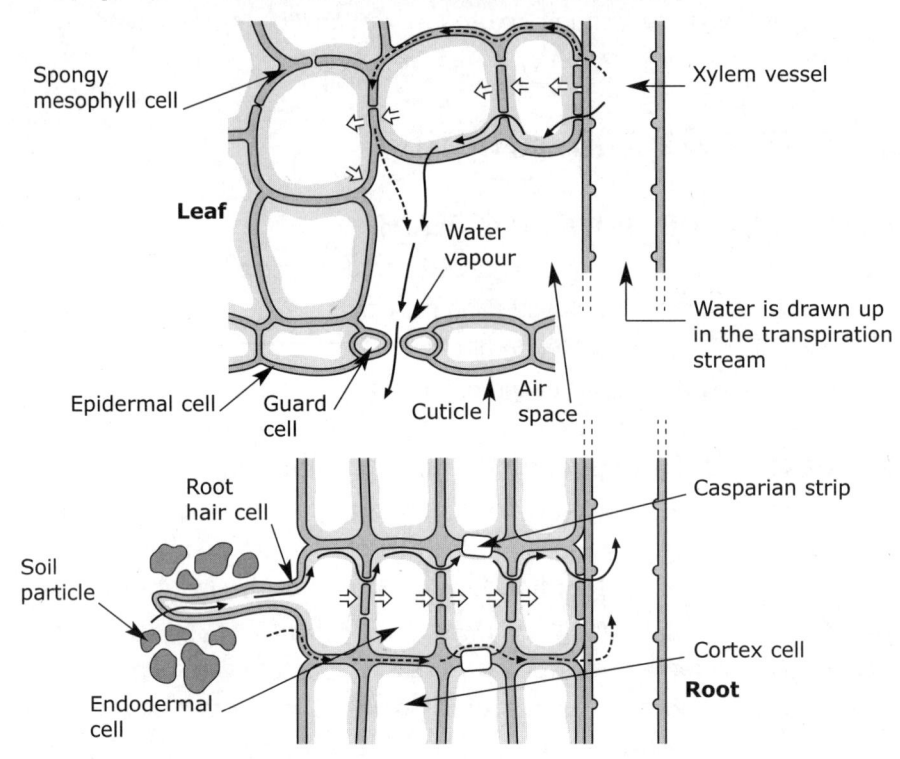

Labels: Spongy mesophyll cell, Xylem vessel, Leaf, Water vapour, Water is drawn up in the transpiration stream, Epidermal cell, Guard cell, Cuticle, Air space, Root hair cell, Casparian strip, Soil particle, Cortex cell, Endodermal cell, Root

The Absorption and Use of Carbon Dioxide

Carbon Dioxide is produced by all cells in the plant through respiration. This can be used for the process of photosynthesis if required. If more CO_2 is necessary, gaseous exchange with the atmosphere must occur. Most gaseous exchange occurs through pores in the leaves called **stomata**. Guard cells control the size of stomata. In general, the stomata are opened wide in daylight when CO_2 is required for photosynthesis, (see fig. 3.20).

Fig. 3.20 Stomata

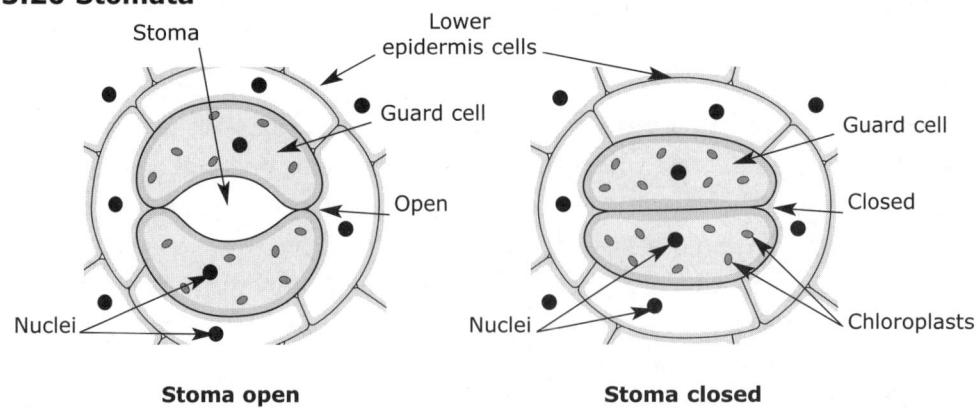

Labels: Stoma, Lower epidermis cells, Guard cell, Open, Guard cell, Closed, Nuclei, Nuclei, Chloroplasts

Stoma open   **Stoma closed**

Stoma and guard cells observed from below the leaf

Formation and Transport of Carbohydrates
Carbohydrate is manufactured in the process of photosynthesis. The transport of carbohydrate around the plant is known as **translocation**. Translocation occurs through the **Phloem sieve tubes** and **companion cells**.

Modified Plant Food Storage Organs
Many plants require the ability to store food from one growing season to the next in order to complete their life cycle. This process is known as **perennation**. Food storage can occur in the modified organs of the root, stem or leaves.

Organ	Modified Structure	Example
Root	Tap Root	Carrot
Stem	Underground stem or Tubers	Potato
Leaf	Bulb	Onion

NUTRITION IN THE HUMAN
Animals have **Heterotrophic nutrition**, i.e. they must capture and consume their food such as plants or other animals. Animals can be classified according to their diet.
(a) **Herbivore**: an animal that feeds on plants only. Examples: Rabbit, Sheep.
(b) **Carnivore**: an animal that feeds on other animals only. Examples: Cat, Hedgehog.
(c) **Omnivore**: an animal that feeds on both plants and animals. Examples: Pig, Human.

Stages of Nutrition
Respiration is a vital process for life and it is carried out in all living cells. Food is essential for respiration and for food to get to all the cells of a multicellular animal it must go through the following stages:
(a) **Ingestion**: The taking in of food to the body through the mouth.
(b) **Digestion**: The mechanical and chemical breakdown of food.
(c) **Absorption**: The products of digestion are passed into the blood for transport. Absorption occurs through the processes of osmosis, diffusion and active transport.
(d) **Assimilation**: The movement of digested food from the blood into the cells.
(e) **Egestion**: The unused, unabsorbed remains of food passed out of the body.

The Digestive System
The Human digestive system consists of a number of organs that:
(a) Mechanically digest food by tearing and crushing food into smaller pieces. Example: mouth and stomach.
(b) Secrete digestive juices to chemically digest and dissolve food. Example: Duodenum.

(c) Provide large vascularised (many blood vessels) surface areas to absorb the products of digestion into the blood. Example: Ileum.
(d) Reabsorb water and concentrate unused remains for Egestion. Example: Large Intestine. (See fig. 3.21.)

Fig. 3.21 Human Alimentary Canal

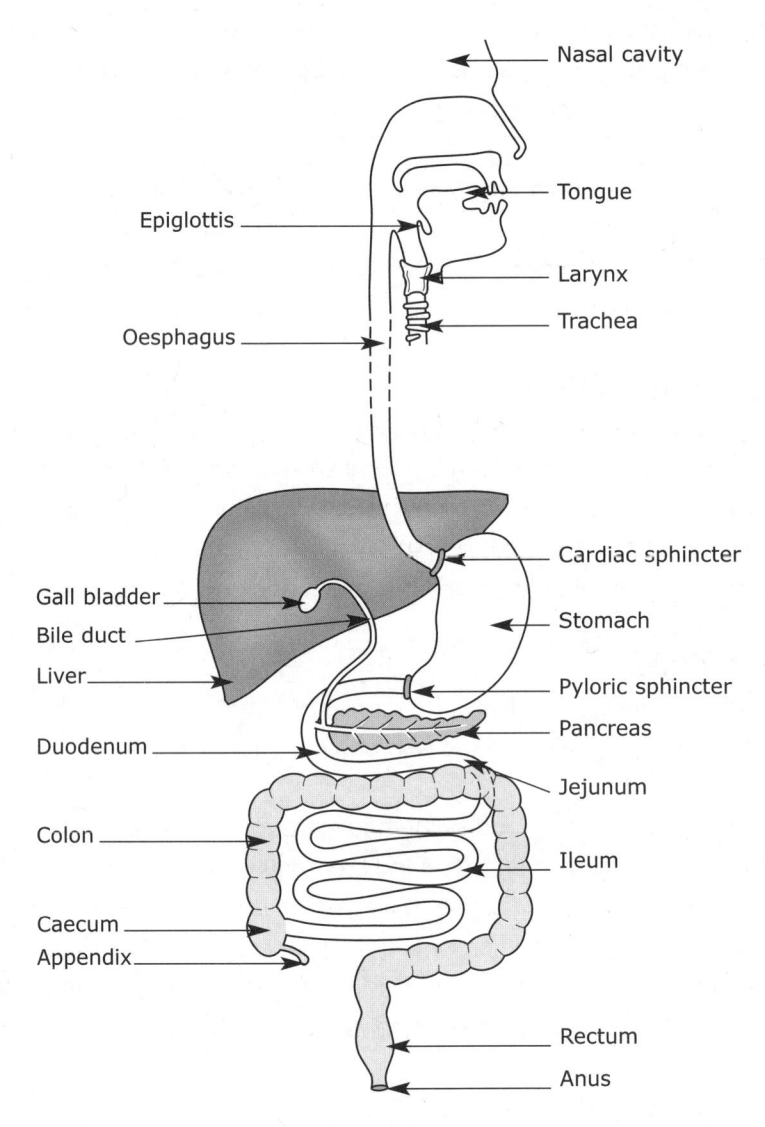

The **Alimentary Canal** is a term used to describe the continuous tube that extends from the mouth to the anus. It consists of the following regions: Mouth, Oesphagus, Stomach, Duodenum, Ileum, Colon, Rectum and Anus. The walls of the alimentary canal contain circular and longitudinal muscles that gradually contract and relax to push food along its length.

> **Peristalsis** is the *involuntary* muscular contractions of the circular and longitudinal muscles that push food through the alimentary canal.

Mechanical digestion begins with the tearing and crushing action of the teeth in the mouth. The process is continued in the stomach where the stomach muscles gradually contract and relax to further crush the food until it has a liquid consistency.
Chemical digestion is carried out by enzymes which break the large food biomolecules down to single units so they can be absorbed into the blood.

Teeth

Teeth play a vital role in mechanical digestion. They crush and tear food, softening it by mixing with saliva. A tooth is a hard structure embedded in the jawbone and adapted to cutting and grinding food.

Dentition

Dentition describes the type and arrangement of teeth in the jaws. The diet of any animal can be determined by an examination of its teeth. Animals can be classified according to their diet.

1. **Herbivore**: an animal that feeds on plants only.
2. **Carnivore**: an animal that feeds on other animals only.
3. **Omnivore**: an animal that feeds on both plants and animals.

There are four different types of teeth which have different locations and functions in the jaw. These are:

Incisors and **canines** at the front of the jaw, used for gripping, cutting and tearing food.
Premolars and **molars** at the back, for crushing and grinding food.

Dental Formula

The dental formula describes the number and type of teeth in one-half of the complete upper and lower jaws.

The human (omnivore) dental formula is given in the table below:

Human	Incisor	Canine	Premolar	Molar
Upper Jaw	2	1	2	3
Lower Jaw	2	1	2	3

Small Intestine

The small intestine is over five metres long. It consists of the duodenum, jejunum and the ileum. The duodenum provides secretions from three sources:

(a) Bile from the gall bladder.
(b) Pancreatic juices from the pancreas.
(c) Digestive juices from the walls of the duodenum.

The ileum is the longest part of the small intestine. The main function of the ileum is the absorption of the products of digestion.

Adaptations of the Small Intestine to Its Functions

(a) It is very long (over 8 m) and its inner lining has finger-like projections called Villi that increase the surface area, (see fig. 3.22).

Fig. 3.22 A Villus and Its Blood Supply

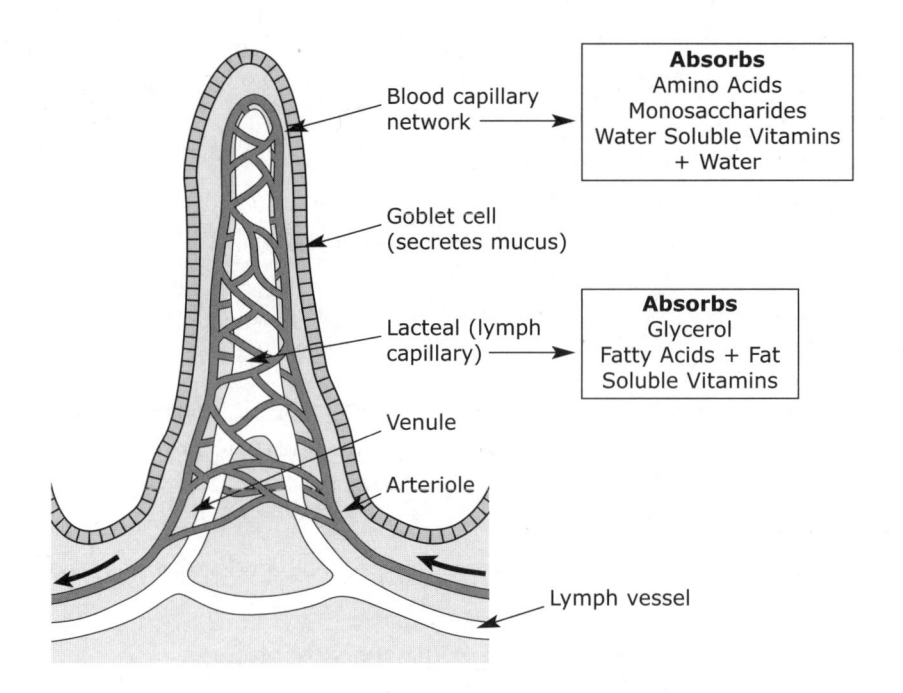

(b) The surface of each villus has smaller projections called microvilli.
(c) The blood capillaries are just below the surface to facilitate absorption.
(d) Cells at the surface have mitochondria providing energy for active transport.
(e) Secretory cells produce large amounts of watery secretions with digestive enzymes.

Examples of Digestive Enzymes and Secretions in the Alimentary Canal

Site of Production	Secretion	Enzyme	Environment pH	Substrate	Products
Salivary Gland (Mouth)	Saliva	Amylase	pH = 8 (Alkaline)	Starch	Maltose
Gastric Gland (Stomach)	Gastric Juice	Pepsin	pH = 1–2 (Acidic)	Protein	Peptides
Pancreatic Glands (Pancreas)	Pancreatic Juice	Lipase	pH = 8 (Alkaline)	Lipids	Fatty Acids + Glycerol
Liver (stored in Gall Bladder)	Bile	Bile Salts Contains no enzymes	pH = 8 (Alkaline)	No substrate It emulsifies Lipids	Smaller droplets of lipids

Large Intestine

The Large Intestine is around 1·5 metres long. It consists of the caecum, appendix, colon and rectum. The remaining mixture of food that enters the large intestine is known as faeces. **Faeces** consists of fibrous plant materials and large amounts of water from the digestive juices. Reabsorption of water from the faeces back into the blood is essential to prevent dehydration.

The large intestine is also a natural habitat for some types of mutualistic bacteria. E. coli is one of the most common resident bacteria in the colon. The bacteria in the colon manufacture some group B vitamins, including Folic Acid and vitamin K.

Adaptations of the Large Intestine to Its Functions

(a) Its length provides increased surface area for absorption.
(b) It is well supplied with blood vessels for reabsorption of valuable materials.
(c) Goblet cells produce large amounts of mucus to ease the passage of faeces along the intestine.

The Liver

The liver is the most active organ in the body. It carries out a number of different functions including:

(a) It is the main storage site for carbohydrates. They are stored in the form of the polysaccharide **Glycogen**. As the body needs energy the liver converts glycogen to glucose and releases it into the blood.
(b) It breaks down excess protein taken in the diet to form **urea**. Urea is released into the blood. The kidney then filters the urea from the blood and uses it to form part of urine.
(c) The liver produces bile.
(d) It breaks down and removes poisons from the blood.

(e) It produces body heat.
(f) It produces the protein **fibrinogen** for blood clotting.

Fibre

Fibre is made up of indigestible cellulose walls of plant material. A diet high in fibre is thought to prevent:
(a) Bowel diseases like cancer.
(b) Obesity.
(c) Coronary heart disease.

3.4 BREATHING SYSTEM AND EXCRETION

Homeostasis

> Animal life is dependent on a constant internal environment. Cells function best in a specific, limited range of conditions. These conditions are both internal and external, in the surrounding fluids of the cells. Homeostasis is the maintenance of these conditions.

Necessity of Homeostasis

Enzymes, which control all metabolic reactions in organisms, are usually very sensitive to factors such as temperature and pH. The regulation of these factors is essential for optimal metabolism in the organism.

In humans, homeostasis is essential for:
(a) Regulation of blood sugar levels.
(b) The control of the concentrations of respiratory gases in the blood.
(c) Regulation of Heartbeat Rate.
(d) Control of the water content in the blood.

One form of homeostasis in plants is the control of gaseous exchange. This occurs by the regulation of the size of the stomata. The guard cells controlling stomatal size are thought to be sensitive to CO_2 concentrations. This allows for the regulation of gaseous exchange to ensure there is sufficient CO_2 for photosynthesis and yet prevent the build up of excess CO_2 when it is not required. **Lenticels** are small pores on the stems of plants that also carry out gaseous exchange. They respond to conditions in a similar manner to stomata.

BREATHING SYSTEM IN THE HUMAN

Breathing is the means by which oxygen is passed from the atmosphere into the blood, and by which Carbon Dioxide and Water are passed from the blood into the atmosphere.

Respiratory System (Breathing System)

The respiratory system consists of:

(a) **The lungs**, which are highly vascular (contain enormous numbers of blood vessels) and contain many **bronchioles**, which end in microscopic air sacs called **alveoli**.

(b) **The air passages** are in the following sequence: mouth + nasal passages, pharynx, larynx, trachea, bronchi, bronchioles and alveoli.

(c) **Breathing muscles**:
   1. The **Intercostal Muscles** join most of the ribs to one another so that a sheet of muscle covers the rib cage.
   2. The **Diaphragm Muscles** form a seal under the lungs separating them from the rest of the lower body organs. (See fig. 3.23.)

Fig. 3.23 Respiratory System

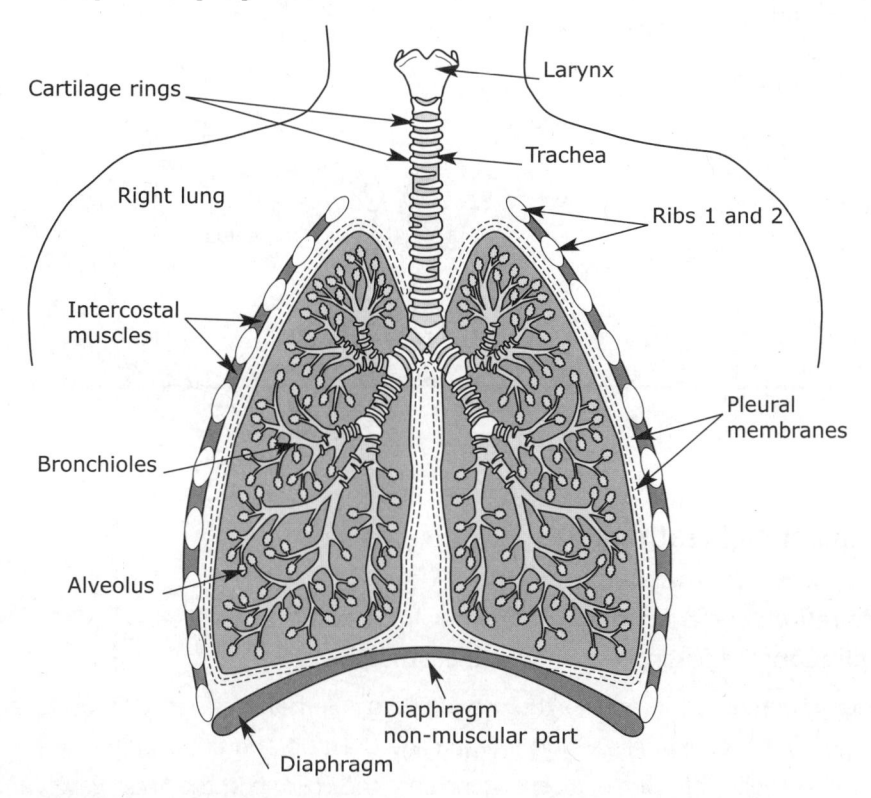

Gaseous Exchange in Humans

This is the movement of oxygen from the air into the blood and the movement of carbon dioxide from the blood into the air. It occurs in the **alveoli** of the lungs. Gaseous exchange occurs by **diffusion**, (see fig. 3.24).

Fig. 3.24 Alveoli and Gaseous Exchange

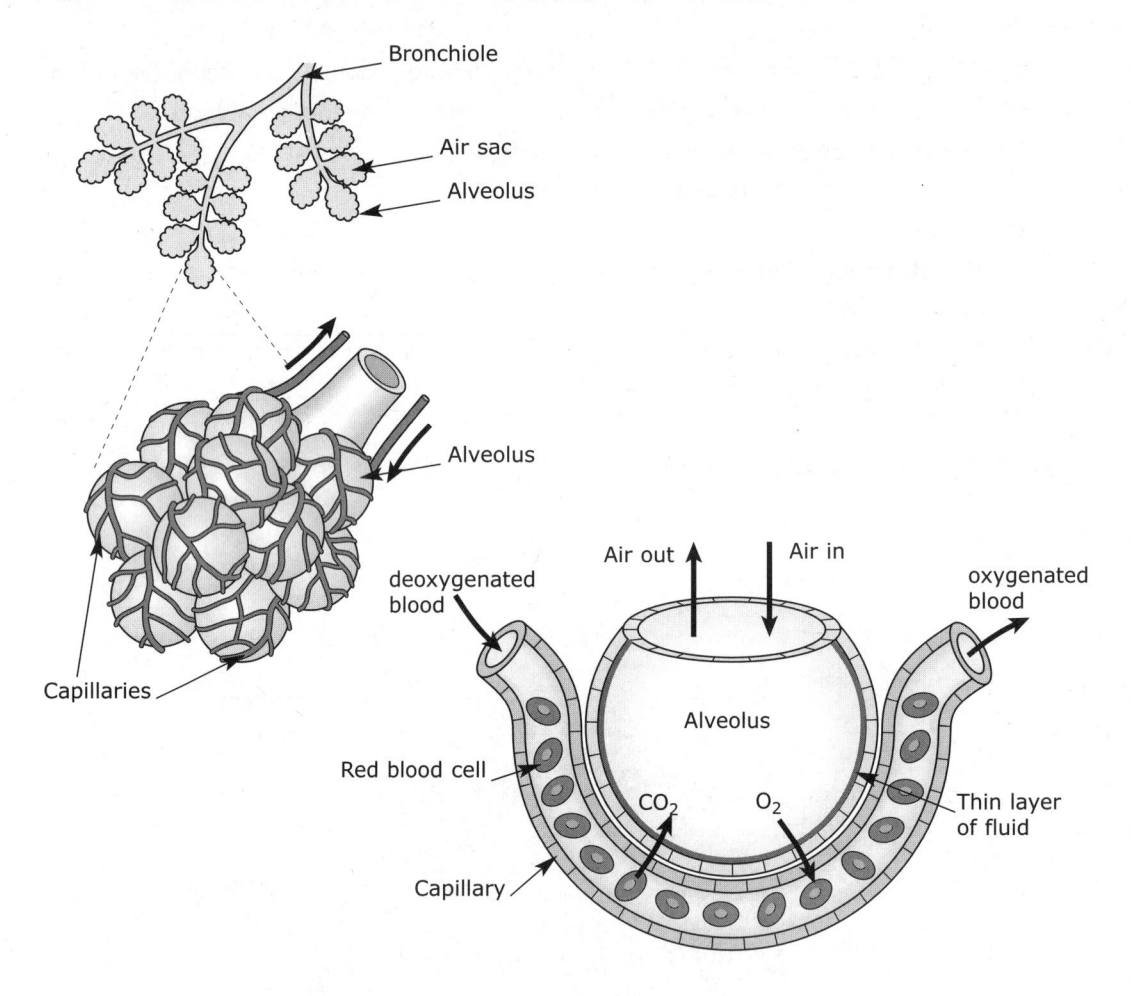

Mechanism of Breathing

Breathing occurs in two stages:

(a) **Inspiration**: the taking in of air from the atmosphere.

(b) **Expiration**: the passing out of air to the atmosphere.

Inspiration is **active**, i.e. it requires the use of energy. Both the Intercostal muscles and the Diaphragm muscles contract causing the rib cage to lift up and out and, the diaphragm to flatten, respectively. Both of these actions increase the volume of the chest cavity and air flows into the lungs.

Expiration is **passive**, i.e. it does not require the use of energy (unless the body undergoes strenuous exercise). The Intercostal muscles relax lowering the ribs, and the Diaphragm muscles relax allowing the Diaphragm to rise up. Both actions cause the volume of the chest to decrease, forcing air out.

Breathing Disorders

Asthma is most commonly caused by an allergic reaction of specialised cells in the lower air passages. These mast cells release chemicals causing the bronchioles to constrict, and fluid and mucus to accumulate in the alveoli. This results in coughing and wheezing.

Causes: Allergens that cause asthma include pollen, fur and house dust. To prevent or reduce the incidence of asthma, it is important to limit exposure to these factors as much as possible.

Treatments: Treatment for asthma can be as simple as reassurance, as anxiety often worsens the effects. Two common medications to ease the symptoms are:
(a) Bronchodilators which cause the bronchioles to dilate.
(b) Steroids which reduce the inflammation.

Control of Breathing

Although we can consciously control breathing it is usually controlled by an unconscious part of the brain the **Medulla Oblongata**. Firstly, when we exercise, the amount of carbon dioxide in the blood increases, due to respiration. Secondly, due to the lack of oxygen, respiration becomes **Anaerobic** producing **lactic acid**. These two substances cause the blood to become more acidic (lowers the pH) and the Medulla Oblongata responds to this acidity by sending nerve impulses to the Diaphragm and Intercostal muscles causing them to contract and relax more quickly and deeply.

THE EXCRETORY SYSTEM IN HUMANS

> **Excretion** is the removal of the waste products of metabolism from the body.

There are three main organs of excretion:
(a) The **Lungs**: excrete CO_2 and H_2O.
(b) The **Kidneys**: excrete urea, uric acid, excess water and salts.
(c) The **Skin**: excretes salts, water and uric acid.

Urinary System

The urinary system consists of two kidneys and their blood vessels, two ureters, the bladder and the urethra, (see fig. 3.25).

Fig. 3.25 Urinary System

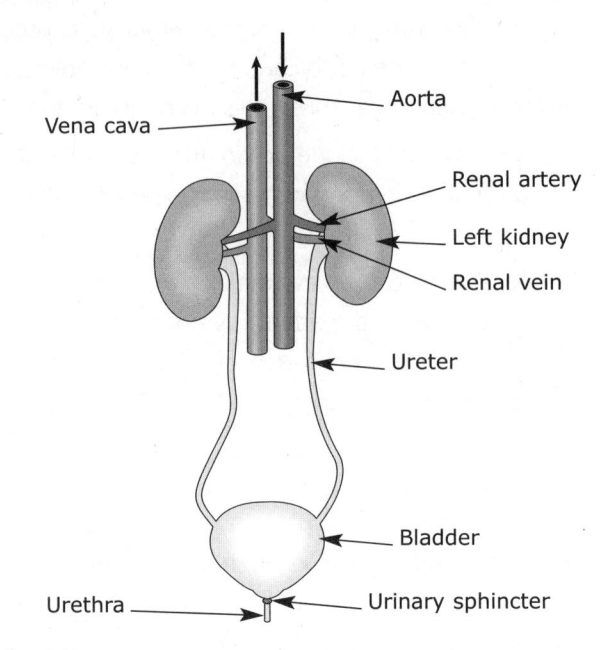

The kidneys have two functions:
1. Excretion.
2. Osmoregulation.

Excretion

The kidneys produce urine which is excreted from the body. Urine consists of urea, excess water and excess salts. A vertical section (V.S.) through the kidney is shown in fig. 3.26.

Fig. 3.26 Vertical Section of Kidney

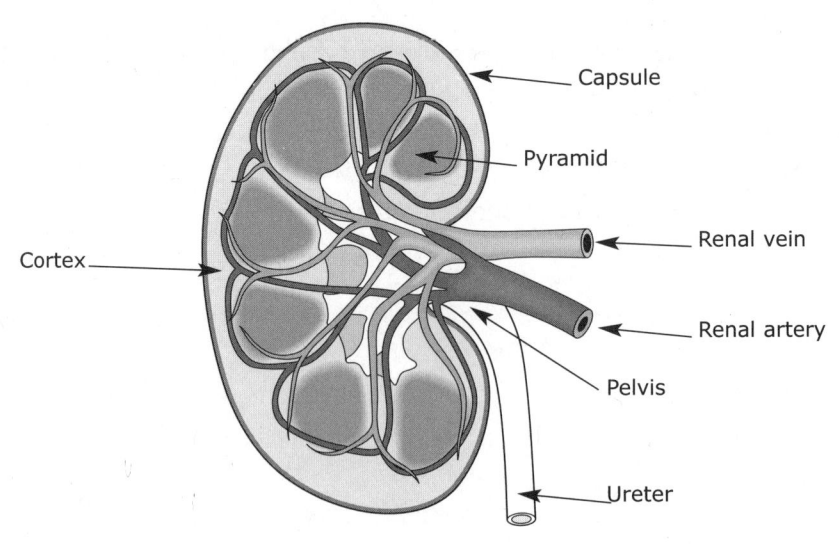

Formation of Urine

Each kidney is made up of millions of filtration units called **Nephrons**, (see fig. 3.27).

Fig. 3.27 Structure of the Nephron

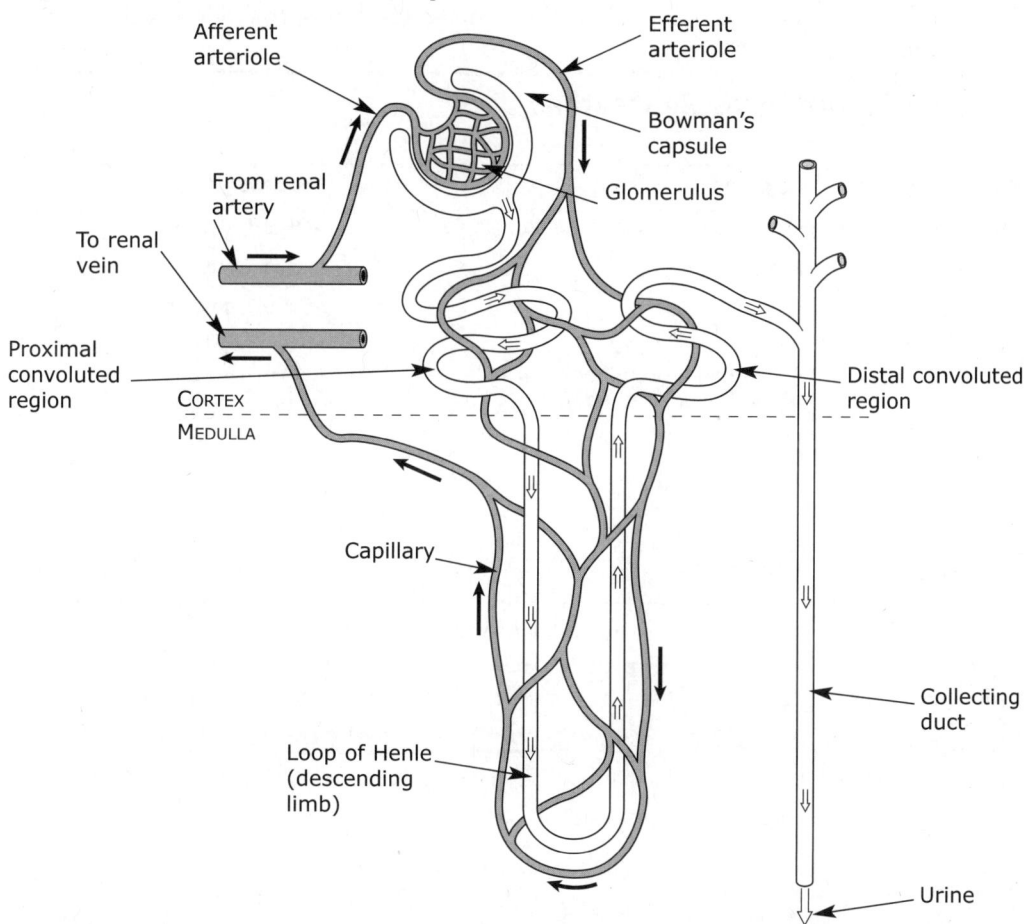

The nephrons are responsible for the formation of urine. The blood in the glomerulus undergoes a process of **ultra filtration** which forces fluid out of the blood into the Bowman's capsule. This fluid does not contain any blood cells or blood proteins as they are too large to leave the glomerulus. The fluid is known as the **glomerular filtrate**. It contains many small molecules that were dissolved in the plasma of the blood. Wastes in the glomerular filtrate include excess salts and excess water, urea and uric acid. Some of the substances that leave the blood are very valuable to the body. These are called **high threshold** substances and would include glucose, amino acids, vitamins, minerals (ions) and water. As the glomerular filtrate flows through the nephron, high threshold substances are **reabsorbed** back into the blood. Reabsorption occurs by diffusion, osmosis and active transport.

> **Reabsorption** is the process where high threshold substances are taken from the glomerular filtrate and returned to the blood. It can only occur by osmosis, diffusion and active transport.
>
> **Secretion** is the process where substances are passed from the kidney cells into the glomerular filtrate, e.g. some ions (H^+) are secreted from the kidney cells into the glomerular filtrate.

Summary of Substances Reabsorbed

Substance	Region	Process
Glucose	Proximal Convoluted Region (PCR)	Active Transport
Amino Acids	PCR	Active Transport
Vitamins	PCR	Active Transport
Salts	PCR	Active Transport
Na^+ and Cl^-	Ascending limb of Loop of Henle	Active Transport
Na^+ and Cl^-	Distal Convoluted Region	Active Transport
Water	PCR	Osmosis
	Loop of Henle	Osmosis
	Collecting Duct	Osmosis

Osmoregulation

> Osmoregulation is the control of the salt-water balance in the body.

Osmoregulation is vital to keep the internal environment in the body constant. Too much water in the blood would lead to cells absorbing excess water by osmosis. Too little water or too much salt in the blood would lead to excess loss of water from the cells by osmosis. Either condition would destroy the cells' ability to function.

ADH

Diuresis is the production of excess watery urine. The Antidiuretic hormone (ADH) prevents the production of large amounts of watery urine. If there is too little water (or too much salt) in the blood the **pituitary gland** produces more ADH. It causes the **collecting ducts** of the nephrons to become more permeable, so more water can be reabsorbed from the urine back into the blood before it leaves the kidneys.

3.5 RESPONSES TO STIMULI

RESPONSES IN THE FLOWERING PLANT

> A **Tropism** is the response of a plant to an external stimulus.

There are different types of Tropisms:
(a) Phototropism is the response to Light.
(b) Geotropism is the response to Gravity.
(c) Hydrotropism is the response to Water.
(d) Thigmotropism is the response to Touch.
(e) Chemotropism is the response to Chemicals.

Phototropism is the response of a plant to light. The Shoots of plants are positively phototropic. If exposed to unilateral light the shoot always grows towards it. This ensures the plant leaves have maximum light for photosynthesis. Roots are negatively phototropic. The root response is to grow away from unilateral light. This response causes the root to grow down into the soil. This will provide anchorage and a source of minerals and water.

Geotropism is the response of a plant to gravity. Roots are positively geotropic while shoots are negatively geotropic.

GROWTH REGULATORS

> A growth regulator is a chemical produced in the growing tips (meristematic cells) of plants. The chemical is then transported from cell to cell by active transport to the site of response where growth is modified.

Auxin (IAA) is one growth regulator thought to play a significant role in phototropism. The process of phototropism is thought to occur as follows:
(a) If a plant is exposed to unilateral light, auxin is produced in the growing tips and is transported down the stem.
(b) Lateral movement of the auxin occurs from the illuminated side to the shaded side.
(c) The increased concentration of auxin causes cell elongation on the shaded side.
(d) Light on the illuminated side causes any auxin present to degenerate and become inactive. See fig. 3.28.

Fig. 3.28 Phototropism

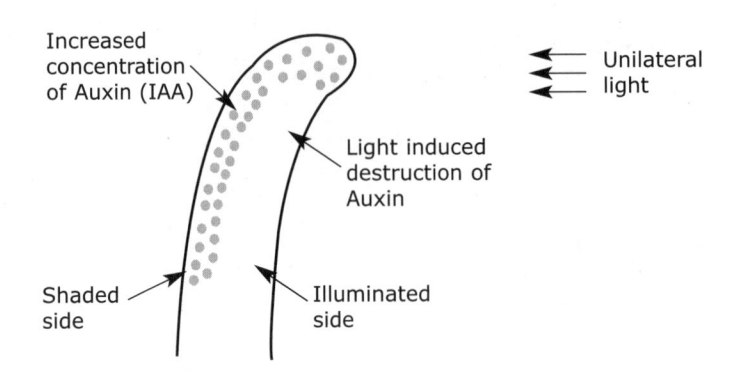

Increased concentration of Auxin (IAA)

Unilateral light

Light induced destruction of Auxin

Shaded side

Illuminated side

Note: **Growth Inhibitors** are thought to play a role in geotropism at least. Abscisic Acid is an inhibitor which has been detected in shoots responding to gravity.

Uses of Growth Regulators in Industry

Growth Regulator	Effects	Applications
Auxin (IAA)	(a) **In Stems:** promotes Cell enlargement, Cell division.	(a) Speeds up primary and secondary growth in plants.
	(b) **In Roots:** promotes root development in low concentrations.	(b) Used as rooting powders for plant cuttings.
Gibberellins	(a) **In Stems:** promote elongation between nodes.	
	(b) **In Seeds:** promote germination.	(b) Used to promote the malting of barley.

MANDATORY ACTIVITY

To Investigate the Effect of IAA Growth Regulator on Plant Tissue

1. Five solutions of IAA in distilled water are set up as shown in the table below.
2. Place a sheet of filter paper in each of 5 petri dishes.
3. Label each of the dishes A, B, C, D and Control.
4. Pour 5 ml of each solution into the corresponding petri dish.
5. Place 10 Cress seeds into each dish.
6. Place the lids on the petri dishes and leave for three days at 20°C.
7. Measure the lengths of the roots on each of the 10 seedlings in each dish and calculate an average.
8. Record the results.

Solution	Conc. of IAA (mg/litre)
A	100
B	1
C	0·01
D	0·000001
Control	0

RESPONSES IN HUMANS

There are two systems of sensitivity in animals:

(a) **Nervous System.**

(b) **Endocrine System.**

Nervous System

The Nervous system consists of:

1. **Central Nervous System (CNS)**: the brain and spinal cord.
2. **Peripheral Nervous System (PNS)**: all the nerves attached to the central nervous system.

Central Nervous System

The **brain** consists of two hemispheres. The larger parts include a cerebrum, cerebellum and a medulla oblongata. The main parts of the brain are listed below, (also see fig. 3.29).

Fig. 3.29 Human Brain

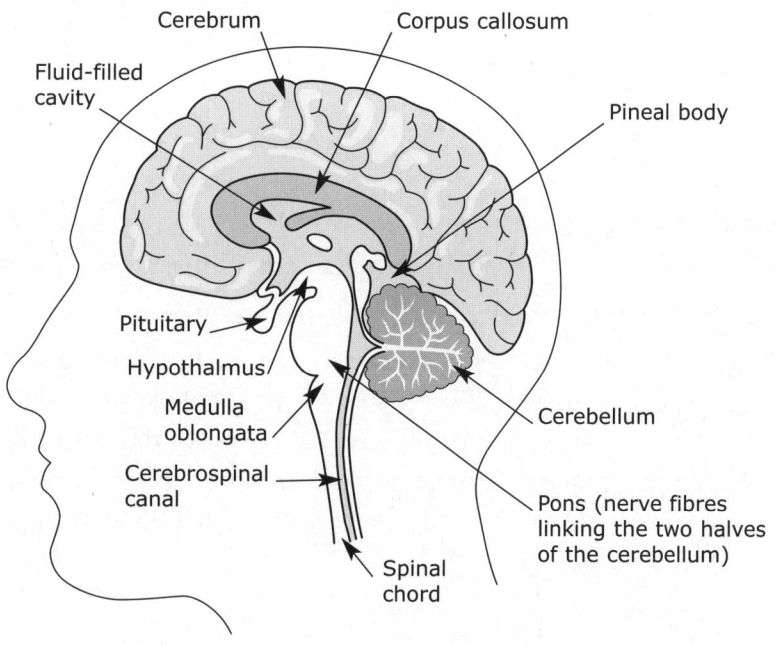

(a) **Cerebrum**: carries out conscious thought processes and voluntary actions.
(b) **Cerebellum**: controls balance and muscle coordination.
(c) **Medulla oblongata**: controls breathing and heartbeat.
(d) The **Hypothalamus** is mainly concerned with homeostasis, i.e. the maintenance of a constant internal environment. It monitors levels of sugars and hormones in the blood.
(e) The **Pituitary gland** controls the secretions of most endocrine glands in the body.

The **spinal cord** extends down through the vertebral column of the back. Pairs of peripheral nerves are attached to the spinal cord along its length, (see fig. 3.30). The spinal cord has two main areas:

(a) White matter, on the outside, which is made up of nerve fibres. Nerve fibres carrying impulses away from the body are axons. Fibres carrying impulses into the body are dendrons.
(b) Grey matter, on the inside, consists mainly of cell bodies.

Fig. 3.30 Spinal Cord

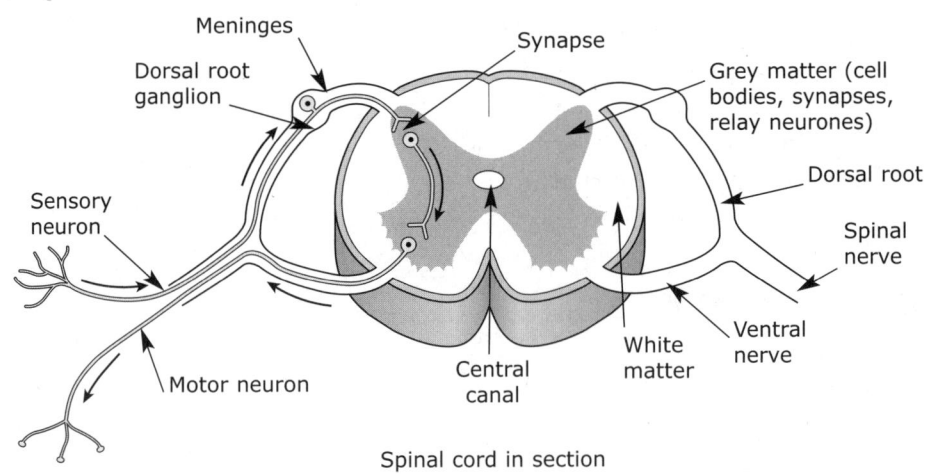

Spinal cord in section

Reflex Action (Arc)

A reflex action is an automatic response to a stimulus that does not involve the brain.

Function: It provides a quicker response to protect the body.

Example: If our hand touched an object that was too hot, a message is immediately sent along a sensory neuron to the spinal cord. At the spinal cord the message splits in two. One message begins to travel up the spinal cord to the brain. The second message travels directly out along a motor neuron to muscles in the arm causing them to contract, pulling the arm away. When the message travelling up the spinal cord reaches the brain we feel the sensation of pain, (see fig. 3.31).

Fig. 3.31 Reflex Action

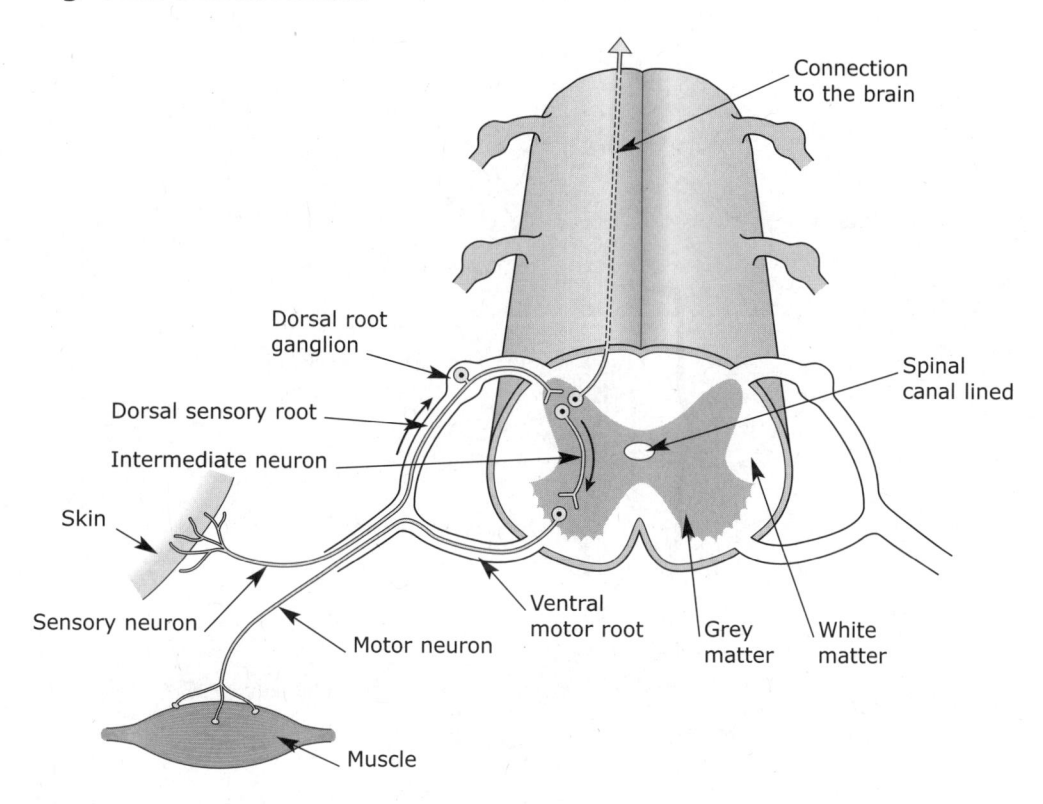

Nerve Cells (Neurons)

There are two main types of nerve cells:

1. **Sensory neurons** that bring messages from sense receptors in the body into the CNS, (see fig. 3.32(a)).

Fig. 3.32(a) Sensory Neuron

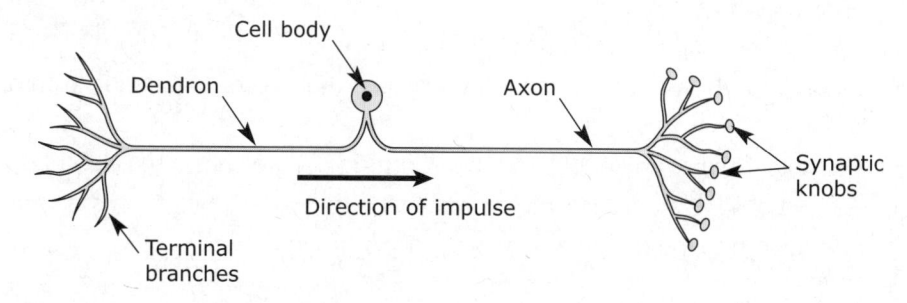

2. **Motor neurons** that bring messages from the CNS out to effectors in the body, (see fig. 3.32(b)).

Fig. 3.32(b) Motor Neuron

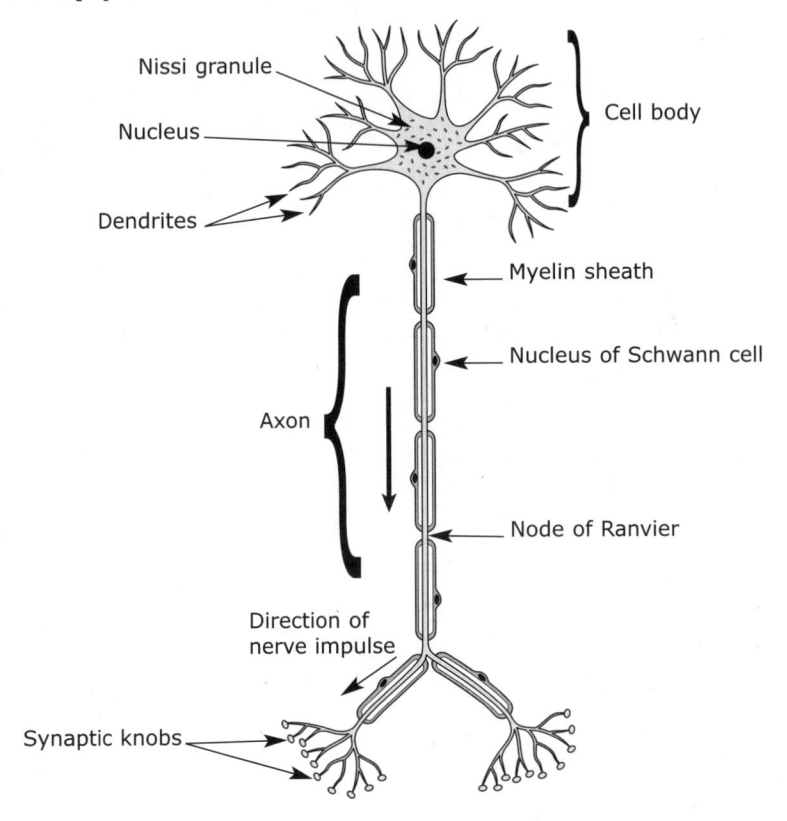

Diagram labels: Nissi granule, Nucleus, Dendrites, Cell body, Myelin sheath, Nucleus of Schwann cell, Axon, Node of Ranvier, Direction of nerve impulse, Synaptic knobs

Note: A third type of neuron, known as an **inter neuron**, is located in the spinal cord and acts as a link between a sensory neuron and a motor neuron in some reflex arcs.

Functions of Neuron Organelles

(a) Myelin sheath: increases the speed of nerve impulse.
(b) Schwann cell: secretes the myelin sheath which provides a faster rate of impulse transmission.
(c) Axon: carries impulses away from the cell body.
(d) Synaptic Knob: secretes a chemical transmitter that passes an impulse from one neuron to the next.
(e) Dendrite: initiates an impulse in a neuron sending it towards the cell body.
(f) Acetylcholine: is a chemical messenger that passes an impulse from the synaptic knob of one neuron to the dendrite of another across a synapse.

Movement of Nerve Impulse

The transmission of an impulse through a neuron is **electrical**. Movement of electrically charged atoms (Ions) from the inside to the outside of the cell membranes causes the impulse to flow along the length of the neuron.

Transmission of an impulse from one neuron to another is **chemical**. Neurotransmitter vesicles at the synaptic knobs release chemical messengers across the space between the neurons known as the synapse. Examples of neurotransmitters are Acetylcholine (ACH) and Dopamine. The neurotransmitters diffuse rapidly across the synapse to receptors on the next neuron. Once the receptor is activated, the impulse begins, and the neurotransmitter becomes inactive. This inactive form diffuses back across the synapse to the synaptic knob for reuse, (see fig. 3.33).

Fig. 3.33 Synapse

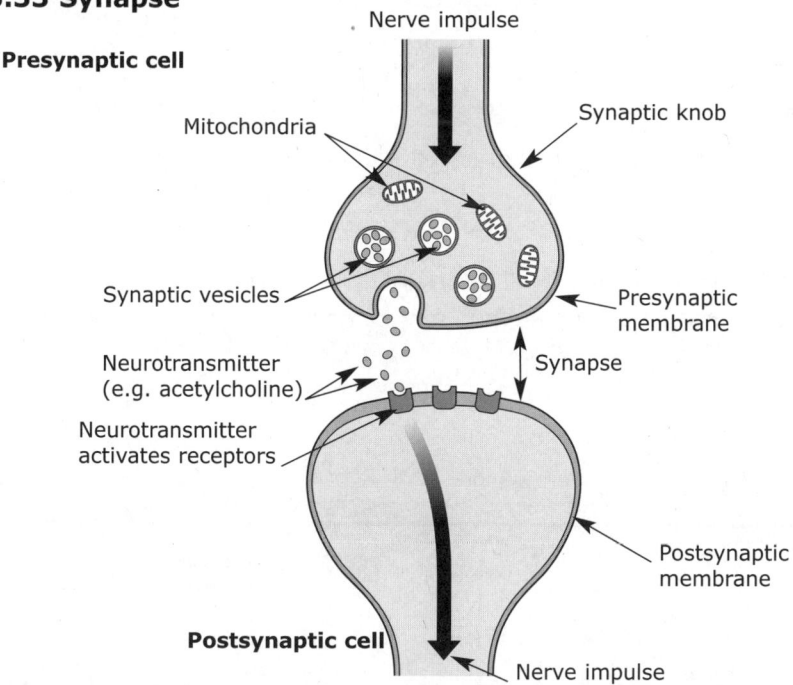

Synapse: is a space between two neurons that are linked by chemical messengers. It allows for:
(a) Impulses to be passed from one neuron to a number of neurons.
(b) The protection of the response system from overstimulation, i.e. the supply of chemical messenger can be temporarily exhausted, ending the trasmission of the impulse.

Parkinson's Disease

This is a neurodegenerative disease that affects voluntary control of muscles in the body.

Symptoms: It normally develops late in life and leads to progressive muscle stiffness, tremors and slowness of movement. In later stages of the disease a general loss of motor coordination occurs.

Causes: Some parts of the brain (Substantia Nigra) do not produce sufficient amounts of the neurotransmitter dopamine. Dopamine is responsible for the stimulation of motor neurons. When dopamine production is depleted, the motor neurons are unable to control movement and coordination.

Treatment and Prevention: There is no known cure for Parkinson's disease at present. Two possible treatments are being investigated:

(a) Dopamine cannot be given to a patient directly, as it cannot pass the blood-brain barrier. The drug Levodopa can, and it is converted to dopamine in the brain. Unfortunately, high concentrations of Levodopa can have harmful side effects.

(b) Stem cell research is exploring the possibility of replacing damaged cells with newly developed nerve cells.

Sense Organs

The three main sense organs are the eye, the ear and the skin.

Eye

The eye is sensitive to light. Images of reflected light from objects are focused on light sensitive cells in the retina. Messages are then sent to the brain to create the sense of sight, (see fig. 3.34).

Fig. 3.34 Eye

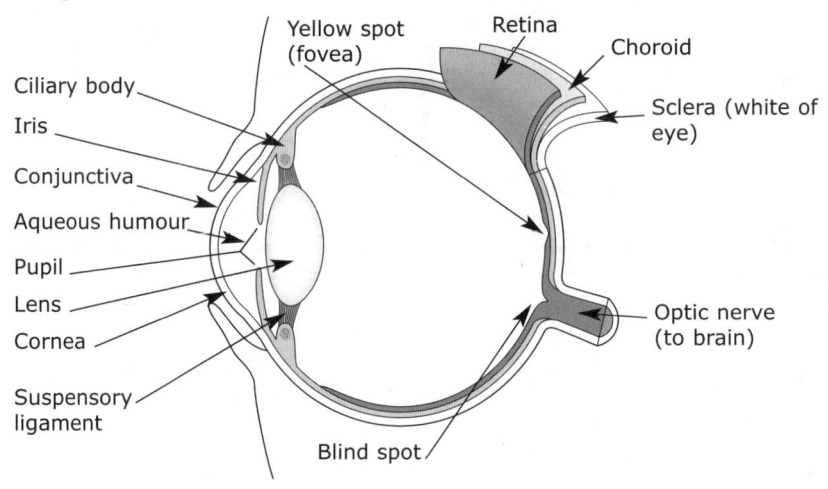

Lens: focuses light onto the retina.

Cornea: protects the front of the eye and allows light to enter.

Iris: controls the amount of light entering the eye.

Choroid: supplies blood to the eye.

Sclera: protects the eye.

Retina: is light sensitive. There are two types of light-sensitive cells in the eye, Rods and Cones.
(a) Rods are not sensitive to colour and are used in poor light conditions.
(b) Cones are sensitive to colour and are used during the day.

Accommodation

> Accommodation is the changing of the shape of the lens to focus light onto the retina.

The ciliary muscle (body) is a circular muscle around the lens. When viewing distant objects the ciliary body relaxes and stretches the lens. When looking at near objects the ciliary body contracts allowing the lens to become thicker.

Eye Defects
There are two main eye defects:
(a) Myopia (Short sight).
(b) Hyperopia (Long sight).

Myopia
Myopia is a condition where an individual can see close objects clearly, but distant objects are blurred. Myopia occurs when the lens focuses the image in front of the retina, resulting in a blurred image when the light strikes the retina. Myopia can be corrected using a **concave** lens, (see fig. 3.35).

Fig. 3.35 Myopia

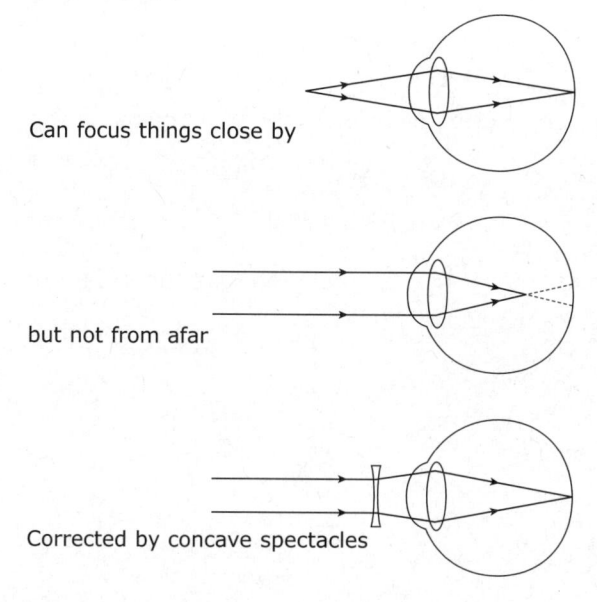

Can focus things close by

but not from afar

Corrected by concave spectacles

Hyperopia

Hyperopia is a condition where an individual can see distant objects clearly, but close objects are blurred. Hyperopia occurs when the lens focuses the image behind the retina, resulting in a blurred image when the light strikes the retina. Hyperopia can be corrected using a **convex** lens, (see fig. 3.36).

Fig. 3.36 Hyperopia

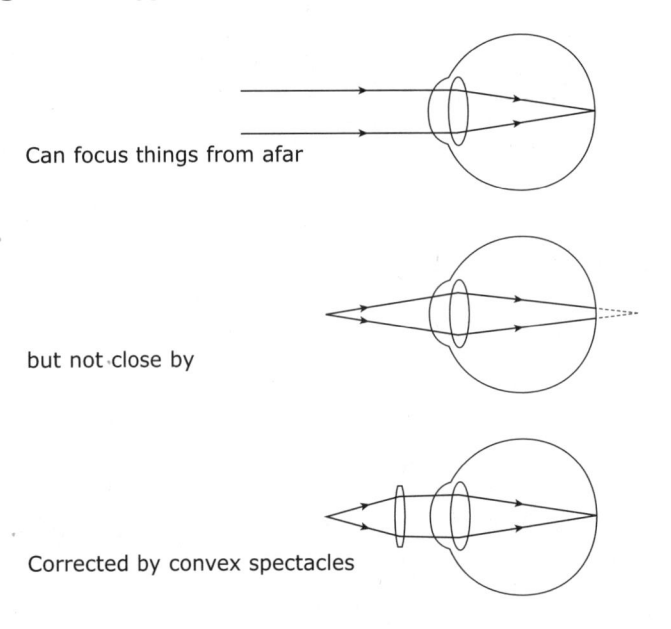

Can focus things from afar

but not close by

Corrected by convex spectacles

Binocular Vision

Humans have two eyes at the front of the head providing binocular vision. Because the eyes are separated each one provides a slightly different view of any object being observed. The views from different angles provide enough information for the brain to develop a three dimensional (3-D) image of the object. The 3-D image provides the sense of depth and distance.

Ear

The ear is concerned with both hearing and balance. The **cochlea** is responsible for hearing and the **semicircular canals** for balance, (see fig. 3.37).

Fig. 3.37 The Ear

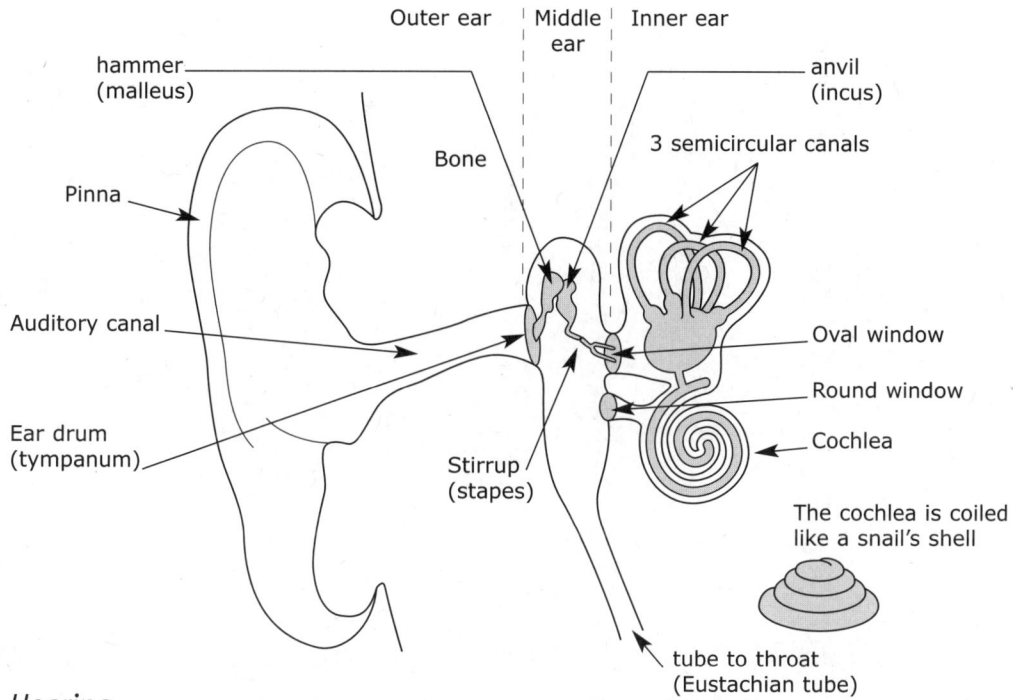

Outer ear | Middle ear | Inner ear

- hammer (malleus)
- anvil (incus)
- Bone
- 3 semicircular canals
- Pinna
- Auditory canal
- Oval window
- Round window
- Ear drum (tympanum)
- Stirrup (stapes)
- Cochlea
- The cochlea is coiled like a snail's shell
- tube to throat (Eustachian tube)

Hearing

Sound is funnelled into the ear by the pinna. It causes the tympanum (eardrum) to vibrate. This movement is magnified by the three ossicles (bones), the malleus, incus and stapes. The stapes vibrates against a membrane called the fenestra ovalis. These movements in turn cause the fluids, perilymph and endolymph, to vibrate inside the cochlea. The vibrations stimulate sensory nerve cells which send impulses to the brain along the auditory nerve.

Balance

Movements of the fluid, endolymph, in the Semicircular canals of the inner ear are responsible for the sense of balance. Movement of the head in any particular direction will cause the movement of endolymph in one or more of the canals. Sensory neurons, sensitive to this movement, are located in the ampullae of the semicircular canals. Impulses are then passed to the brain by the Auditory nerve.

Skin

The skin acts as:
(a) An excretory organ.
(b) A heat regulating organ.
(c) A sense organ. See fig. 3.38.

Fig. 3.38 The Skin

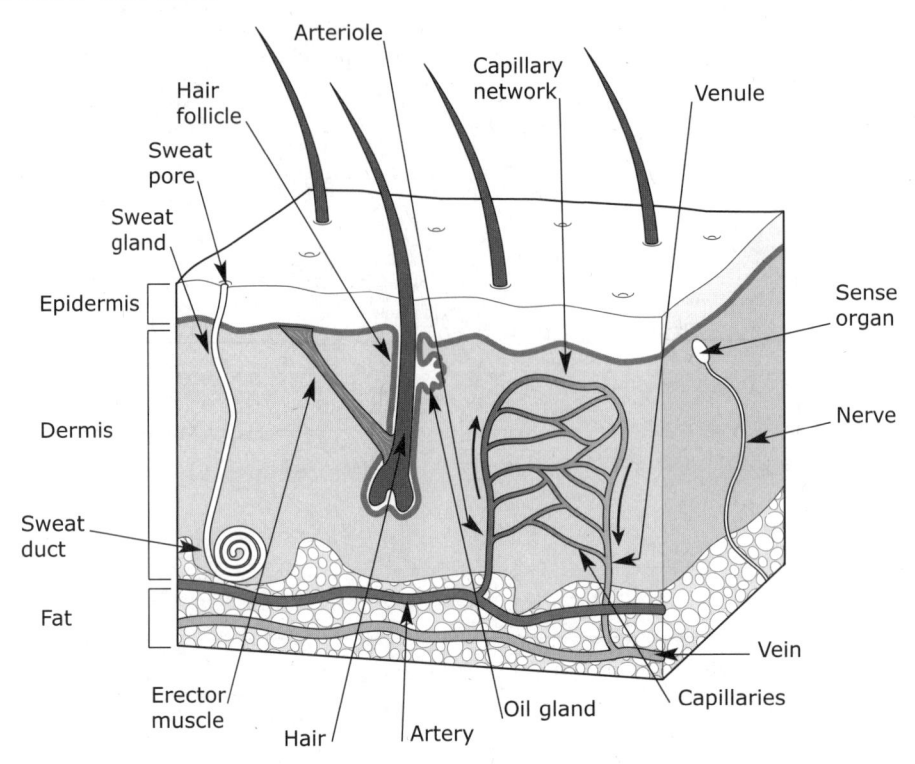

Heat Regulation

When the body is too cold arterioles near the skin surface contract keeping blood away from the surface, reducing heat loss. The skin whitens. Also, erector muscles contract causing the hairs to stand up and trap a layer of air to act as an insulator.

If the body is too warm arterioles widen to allow blood nearer the skin surface. This increases the rate of heat loss from the blood. The skin reddens. The sweat glands release sweat. As the sweat evaporates it carries away heat energy from the body.

Endocrine System

The Endocrine System is a system of coordination in Mammals. It consists of **ductless glands** that produce **chemical messengers** called hormones. Hormones are transported in the **blood** to a **specific target** where they produce a specific effect(s).

> A **Hormone** is a chemical messenger produced in small amounts by an Endocrine Gland. It is transported in the blood to a particular site causing a specific effect.

Endocrine and Exocrine Glands

Endocrine glands are ductless glands that release their cellular secretions (hormones) directly into blood capillaries.

Exocrine glands release their cellular secretions into a collecting duct before their release. Sweat and Salivary glands are examples of exocrine glands.

Summary of Endocrine Glands in the Human

Gland	Location	Hormone	Function
Thyroid	Around larynx	Thyroxine	Controls metabolic rate of body cells
Parathyroids	Behind thyroid	Parathyroid hormone	Controls Calcium levels in the body
Adrenal	Above kidneys	Adrenaline	Prepares the body for high physical performance
Islets of Langerhans	In the pancreas	Insulin	Lowers blood glucose levels
Ovaries	Lower abdomen	(a) Oestrogen (b) Progesterone	Builds up lining of uterus Causes ovulation
Testes	Scrotum	Testosterone	Secondary sexual characteristics
Pituitary	Below forebrain	Somatotrophin	Stimulates body growth

Insulin

A lack of insulin causes the blood glucose level to rise because the glucose cannot be converted to glycogen. If the amount of glucose in the blood rises above a certain level the kidneys cannot reabsorb it all. The excess glucose is excreted in the urine. This is known as **hyperglycaemia** and causes the disease **diabetes mellitus**. This is commonly known as insulin dependent diabetes.

Symptoms: Lack of energy, persistent thirst and sometimes dizziness.

Treatment: This involves a carefully balanced diet related to physical activities to reduce insulin dependence. In many cases the individual injects monitored quantities of insulin directly into the blood. This acts as a supplement to provide the correct dosage necessary to maintain a healthy balance of blood glucose.

Note: Too much insulin in the blood causes a fall in blood glucose levels and can lead to **hypoglycaemia**.

Symptoms: Unconsciousness. In severe cases coma and death can occur.

Hormone Supplements

Menopause occurs in most females between the ages of 45 and 55 years. It results in the lowering of oestrogen and progesterone levels in the body. The effects of these hormonal changes are hot flushes, depression, anxiety, and a significant decrease in bone density. This decrease in bone density can lead to a serious condition known as osteoporosis. **Hormone Replacement Therapy (HRT)** can reduce the effects of menopause. It involves the taking of supplementary doses of oestrogen and progesterone.

HRT is not suitable for all individuals. Recent research has linked HRT with incidences of breast cancer in some females.

Erythropoietin (EPO)

EPO is a naturally occurring hormone produced in the kidneys to regulate red blood cell formation in bone marrow. The illegal use of supplementary EPO is known to occur in total body endurance sports such as road cycling and distance running. Excess EPO increases red blood cell production to unnatural levels increasing the oxygen carrying capacity of the blood. Research has shown that performance can be improved by up to 15% in endurance events. Excessive use of EPO thickens the blood causing stresses in the circulatory system. Clotting can occur in smaller blood vessels. In extreme cases cardiac arrest can occur.

Feedback Mechanisms

All organisms that require stable internal body conditions (homeostatic organisms) use negative feedback in their control systems. The endocrine system has many examples of negative feedback inhibition. The female menstrual cycle begins when the pituitary gland secretes the hormone FSH. This stimulates a graafian follicle to develop in the ovary. As the graafian follicle matures it produces the hormone oestrogen. Rising levels of oestrogen in the blood inhibit the pituitary gland from further production of FSH. This prevents the development of any more graafian follicles in the ovary, (see fig. 3.39).

Fig. 3.39 Negative Feedback Inhibition

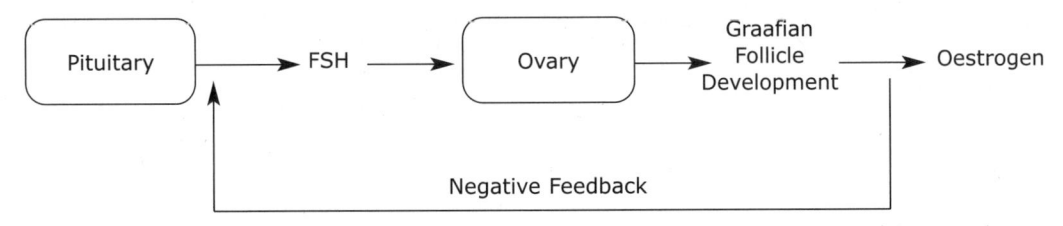

Pituitary → FSH → Ovary → Graafian Follicle Development → Oestrogen

Negative Feedback

High levels of oestrogen inhibit the pituitary from producing more FSH

Differences between Endocrine and Nervous Systems

Nervous System	Endocrine System
1. Communication is by electrical-chemical impulses along nerve fibres.	1. Communication by chemical messengers in the blood.
2. Impulses targeted to specific sites.	2. Messages can be sent to many regions in the body.
3. Causes muscles to contract or glands to secrete.	3. Causes change in chemical reactions (metabolism).
4. Effects usually short-lived and reversible.	4. Generally long-lasting effects.

Musculoskeletal System

The skeleton in vertebrates (animals with backbones) is an **endoskeleton**. It is a rigid framework of bone and cartilage. The endoskeleton is inside the body. Muscles involved in movement are outside the skeleton, (see fig. 3.40).

Fig. 3.40 Human Skeleton

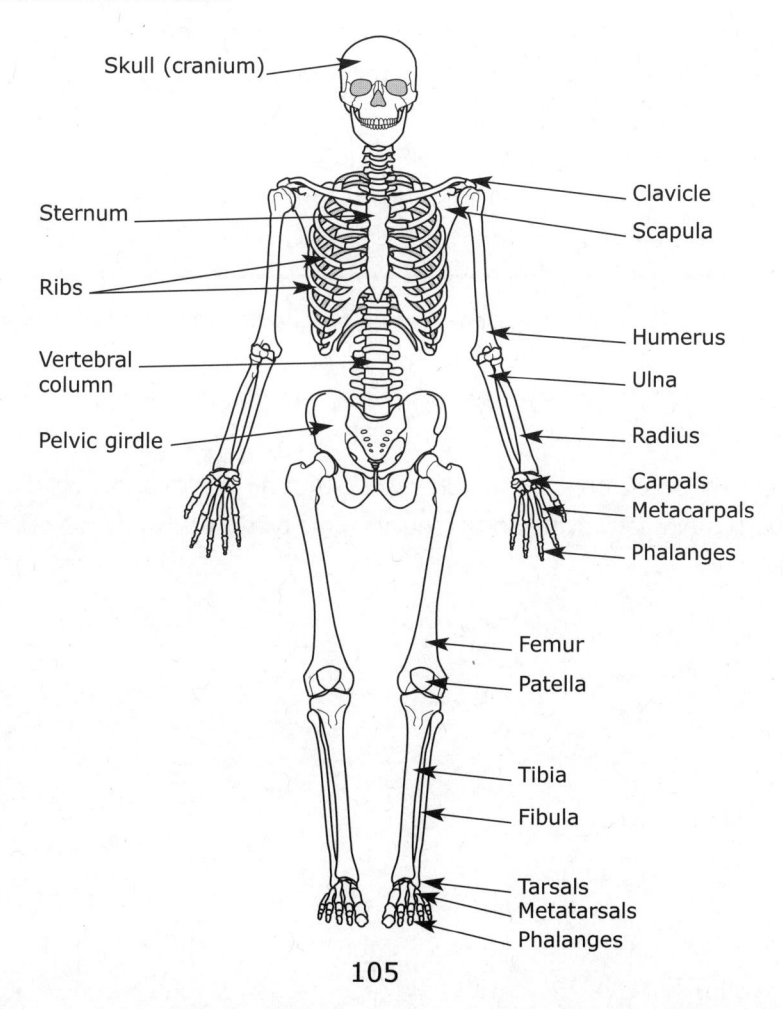

Labels: Skull (cranium), Clavicle, Scapula, Sternum, Ribs, Humerus, Ulna, Vertebral column, Radius, Pelvic girdle, Carpals, Metacarpals, Phalanges, Femur, Patella, Tibia, Fibula, Tarsals, Metatarsals, Phalanges

Functions of the skeleton:
(a) Support: It provides shape and support to the soft body.
(b) Protection: It protects internal organs, e.g. the heart and lungs.
(c) Movement: It provides solid points of attachment for muscles to act on.

Bone

Bone is made up of organic and inorganic matter. The organic matter consists of living **cells** and **protein** (collagen). The inorganic matter consists of the minerals **Calcium carbonate** and **Calcium phosphate**.

There are two main types of bone:
(a) Compact bone.
(b) Spongy bone.

Compact bone is made up of Haversian systems packed together. Each Haversian system is made up of blood capillaries surrounded by concentric rings of tightly packed mineral bars called **lamellae**. Embedded in the lamellae are bone cells in small chambers called **lacunae**. Bone cells are responsible for laying down lamellae and producing new bone if a bone breaks. **Canaliculi** are blood capillaries that supply bone cells with nutrients.

There are three types of bone cells:
1. Osteocytes: are non-dividing inactive bone cells.
2. Osteoblasts: are actively dividing, laying down new lamellae.
3. Osteoclasts: reduce the size of bone by removing lamellae.

Most compact bones are formed by ossification. In the foetus the original skeleton of cartilage is filled with inorganic salts by the osteoblasts to form hard bone. Bone is constantly changing. Osteoblast and osteoclast activity form an equilibrium that provides sustained bone growth and maintenance.

In long bones of the skeleton, compact bone surrounds a central core of **yellow bone marrow**. This contains fatty tissue and produces some types of white blood cells, (see fig. 3.41).

Fig. 3.41 Macroscopic Anatomy of a Long Bone

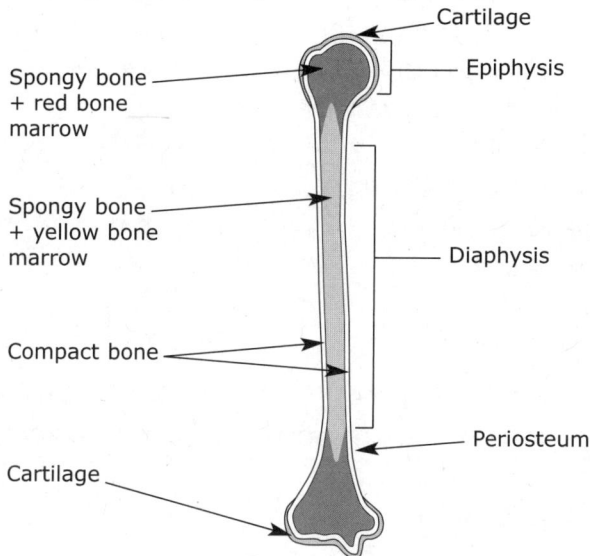

- Cartilage
- Spongy bone + red bone marrow
- Epiphysis
- Spongy bone + yellow bone marrow
- Diaphysis
- Compact bone
- Periosteum
- Cartilage

Spongy bone consists of a network of hardened bars surrounded by **red bone marrow**. Red bone marrow is a soft tissue that is made up of cells that produce red blood cells and some white blood cells.

Main bones in the body

Forelimb (Arm): The bones in the forelimb are: Humerus, Radius and Ulna, Carpals (wrist), Metacarpals (hand) and Phalanges (fingers), (see fig.3.40).

Hindlimb (Leg): The bones in the hindlimb are: Femur, Tibia and Fibula, Tarsals (ankle), Metatarsals (foot), Phalanges (toes).

Cartilage

Cartilage is a firm but flexible tissue, consisting of cells and some protein fibres. There are three types:

(a) **Hyaline cartilage** covers the surfaces of bones in movable joints. It contains some collagen (protein) fibres. Its functions are to reduce friction in movable joints and to act as a shock absorber.
(b) **Elastic cartilage** is very flexible and provides shape in the outer ear.
(c) **Fibro-cartilage** is permeated with many collagen fibres. This provides great strength. This cartilage forms the discs between the vertebrae. It allows for movement and acts as a shock absorber.

Note: A slipped disc refers to back injury where a disc is pinched between two vertebrae. The outer cartilage of the disc ruptures and softer inner cartilage protrudes. This increases pressure on spinal nerves around this region and results in severe pain.

Joints

A joint is any point where two bones meet. There are three main types of joint:

(a) **Fixed Joint**: Example: Bones in the skull that have no movement.
(b) **Slightly Movable**: Example: Vertebrae in the backbone.
(c) **Synovial Joint**: Examples:
   1. Ball and Socket Joint (hip, shoulder).
   2. Hinge Joint (knee, elbow, fingers).
   3. Gliding Joint (wrist, ankle).
   4. Pivot Joint (neck).

Synovial Joint

A synovial joint is freely movable. The parts of the two bones involved in the joint are covered with a layer of smooth cartilage. The synovial membrane produces **synovial fluid** which lubricates the joint.

Ligaments hold bones together in a joint.

Tendons attach muscles to bone to facilitate movement.

Antagonistic Muscles

Voluntary muscles are attached to the skeleton and used for the movement of limbs. They work in pairs called **antagonistic pairs** that coordinate movement. Example: The triceps and biceps of the upper arm. The biceps contracts and the triceps relaxes to raise the lower arm. To lower the arm the triceps contracts and the biceps relaxes.

Arthritis

There are two common forms of Arthritis:

(a) Osteoarthritis.
(b) Rheumatoid Arthritis.

Osteoarthritis

Symptoms: It is a degenerative disease of the cartilage in movable joints. Much pain and stiffness can occur.

Causes: Obesity, low bone density and a genetic influence are all linked to the disease.

Treatment/Prevention: Consistent light exercise of the affected joints can delay the onset of the symptoms. Treatments to alleviate the symptoms include weight loss and the use of painkillers and anti-inflammatory drugs.

Rheumatoid Arthritis

Symptoms: It is a chronic inflammation of affected joints. Many joints are often affected at the same time.

Cause: It is caused when the immune system begins to attack normal tissues at the joints.

Treatment: This includes the use of anti-inflammatory drugs, exercise and in severe cases the replacement of joints.

DEFENCE AND THE IMMUNE SYSTEM

The first form of defence in humans prevents the entry of pathogens into the body. These first and second lines of defence form what is known as **Natural Immunity**.

The first line of defence consists of:

(a) **The Skin**: The skin is impregnated with keratin, which is an impermeable barrier. Sweat from sweat glands and a natural flora of bacteria inhibits the establishment of pathogens on the surface.

(b) **The Respiratory System**: The Nasal passages are lined with hairs to filter incoming air. The trachea and bronchi are lined with a sticky mucus and cilia to trap any unwanted particles in the air.

(c) **The Digestive System**: The hydrochloric acid in the stomach can destroy pathogens taken in with food.

The second line of defence is the response of the body once the first line fails and pathogens have a point of entry into the body.

The second line of defence consists of:

(a) **Blood Clotting**: This is a rapid response that seals a wound.

(b) **Phagocytic White Blood Cells**: These accumulate at the damaged site and attack any foreign objects.

If a pathogen evades the Natural Immunity of the body the use of **Induced** or **Acquired Immunity** is then necessary. A few important terms are defined below:

> **Antigen**
> Any foreign object (usually a pathogenic bacteria) in the body which causes the production of antibodies to destroy it, is known as an antigen.
> **Lymphocyte**
> A lymphocyte is a white blood cell stored in the lymphatic system that produces antibodies to destroy antigens.
> **Antibody**
> An antibody is a specific protein produced by Lymphocytes in response to the presence of an antigen.
> **Vaccine**
> A vaccine is a diluted or dead non-disease causing dose of a pathogen. It stimulates antibody production. Vaccination activates immune response before infection occurs.

There are two forms of Induced Immunity:

(a) **Active Induced Immunity** where antibody production is stimulated by exposure to a particular antigen. There are two forms:

1. Antibody production stimulated by exposure to a particular pathogen by natural means.
   2. Antibody production stimulated by the administration of a vaccine.
(b) **Passive Induced Immunity** where antibodies are supplied from an external source to fight disease. There are two examples:
   1. Antibodies are injected into the body immediately after injury, e.g. anti-tetanus injection.
   2. Maternal antibodies diffusing across the placenta to the foetus. Similarly, antibodies in breast milk provide immunity for the offspring.

Role of Lymphocytes in Immunity

There are two main types of lymphocytes in the body. These are known as B and T cell types.

B Lymphocytes

B Lymphocytes are produced in the bone marrow and migrate to the lymph nodes. When exposed to an antigen the B cells replicate. Most of the cells produced provide large quantities of antibodies to destroy the antigen. Some of the cells produced remain in the lymph nodes as memory cells. They provide a very rapid response if a second exposure occurs to the antigen.

T Lymphocytes

T Lymphocytes are produced in the thymus gland and then migrate to the lymph nodes. There are three main types, each having different roles in the immune response.
(a) **Helper T Cells** divide when exposed to an antigen. Some of the cells form memory cells while others activate the different types of T cells enhancing their effectiveness.
(b) **Killer T Cells** attack large pathogens such as unicellular parasites. They can also destroy cancer cells or cells containing viruses. Killer T Cells act by puncturing the cell membranes of pathogens.
(c) **Supressor T Cells** regulate the immune system. They can suppress immune responses when appropriate.

Viruses

Structure

Viruses are minute micro-organisms that consist of an outer protein coat and some nucleic acid (DNA or RNA). Viruses are a unique life form in that they:
(a) do not have a cellular structure with organelles,
(b) contain only one type of nucleic acid, either DNA or RNA,
(c) cannot reproduce without host cells.

Reproduction

Viruses are obligate parasites, that is, they cannot reproduce outside their host. The viral nucleic acid takes control of the protein synthesis enzymes of the host cell. The host cell then exclusively manufactures copies of the virus.

Importance of Viruses

Human diseases caused by viruses include rabies, the common cold, AIDS and measles. Viruses also attack plants. Tobacco and tomato plant crop yields can be seriously reduced by the tobacco mosaic virus. Bacteria are also susceptible to viral attack. Any virus that destroys bacterial cells is called a **bacteriophage**.

3.6 REPRODUCTION AND GROWTH

SEXUAL REPRODUCTION IN THE FLOWERING PLANT

The flower is the reproductive organ of the flowering plant, (see fig. 3.42).

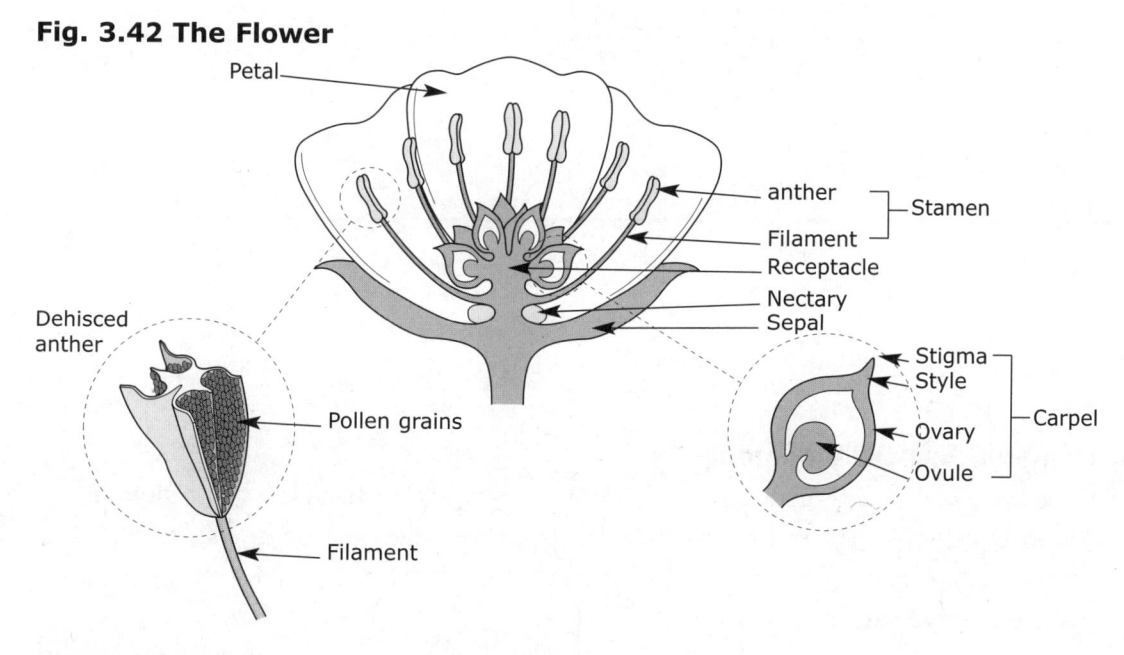

Fig. 3.42 The Flower

It consists of:
(a) The Sepals: are green and protect the developing flower bud.
(b) The Petals: are brightly coloured and can produce scent and nectar.
(c) The Stamens: produce the male pollen.
(d) The Carpels: produce the female embryo sac.

Pollen Development

Pollen is produced in the anther of the stamen. The anther contains four pollen sacs. The inner layer of each sac is called the tapetum and it nourishes the developing pollen. **Diploid Mother cells**, in the sac, divide by meiosis to form four haploid cells. Each haploid cell forms a pollen grain. The nucleus of the pollen grain divides once by mitosis to form a vegetative nucleus and a generative nucleus, (see fig. 3.43).

Fig. 3.43 Pollen Formation

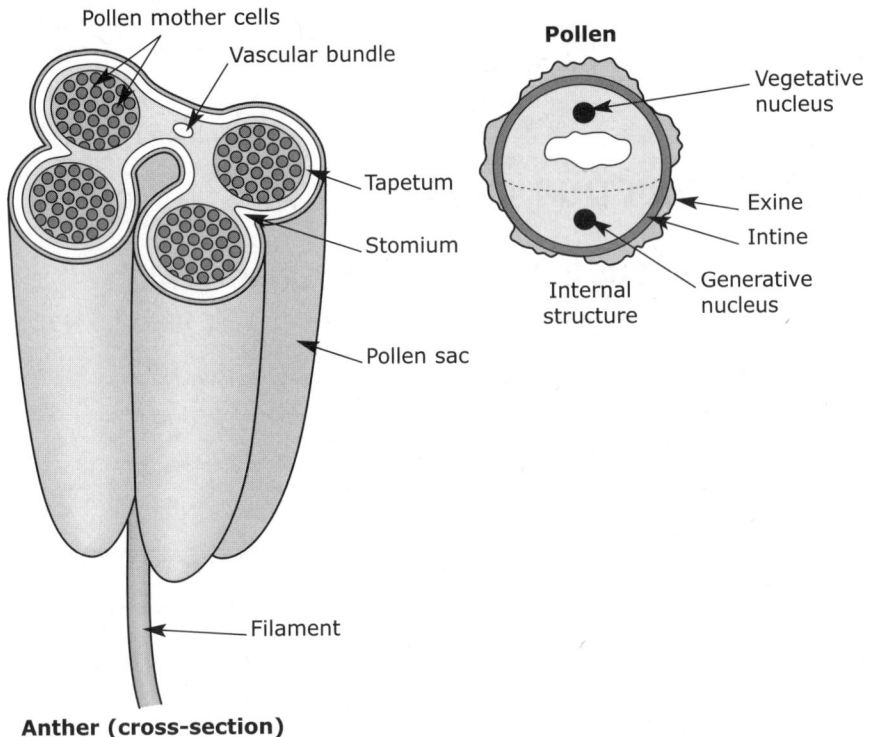

Anther (cross-section) labels: Pollen mother cells, Vascular bundle, Tapetum, Stomium, Pollen sac, Filament.

Pollen internal structure labels: Vegetative nucleus, Exine, Intine, Generative nucleus.

Embryo Sac Development

The ovary of the carpel contains one or more ovules. Inside each ovule a single **diploid Mother cell** divides by meiosis to produce four haploid cells. Three degenerate and the nucleus of the one remaining divides by mitosis three times. The cell with its nuclei is known as the **embryo sac**.

Sexual reproduction occurs in four stages:
(a) Pollination.
(b) Fertilisation.
(c) Seed Dispersal.
(d) Germination.

Pollination

> Pollination is the transfer of mature pollen from the stamen to the stigma of the carpel.

There are two main types of pollination:
1. **Self-pollination**: The plant uses its own pollen for fertilisation.
2. **Cross-pollination**: The plant uses pollen from another plant for fertilisation. There are two types:
    (a) Insect/Animal Pollination.
    (b) Wind Pollination.

Characteristics of Wind and Insect/Animal Pollinated Plants

Wind Pollinated	Insect/Animal Pollinated
1. Large quantities of light pollen produced.	1. Small numbers of large sticky pollen produced.
2. No perfume and little colour in flower.	2. Coloured perfumed flowers produced.
3. Anthers and stigmas hang outside the flower.	3. Anthers and stigmas are protected inside the flower.
4. No nectar produced.	4. Nectar produced.

Fertilisation

> Fertilisation is the fusion of two haploid gametes to form a diploid zygote.

Fertilisation in the Flowering Plant

The pollen grain germinates and the generative nucleus divides by mitosis to produce two male gamete nuclei (n). The tube nucleus grows down through the style and moves towards the micropyle by **chemotropism**. At the micropyle the tube nucleus disintegrates and the two male gamete nuclei enter the embryo sac via the micropyle.

Fertilisation in the flowering plant is known as **double fertilisation** because fusion of first male gamete nucleus with female egg produces the zygote (2n). Fusion of second male nucleus with the two polar nuclei forms a triploid (3n) endosperm nucleus, (see fig. 3.44).

Fig. 3.44 Fertilisation

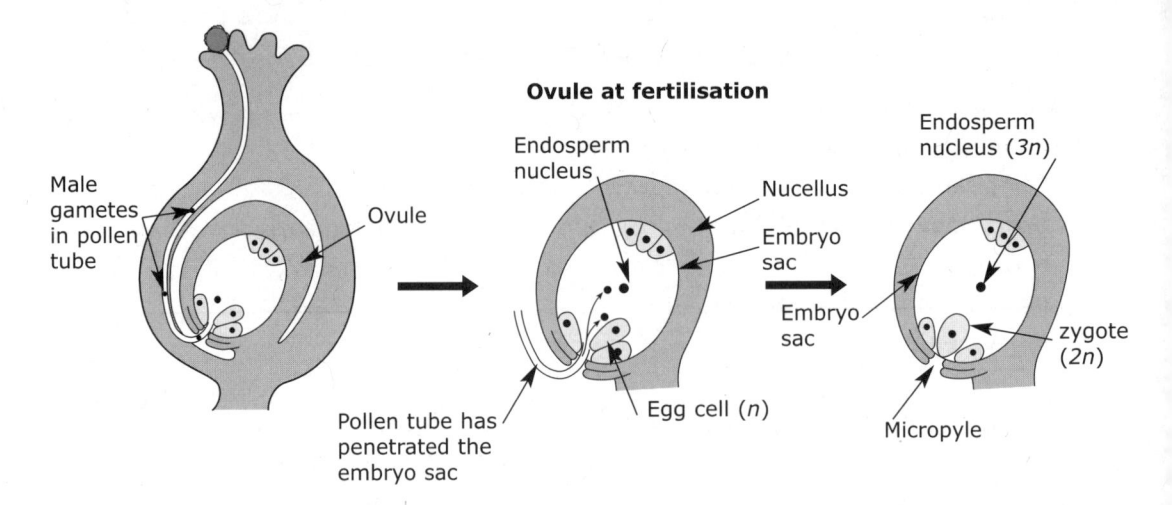

Seed

The seed is formed after fertilisation. The seed is a form which allows the plant to:
(a) Survive the unfavourable season for young seedling growth.
(b) Ensure dispersal of offspring.

Two types of seed can be produced depending on the location of stored food for the embryo:
1. Non-endospermic seed stores food reserves in the cotyledon(s).
2. Endospermic seeds store their food in the endosperm. (See fig. 3.45.)

Fig. 3.45 Endospermic and Non-endospermic Seeds

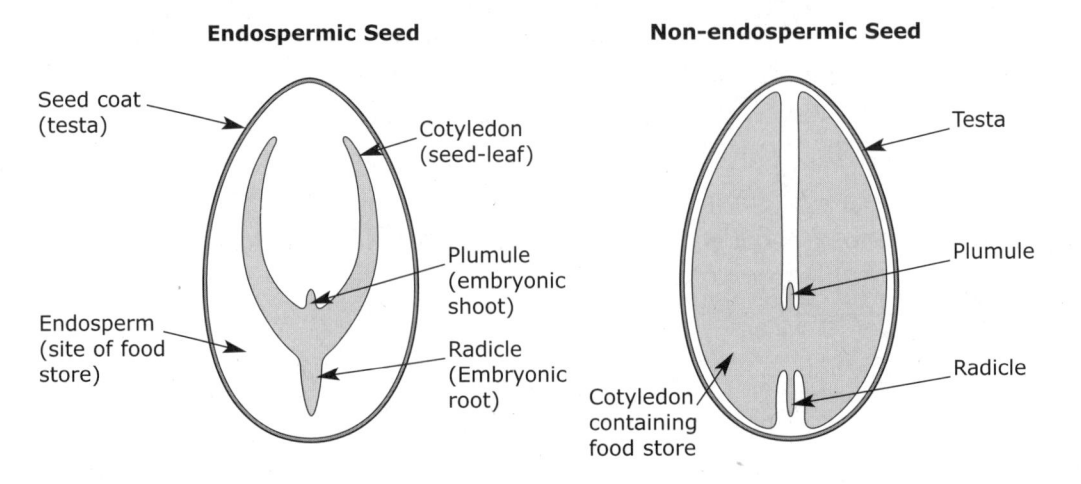

Fruits

Fruits are formed to disperse the seeds. Fruits that are formed from the ovary wall of the carpel alone are **true fruits**. Fruits that are formed from any other part of the flower are known as **false fruits**.

Reasons for Dispersal

Seeds are dispersed away from the parent plant to avoid **competition** for light, minerals, water and space.

Methods of Seed Dispersal

There are four methods of seed dispersal:

(a) **Wind**: The seeds of the sycamore tree have winged fruits which makes the seed spin on release. This slows the rate of fall and carries the seed away from the parent plant.

(b) **Animal**: The blackberry bush produces seeds with succulent fruits. Animals consume the seeds, depositing them undigested much later. The seeds are dispersed with the natural fertiliser of the animal faeces.

(c) **Water**: Water Lily plants produce seeds with a spongy buoyant fruit. This allows the water to carry the seeds away from the parent plant.

(d) **Self**: Pea plants produce their seeds inside pods. Tension increases as the pods dry out. Eventually the pod bursts, flicking the seeds away from the parent plant.

Germination

> This is the beginning of the process of development of a seed to an adult plant.

Germination requires the presence of three factors:
1. **Water.**
2. **Oxygen.**
3. **Temperature**.

Germination begins when the seed absorbs water into its cells. This provides the medium for the seed enzymes to function. The enzymes digest the food stores (in the cotyledons or the endosperm) breaking them down to single units so they can be **translocated** to the growing embryo. Starch is converted to glucose. Protein is converted to amino acids. Lipids are converted to fatty acids and then glucose. Much of the glucose produced is used for the process of respiration. Initially, anaerobic respiration occurs but as energy demands increase respiration becomes aerobic. The energy released is used to fuel the processes of germination.

Stages of Seedling Growth

The radicle is first to emerge from the seed. It grows downwards into the soil developing a root system and root hairs. The seedling now has anchorage and a source of water and minerals. The plumule then emerges, pushing above the soil. The plumule develops to form the stem and leaves. Once photosynthesis can occur the seedling then manufactures its own food.

MANDATORY ACTIVITY

To Investigate the Effect of Water, Oxygen and Temperature on Germination

1. Soak 20 dried pea seeds in water for 24 hours.
2. Place 5 soaked seeds on moist cotton wool in Test Tube A and leave in an incubator at 30°C.
3. Place 5 soaked seeds on moist cotton wool in Test tube B and leave in a fridge at 4°C.
4. Place 5 soaked seeds on moist cotton wool in test tube C with Alkaline Pyrogallol (to remove O_2). Seal with a stopper. Leave in an incubator at 30°C.
5. Place 5 **dry** pea seeds on dry cotton wool in test tube D and leave in the incubator at 30°C. (See fig. 3.46.)

Fig. 3.46 To Investigate the Effect of Water, Oxygen and Temperature on Germination

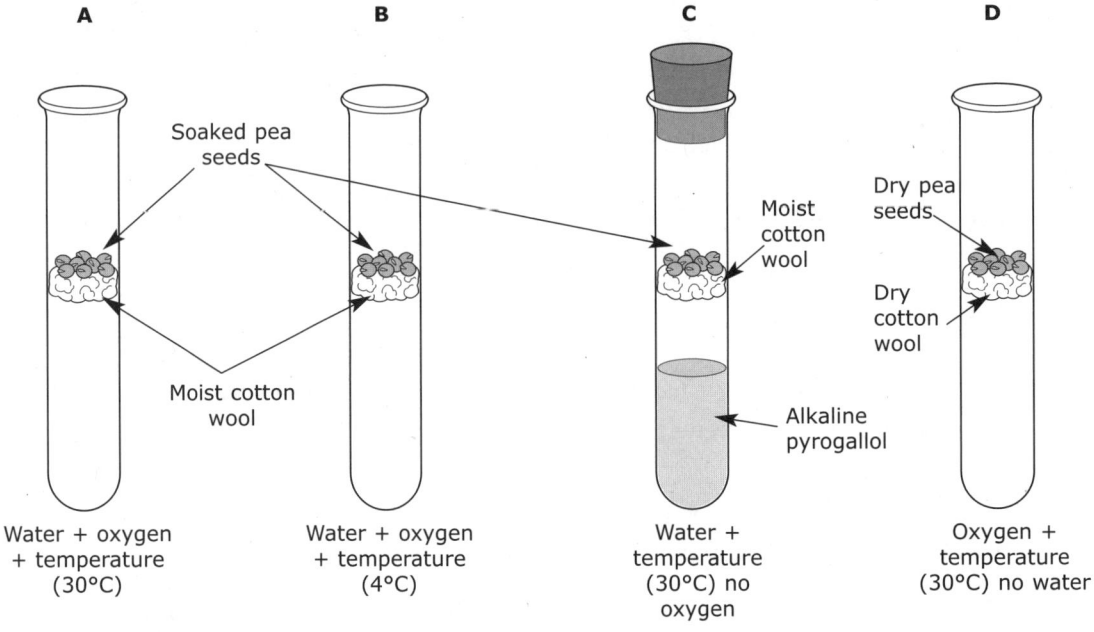

A	B	C	D
Water + oxygen + temperature (30°C)	Water + oxygen + temperature (4°C)	Water + temperature (30°C) no oxygen	Oxygen + temperature (30°C) no water

Tube A: Soaked pea seeds on moist cotton wool.
Tube B: Soaked pea seeds on moist cotton wool.
Tube C: Soaked pea seeds on moist cotton wool, with alkaline pyrogallol at the bottom, sealed with a stopper.
Tube D: Dry pea seeds on dry cotton wool.

Results: The seeds in A germinate normally. The seeds in B, C and D do not germinate.

MANDATORY ACTIVITY

To Investigate the Digestive Activity of Seeds during Germination

1. Soak some dried pea seeds in water for 24 hours.
2. Prepare 2 petri dishes of Starch dissolved in agar solution and allow to set.
3. Remove the testa of the pea seeds and separate the cotyledons.
4. Boil some of the cotyledons in water for 10 minutes.
5. Press the live cotyledons onto the starch agar surface of one of the plates and label the dish.
6. Press the boiled cotyledons onto the second plate and label.
7. Leave both plates for 48 hours at 30°C.
8. After 48 hours pour Iodine solution over both plates covering the agar.
9. Rinse off the excess iodine after a few minutes and examine the plates.

Results: Yellow areas on the starch agar around the live seeds indicate the absence of starch. Blue/black areas indicate the presence of starch, (see fig. 3.47).

Fig. 3.47 To Show the Digestive Activity of Seeds during Germination

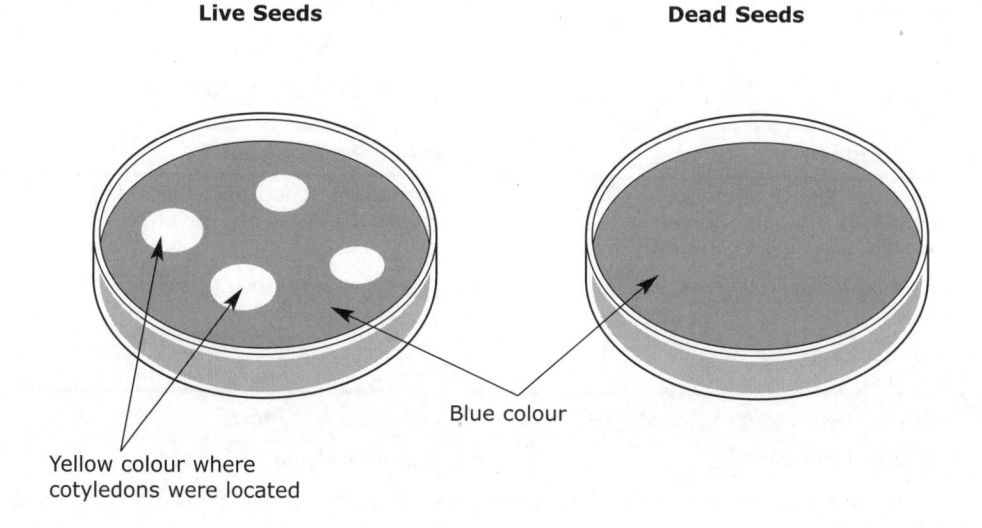

Live Seeds   **Dead Seeds**

Blue colour

Yellow colour where cotyledons were located

Dormancy

> Dormancy is a condition where seeds do not germinate even though the factors of oxygen, temperature and water are present.

Dormancy is used to ensure that a seed germinates at a time when climatic conditions are optimal.

Examples: Apple seeds do not germinate until after a long period of cold. This ensures the seeds only germinate in spring, after winter. Earlier germination would expose the vulnerable seedlings to hazardous winter temperatures.

Certain cactus plants in deserts produce seeds with inhibitors in their seed coats. The seeds will only germinate when there is enough water to wash the inhibitor out of the seed. This helps ensure that germination will only occur in conditions of heavy, prolonged rainfall. Sufficient water is essential for the seedlings to establish themselves before drought conditions return.

Vegetative Propagation

> This is asexual reproduction in flowering plants. It does not involve the production of gametes or seeds and the offspring are genetically identical to the parent.

Different organs can be used for vegetative propagation such as:

(a) **Stem**: The potato plant produces a modified underground stem tuber.

(b) **Root**: The carrot is a modified tap root.

(c) **Bud**: The onion is a modified bud.

(d) **Leaf**: Begonia produces a modified leaf for asexual reproduction.

Comparison of Sexual Reproduction with Vegetative Propagation

Sexual Reproduction	Vegetative Propagation
1. There is genetic variation in the offspring. This provides a greater chance of individuals surviving in adverse conditions.	All offspring are genetically identical. A disease that affects one will affect all.
2. Seeds will be dispersed to avoid competition.	Offspring grow very close to parents increasing competition.
3. Seeds may remain dormant in adverse conditions.	Plants may survive adverse conditions by their modified roots, stem or leaves.
4. Plants may take years to grow to maturity.	Plants develop very rapidly.
5. Many seeds are wasted.	No wastage involving lost seeds.
6. Offspring can never be genetically identical to the parent.	Plants of a particular variety can be maintained.

Artificial Propagation

Horticulturists use methods of vegetative propagation that do not occur in nature.

(a) **Budding**: A vegetative bud (scion) is cut away from a plant. The bark of the new plant (stock) is cut to expose the cambium tissue and the vegetative bud inserted. New xylem and phloem tissues connect the two parts.

(b) **Grafting**: An entire branch or stem (scion) is cut from one plant and attached to a newly cut stem of equal diameter of a second plant (stock). It is important that the cambia, of both parts, are in contact. New xylem and phloem then develop linking both parts.

(c) **Cuttings**: A healthy branch is cut from a parent plant at a point between two nodes. The cut section is dipped in rooting powders and planted in very moist fresh soil. New roots develop from the base of the cutting.

(d) **Micropropagation**: This is also known as tissue culture propagation. Very small pieces of tissue (explants) are cut from the parent plant and are cultured in a sterile nutrient medium in a controlled environment. Growth regulators are then used to stimulate the production of roots and leaves in each sample.

SEXUAL REPRODUCTION IN THE HUMAN

In mammals the male reproductive organs produce haploid (n) motile sperm. These are passed to the female through the penis. Fertilisation is internal. It occurs in the oviduct of the female when the sperm fuses with the haploid (n) female egg or ovum. The diploid (2n) zygote produced, divides repeatedly by mitosis finally implanting into the uterus wall. The embryo develops in the uterus for 38 weeks until birth.

Male Reproductive System

Testes: The testes produce haploid sperm in the seminiferous tubules. Diploid cells known as primary spermatocytes divide by meiosis to form haploid sperm cells. The sperm are stored in the epididymis. The testes are enclosed in an external scrotum, which maintains the testes at 2°C below body temperature. This is essential for sperm production, (see fig.3.48).

Fig. 3.48 Male Reproductive System

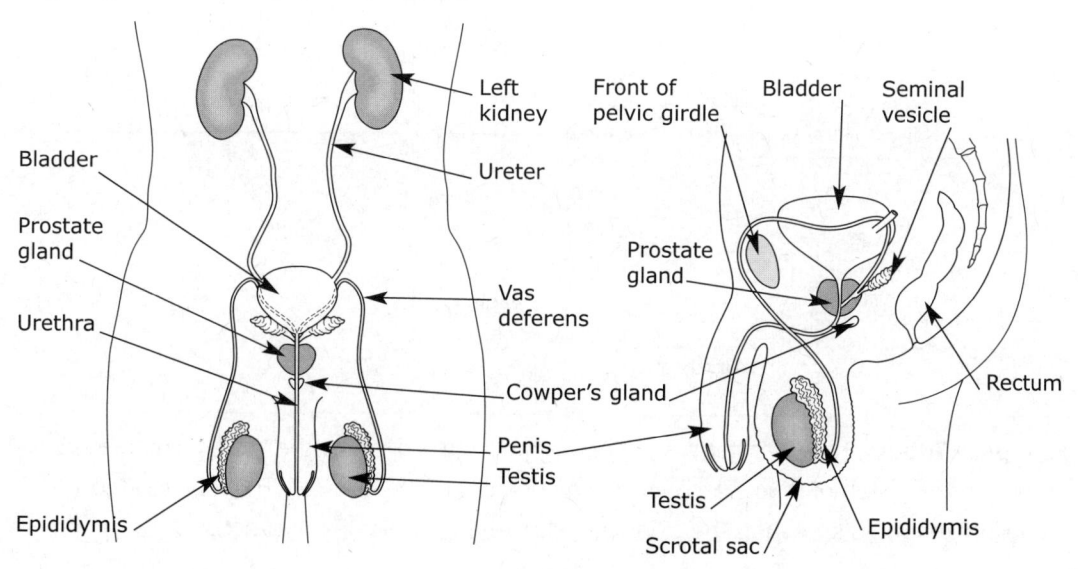

Glands: Three glands produce **nourishment** and a **medium** for the sperm to swim in. These are:
(a) The Seminal Vesicles.
(b) Cowper's Gland.
(c) Prostate Gland.

Penis: The penis is used to expel urine during **excretion**, and, to transfer semen during **copulation**. It is a highly vascular organ that becomes erect due to blood pressure during sexual intercourse.

Testosterone: Testosterone is a hormone produced by the **interstitial cells** in the testes. It stimulates the development of secondary sexual characteristics causing:
(a) The enlargement of the larynx to deepen the voice.
(b) The growth of facial and pubic hair.
(c) Muscular development.
(d) Enlargement of the penis.

Female Reproductive System

Ovaries: The ovaries are suspended at the base of the abdominal cavity by ligaments. Haploid eggs or ova (n) are produced in the ovaries when diploid primary oocytes (2n) divide by meiosis, (see fig. 3.49).

Fig. 3.49 Female Reproductive System

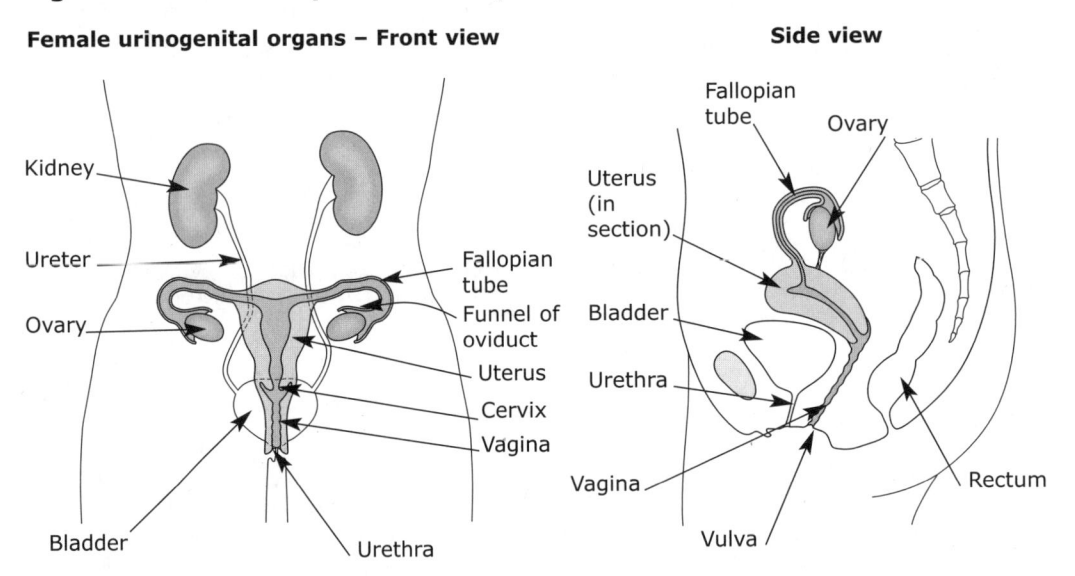

Female urinogenital organs – Front view   **Side view**

Fallopian Tubes: These transfer the mature egg from the ovary to the uterus. The presence of cilia and secretion of mucus facilitate the movement of the egg cell. The lower section of the fallopian tube is known as the oviduct. It is here that fertilisation will occur.

Uterus: The uterus is a thick-walled muscular organ. It has on outer layer of muscle with an inner lining known as the **endometrium**. This consists of a mucous membrane with a rich blood supply.

Vagina: The vagina is a muscular tube linked to the uterus at the cervix. The vagina opens to the exterior at the vulva.

Oestrogen is one of the female sex hormones and is largely responsible for the development of secondary sexual characteristics such as:

(a) The development of the breasts.
(b) Widening of the hips.
(c) Lack of facial hair.
(d) The development of pubic hair.

Copulation

Copulation involves the insertion of the erect penis into the vagina and the ejaculation of semen.

Birth Control

Birth control describes a number of techniques to either plan or avoid conception and pregnancy. Some types are described below:

Type	Method	Principle	(a) Advantages (b) Disadvantages
Natural	Temperature Measurement	During Ovulation body temperature increases by 0·5°C.	(a) No side effects. (b) There can be many reasons for body temperature variation.
Mechanical (Barrier)	Condoms	Prevents sperm access to the uterus.	(a) Good protection against sexually transmitted diseases. (b) Leakages can occur.
Chemical	Combined Pill	Doses of oestrogen and progesterone prevent ovulation.	(a) Stimulates lighter, more regular periods. (b) Can cause nausea.
Surgical	Vasectomy	Vas deferens cut and tied.	(a) Semen is still produced, without sperm. (b) Procedure can be irreversible.

Development after Fertilisation

The zygote divides by mitosis a number of times to form a clump of cells called the **morula**. With further development and growth the **blastocyst** is formed. It is made up of an outer layer of cells known as the **trophoblast** cells and an inner layer of **embryo cells**. Muscular contractions of the fallopian tube and the movement of cilia on the oviduct wall propel the blastocyst gradually into the uterus. The blastocyst obtains nutrition for its cells by active transport of nutrients from the fluids in the fallopian tube, (see fig. 3.50).

Fig. 3.50 Development after Fertilisation

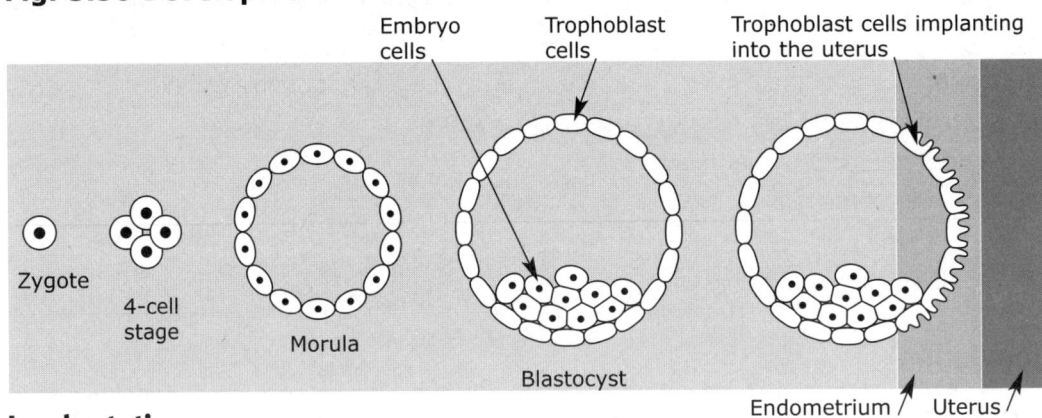

Implantation

After entering the uterus the trophoblast cells produce tiny extensions that grow into the prepared wall (endometrium) of the uterus. The **trophoblast** cells and the **endometrium** of the uterus together begin to form the placenta. The embryo cells grow and differentiate to form the embryo. After implantation, the blastocyst obtains its nutrition by absorption through the trophoblast cells from the endometrium.

Placenta

The placenta is fully formed after 12 weeks of development. It is formed from **both** the trophoblast cells and the endometrium of the uterus.

The placenta acts as a **link** between mother and embryo by:
1. Transporting food, oxygen and some antibodies from mother to embryo.
2. Transporting carbon dioxide and urea from the embryo to the mother's blood.

The placenta acts as a **barrier** between mother and embryo by preventing:
1. the bloods from mixing,
2. the transfer of blood proteins,
3. the transfer of hormones.

The placenta **produces the hormones** oestrogen and progesterone after the 18th week of pregnancy. Both these hormones stimulate further development of the uterus wall and prevent the production of FSH by the pituitary.

Development of the Embryo to the Thirteenth Week

3rd week: The brain, spinal cord and nervous system are developing.
4th week: Circulation has developed and heartbeat is present. The embryo is 1·5 cm in length. Muscles and buds (developing limbs) appear.

8th week: All organs are developed in miniature. The foetus is now 2·5 cm long.

13th week: Foetus becomes active. The placenta and amniotic cavity are fully formed. The foetus is 7 cm long and weighs around 30 g, (see fig. 3.51).

Fig. 3.51 Placenta and Amniotic Sac

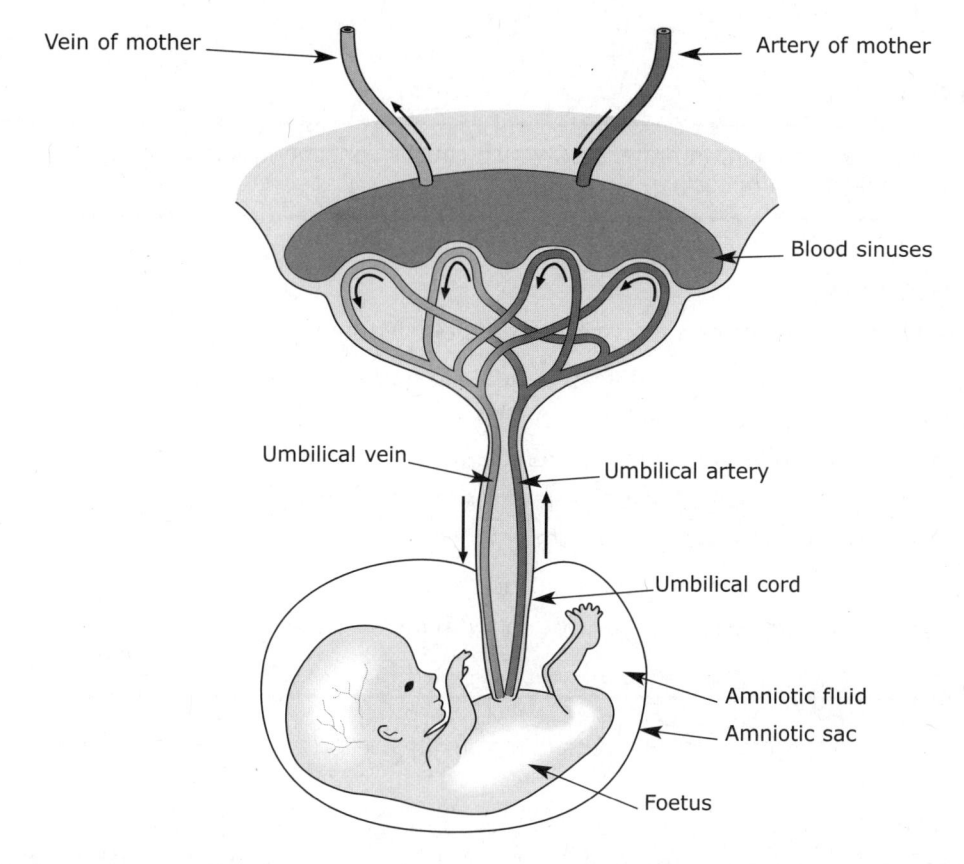

Birth (Parturition)

Parturition means giving birth. The process begins when the pituitary produces the hormone **oxytocin**. This causes the walls of the uterus to begin to contract rhythmically. The baby should be upside down with the head at the cervix. The amniotic sac ruptures releasing the amniotic fluid. As the contractions continue, the cervix and vagina dilate in preparation for the passage of the baby. Further contractions force the head out through the vagina. After a short period the baby is passed out through the vagina. The baby is briefly held upside down to allow the amniotic fluid to drain out from its lungs and air passages so breathing of air can begin. The umbilical cord is tied at the navel to prevent excessive blood loss when it is cut. Finally, the remaining umbilical cord and the placenta in the womb is passed out of the uterus forming the afterbirth.

Lactation

This is the production of milk in the mother's breasts to feed and protect the newborn baby. The process begins after birth when the pituitary produces the hormone **prolactin**. It stimulates the mammary glands. The milk produced is very nutritional in that it contains large quantities of protein. It also contains antibodies, produced in the mother's body, which will protect the baby from disease.

Infertility

> Infertility is a condition, in either sex, which causes conception and pregnancy to be very difficult or impossible.

Male Infertility

In males a **low sperm count** is a common source of infertility.

Cause: Scientists have observed a distinct decrease in human sperm counts across the population over the last century. Reliable scientific evidence links the accumulation of **synthetic organic pollutants** in the environment to this observation. Tests have shown that some pesticides are directly linked to sterility in males. Common industrial chemicals such as benzene are also thought to affect sperm production.

Treatment: Further research is necessary to find specific causes. Only then can steps be taken to prevent further release of the pollutants into the environment.

Female Infertility

Causes: Blockages in the fallopian tubes are a cause of sterility in females. Two common causes are:

(a) A functional blockage such as a mucous plug.
(b) A structural blockage such as scarring.

Treatment: The closer the location of the blockage to the uterus the greater the possibility of successful treatment. **Hysteroscopy** involves the insertion of a lighted viewing instrument into the uterus through the vagina and cervix. The exact nature of the blockage can then be determined and treatment, usually surgery, can be prescribed.

Fibroids (Leiomyomata uteri)

Description/Symptoms: Uterine fibroids are often found in females of reproductive age. They are benign (non-cancerous) growths that develop in the muscular wall of the uterus. Fibroids can vary in size from tiny to the size of a melon, or larger. Their size and location can result in problems of pain and heavy bleeding. Fibroid tumours can reduce fertility and cause difficulties in pregnancy including miscarriage.

Treatment: There are three main courses of treatment for acute fibroids:
(a) **Hysterectomy**: This is the complete surgical removal of the uterus and perhaps the ovaries. It is the least preferred option. It is usually used in post menopausal females when other procedures have failed.
(b) **Myomectomy**: This is the surgical removal of the fibroids. It is usually reserved for females who wish to preserve fertility. Myomectomy is usually the preferred treatment if pharmaceutical management has failed.
(c) **Fibroid Embolisation**: This procedure involves the insertion of tiny plastic or gelatin sponge granules into the artery supplying blood to the fibroid. This restriction of blood flow causes the fibroid to shrink. In many cases the treatment has successfully reduced bleeding and alleviated pain.

In-vitro Fertilisation

In-vitro fertilisation is used as a solution to infertility caused by permanent blockage of the oviducts. Supplementary FSH and LH may be provided to stimulate multiple egg production in the female. The mature female egg cells are then removed from the ovary or fallopian tube. The eggs are placed in an in-vitro culturing solution. Fertilisation with the male sperm then occurs outside the body. The developing fertilised eggs are then implanted back into the uterus.

Hormonal Control in the Menstrual Cycle

Hormonal control in the menstrual cycle is a complex process. It is summarised below in order of events as they occur in the cycle, (see fig. 3.52).

1. The pituitary gland secretes the hormone FSH.
2. FSH stimulates a Graafian Follicle to mature in the ovary.
3. FSH stimulates cells in the ovary to produce the hormone Oestrogen.
4. Oestrogen causes the lining of the uterus to build up.
5. As the concentration of oestrogen rises in the blood it stops the pituitary producing FSH thus preventing any more graafian follicles maturing until the cycle is complete.
6. Oestrogen stimulates the pituitary to produce LH.
7. LH causes ovulation, releasing the egg from the ovary. The remaining cells of the Graafian follicle form the Corpus Luteum in the ovary.
8. The corpus luteum produces the hormone Progesterone. It causes further build-up of the uterus wall.
9. Progesterone further inhibits the production of FSH by the pituitary. High levels of progesterone in the blood inhibit the production of LH.
10. When the level of LH drops in the blood the corpus luteum begins to break down. This causes a drop in the progesterone level in the blood.

11. A drop in progesterone levels causes the built-up uterus wall to break down which begins menstruation.

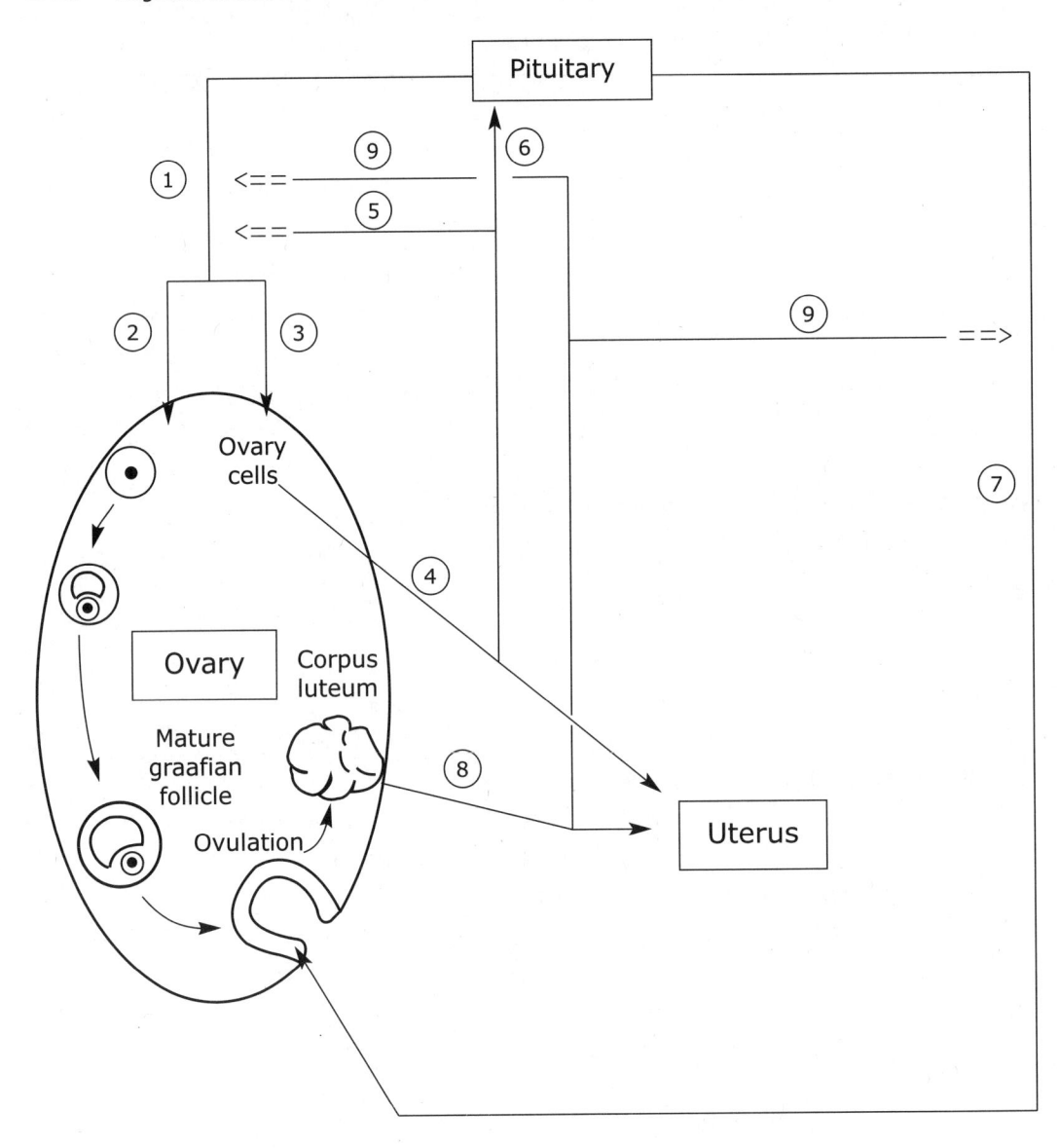

A comparison of the hormone levels, graafian follicle development and the uterus wall during the menstrual cycle is shown in fig. 3.53.

Fig. 3.52 Hormonal Control in the Menstrual Cycle

==> = Negative feedback inhibition

Fig. 3.53 Comparison of Hormone Levels, Graafian Follicle Development and the Uterus Wall during the Menstrual Cycle

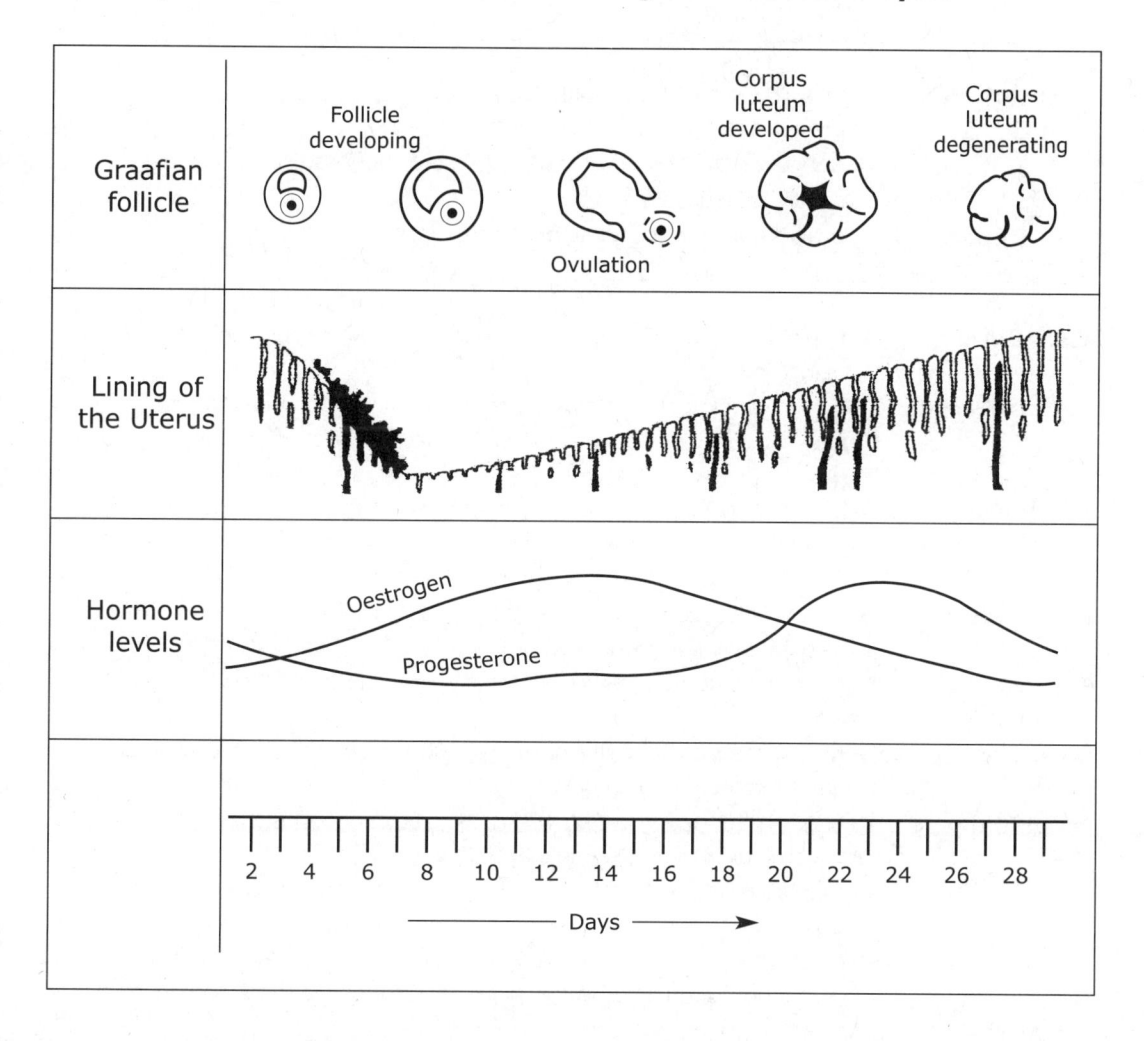

GLOSSARY OF TERMS

Def.	provides a specific definition for each
Ex.	provides suitable examples where required
*	denotes definitions that have previously been asked at Leaving Certificate level
Expan.	provides important relevant information to a definition

Abscisic Acid   **Def.** a plant hormone that inhibits growth. It is also responsible for leaf fall and dormancy in seeds.

Accommodation   **Def.** the changing of the shape of the lens to focus light onto the retina.
Expan. Contraction and relaxation of the ciliary muscle controls the shape of the lens.

Acetylcholine   **Def.** a chemical transmitter that relays messages across synapses between nerve cells.
Expan. The transmission of messages along nerve cells is electrical. Between two nerve cells (synapse) the message is in chemical form.

Acoelomate   **Def.** a triploblastic metazoan that does not possess a coelom. Ex. Flatworm (Dugesia) + Liver fluke (Fasciola).

Acquired Immunity   **Def.** immunity from a pathogen or its toxins due to the active production of antibodies.

Active Site   **Def.** temporary point of attachment for substrate on the surface of an enzyme, before it is converted to products.

Active Transport*   **Def.** this is the movement of a substance, across a cell membrane against the diffusion gradient. It requires energy (ATP) to occur.
Expan. Plant root hairs take in minerals from the soil by active transport. Plant roots need oxygen in the soil so that enough energy (ATP) will be produced from aerobic respiration to carry out active transport of minerals. Reabsorption of many high threshold substances in the nephrons of the kidney also occurs by active transport.

Adaptation*   **Def.** the way in which organisms become adapted (in behaviour or structure) to survive better in their community. Ex. A frog in a freshwater pond habitat has long muscular legs for jumping on land and webbed feet for swimming.

ADH   **Def.** (Antidiuretic Hormone) a hormone involved in osmoregulation. It is secreted by the pituitary and stimulates the collecting ducts in the kidneys to become more permeable to water.

Adrenaline   **Def.** a hormone produced by the Adrenal Glands. It causes the release of glucose into the muscles providing emergency reserves of energy.

Adventitious Roots   **Def.** roots that have developed from some part of the plant other than the original radicle (root). Ex. Grass roots or gripping roots on the stem of ivy.

AIDS   **Def.** (Acquired Immune Deficiency Syndrome) a lethal, incurable, viral disease in humans, transmitted through body fluids.

Alleles* **Def.** different genes that control the same trait and have the same locus on homologous chromosomes. Ex. In pea plants T = tall stem, t = short stem.

Alternation of Generations* **Def.** in advanced plants (fern or moss upwards) the life cycle is divided into two parts, a diploid Sporophyte plant that produces haploid spores and a haploid Gametophyte plant that produces gametes.

Expan. In the fern the sporophyte is the fern plant, the gametophyte is the prothallus. In the flowering plant, the plant itself is the sporophyte stage that produces two gametophytes. The male gametophyte is the pollen grain and the female gametophyte is the embryo sac.

Amoeba **Def.** a unicellular free living animal found in fresh water. It is classified in the phylum Protozoa.

Anabolism **Def.** chemical reactions in organisms where simple substances are used to produce complex substances. Energy is required for this process. Ex. photosynthesis.

Expan. In photosynthesis simple substances (CO_2 and H_2O) are used to make a complex substance, glucose ($C_6H_{12}O_6$). The presence of sunlight energy is necessary for the reaction to occur.

Angiosperms* **Def.** flowering plants that produce seeds enclosed in a fruit during sexual reproduction. They have a root, stem and leaves and a well-developed transport system (xylem + phloem). Ex. Elm, Rose, Grass.

Annelida **Def.** a phylum of triploblastic coelomate animals with the following characteristics: bilateral symmetry, **segmentation**, possesses a **circulatory system**, has **setae** and has a mouth and anus. Ex. Earthworm (Lumbricus terrestris).

Antibiotics* **Def.** chemicals produced by micro-organisms that prevent the reproduction of fungi and bacteria, finally killing them.

Expan. Antibiotics are commonly prescribed by doctors to rid the body of bacterial or fungal diseases.

Antibody* **Def.** a protein, produced in the lymphatic system by lymphocytes, which is specific for any one antigen. Their function is to fight disease (pathogens).

Antigen **Def.** a foreign substance that stimulates antibody production. Ex. toxins from disease-causing organisms.

Apical* Dominance **Def.** the terminal bud of woody angiosperms restricts the growth of lateral buds below it, by producing large amounts of Auxin.

Expan. If the terminal bud is removed the lateral buds below grow much more quickly, providing new active twigs and giving a more bushy appearance to the plant.

Arthropoda* **Def.** a phylum of triploblastic coelomate animals that have a segmented exoskeleton, and jointed limbs. Ex. cockroach, crab, lobster, woodlice, flies, grasshoppers, spiders, millipedes.

Expan. Because of the limitations posed by the impermeable rigid exoskeleton many adaptations have been developed. Antennae enhance sensitivity by smell and touch. Spiracles in the exoskeleton facilitate gaseous exchange. A process of ecdysis (shedding of the exoskeleton) facilitates growth. Muscles are arranged inside the skeleton as opposed to vertebrates where muscles are arranged outside bones.

Aseptic Technique **Def.** steps used when culturing bacteria and fungi for safety, and to prevent unwanted contamination of the growth medium (sterile nutrient agar).

Asexual Reproduction	**Def.** a form of reproduction that involves one parent only. It does not involve the formation of gametes or spores i.e. it does not involve meiosis. The offspring are always genetically identical to the parent.
Atmometer	**Def.** a device used to measure the rate of evaporation from the surface of a porous pot. It can be used to investigate the external conditions that affect the rate of evaporation. Ex. wind, temperature.
ATP	**Def.** made up of Adenine (an amino acid), ribose (a sugar) and three phosphate molecules. It stores energy in chemical form between the phosphates. **Expan.** ATP is converted to ADP + P to release energy. If energy is to be stored ADP + P form ATP.
Autosomes	**Def.** chromosomes that control other traits in the body apart from the sex of the individual. **Expan.** In humans there are 22 pairs of autosomes and one pair of sex chromosomes.
Auxin (Indole Acetic Acid, IAA)	**Def.** plant hormone produced by growing tips. It stimulates: 1. cell elongation, 2. fruit formation, 3. root formation, 4. apical dominance.
Available Soil Water*	**Def.** the water in soil that can be absorbed by the roots of plants.
Axon	**Def.** long extension of a nerve cell that carries messages away from the cell body.
Balanced Diet	**Def.** a variety of foods that contain the correct amounts of carbohydrates, protein, lipids, vitamins and minerals for a healthy body.
Benedict's Reagent	**Def.** used to test for glucose or any reducing sugar. It changes from blue to a brick red for a positive result. **Expan.** When testing, the solution in the test tube must be boiled for 10 minutes before a result is seen. If a very small amount of glucose is present it turns green in colour.
Bicarbonate Indicator*	**Def.** reagent used to indicate gaseous exchange by change of colour. **Expan.** When neutral it is orange or red. If Carbon Dioxide increases it becomes acidic and turns yellow. If Carbon Dioxide is removed it becomes alkaline and turns purple.
Binary Fission	**Def.** a form of Asexual Reproduction where one cell divides by mitosis to form two identical daughter cells. It is the means by which Amoeba and bacteria reproduce.
Binocular Vision	**Def.** the combined use of two eyes to produce an image that is accurate in terms of distance and size.
Blind Spot	**Def.** point of attachment of the optic nerve to the retina. It is not sensitive to light.
Bowman's Capsule	**Def.** cup-shaped part of a nephron that surrounds the glomerulus and is located in the cortex of the kidney. Ultra filtration of the blood occurs at this point producing the glomerular filtrate.
Capillarity (Capillary Action)	**Def.** the means by which water rises up vessels of very small diameter. It occurs in the xylem vessels of plants. **Expan.** This is regarded as one of the forces responsible for the upward movement of water in the plant (Transpiration Stream).
Chemotropism	**Def.** the way in which male gametes are sensitive and attracted to a female gamete that secretes chemicals. Ex. the sperm in Fucus and Humans.

Expan. In the Fern the sperm swim towards Malic Acid secreted by the egg. In the flowering plant the tube nucleus locates the micropyle, the entry to the Embryo Sac, by chemotropism.

Chiasma* **Def.** during prophase of meiosis I, chromatids of homologous chromosomes may become joined at points called chiasmata (plural). This can lead to crossing over and variation in the offspring.

Chromatid **Def.** during prophase of cell division, each chromosome forms an identical copy of itself and both are joined at the centromere. The two copies are sister chromatids.

Chromosome **Def.** consists of a number of genes made of DNA and protein. It is located in the nucleus of most organisms.

Chromosome Mutation **Def.** a change in the base sequence of a chromosome or a change in the chromosome number of a cell. The effects are usually harmful. Ex. Down's syndrome in humans and polyploidy in plants.

Clinostat **Def.** a rotating device used in experiments investigating geotropism in plants.

Codon* **Def.** a section of DNA or RNA that contains three nucleic acids, the type and sequence of which codes for a specific amino acid.

Coelom **Def.** a fluid-filled cavity present in some triploblastic metazoans. It allows for independent movement of gut and body wall and also provides protection and support.

Coenzyme **Def.** a removable, non-protein, part of an enzyme that is essential for its functioning. Ex. Vit. B.

Cofactor **Def.** a non-removable, non-protein, part of an enzyme that is essential for its functioning. Ex. Calcium.

Cohesion Theory (Transpiration Pull Theory) **Def.** a suction force produced in the leaves due to the transpiration of water. It is of sufficient strength to draw water up the stem from the roots.
Expan. Evidence for this theory is provided by the reduction in the diameter of the tree trunk in actively transpiring trees.

Collenchyma* **Def.** plant tissue consisting of thick-walled living cells found in mid ribs and leaf stalks. Its function is to provide support and strength.

Community* **Def.** this is the group of organisms (plants + animals) that share a habitat. Ex. Grass, leaves, woodmouse and greenfly form part of a community in a woodland habitat.

Comparative Anatomy **Def.** a study of the structural similarities and differences of various organisms. Ex. pentadactyl limb. It is used to support the theory of evolution.

Compensation Point* **Def.** the light intensity at which the rates of photosynthesis and respiration in plants are equal. It occurs at dawn and dusk and there is no gaseous exchange with the atmosphere at this point.

Complete Metamorphosis* **Def.** is when the life cycle of an insect goes through the stages of egg, larva, pupa and adult. The adult is very different in form from the larva. Ex. butterfly (Pieris brassicae).

Conjugation **Def.** sexual reproduction in spirogyra, where a conjugation tube is formed from outward growths of the cell walls. The male and female gametes fuse to form a diploid zygote.
Expan. It is mainly used as a form of survival. The thick-walled zygospore produced can survive adverse conditions.

Cotyledon*   **Def.** an embryonic leaf in seeds that acts as a food store for germination.
Expan. Non-endospermic seeds use the cotyledons as their main source of food. Ex. Pea, Broad Bean. Endospermic seeds use the endosperm as their food source instead of cotyledons.

Cranium   **Def.** fused bones in the head that protect the brain and sense organs.

Crenation   **Def.** the shrinking of animal cells placed in a hypertonic solution due to the loss of water by osmosis.
Expan. It can be demonstrated by placing red blood corpuscles in a 3% salt solution and examining them under a microscope.

Dark Stage (Calvin Cycle)   **Def.** a light-independent stage of photosynthesis that occurs in the stroma of the chloroplast. It produces Glucose from atmospheric Carbon Dioxide.
Expan. ATP and $NADPH_2$ from the light stage are essential for the Dark Stage.

DCPIP   **Def.** a reagent used to measure the amount of Vitamin C present in a sample (quantitative test).
Expan. It measures the volume of the sample that contains 1 mg of Vit. C. Its colour changes from blue to colourless at this point.

Dendrites (Dendrons)   **Def.** extension of a nerve cell that transports messages to the cell body.

Dicot. (Dicotyledon)   **Def.** flowering plant that produces seeds with two cotyledons (food stores). Ex. Pea, Bean, Horse Chestnut.

Dihybrid Cross   **Def.** a genetic cross where two characteristics are being observed. Ex. observing stem height and seed shape, when two pea plants are crossed.

Diploblastic   **Def.** a metazoan that forms its tissues from two germ layers, produced during early development. They are the ectoderm and the endoderm. Ex. Hydra.

Diploid   **Def.** a cell (or nucleus) with the full complement (2n) of chromosomes. Ex. any somatic cell, i.e. stomach cell.

Division of Labour   **Def.** the way in which different cells (or tissues) have specific functions in multicellular organisms. Ex. The holdfast in Fucus anchors it to rock, other cells form air bladders to provide flotation.

DNA (Deoxyribonucleic acid)   **Def.** a nucleic acid that makes up genes and chromosomes. It is located in the nucleus and forms a double helical shape. Its base sequence forms the genetic code.

DNA Replication   **Def.** the process by which DNA (chromosomes) make identical copies of themselves. It allows for the passing of the genetic code faithfully from one generation to the next.

Dominant   **Def.** the gene that is expressed in the phenotype of an organism in the heterozygous condition.
Expan. If T is the gene for tall and t is a gene for a short stem, a plant with the genotype Tt would have a tall stem. The T gene is dominant.

Double Circulation   **Def.** two circulations in mammals where blood is pumped from the heart to the lungs and back (Pulmonary Circulation), also blood is pumped from the heart to the body and back (Systemic Circulation).

Ecdysis   **Def.** the shedding of the protective exoskeleton of Arthropods for growth to occur.
Expan. Many Arthropods are vulnerable just after ecdysis until the body generates a new exoskeleton.

Ectoderm	**Def.** an outer germ layer of metazoans formed during early development. It gives rise to specific organs. **Expan.** In higher animals the ectoderm gives rise to the skin, hair, nails and the nervous system.
Embryology	**Def.** the study of the similarities and differences of developing embryos in various organisms. It is used to support the theory of evolution.
Endocrine Gland	**Def.** ductless gland that produces hormones and secretes them directly into the bloodstream. Ex. Testes.
Endodermis	**Def.** innermost layer of cortex cells in the stem and root of dicot. plants. **Expan.** In the root, endodermal cells have a Casparian strip around the cell wall. It controls the passage of substances into and out of the stele (core).
Endoskeleton	**Def.** an internal support structure of bone or cartilage in vertebrates. **Expan.** In the endoskeleton, muscles are attached outside the bones. In Arthropods, muscles are attached to the inside of the skeleton.
Enzyme*	**Def.** a protein that speeds up chemical reactions (a catalyst) and is produced by living organisms.
Enzyme Action	**Def.** the process of the substrate temporarily joining with the active site of the enzyme to be converted to the product(s).
Evolution	**Def.** the successive altering of species through time in adaptation to changing environmental conditions. This process has produced present-day life forms.
Excretion*	**Def.** the removal of wastes produced from chemical reactions (metabolism) in the body. **Expan.** Respiration is a chemical reaction that occurs in the body. The wastes produced are CO_2 and H_2O. In mammals the body excretes these by breathing.
Exoskeleton	**Def.** external support structure outside the muscles of Arthropods. It is made of chitin.
Expiratory Reserve Volume*	**Def.** the volume of air (about 1,000 cm^3) we can breathe out over and above the tidal volume.
Fermentation	**Def.** anaerobic respiration in plants resulting in the production of Ethyl alcohol (C_2H_5OH) and Carbon dioxide with a small amount of energy (ATP). **Expan.** Fungi (yeast) are used to carry out fermentation in the brewing and baking industries.
Fertilisation*	**Def.** the fusion of two haploid gametes to form a diploid zygote.
Feulgen's Stain (Reagent)*	**Def.** reagent used to stain chromosomes (DNA) purple for viewing with the light microscope.
Fibrinogen	**Def.** a soluble blood protein that is converted to insoluble fibrin at the site of a wound in order to clot the blood.
Fossil	**Def.** the remains of a once-living plant or animal.
Fucoxanthin	**Def.** a brown pigment present with chlorophyll in Fucus. Its function is to carry out photosynthesis in poor light conditions when the plant is submerged.
Gametophyte*	**Def.** the haploid gamete-producing stage in a plant's life cycle. **Expan.** In the fern (Dryopteris) the gametophyte stage is the prothallus. The flowering plant has two gametophytes, the male microspore is the pollen grain and the female macrospore is the embryo sac.

Gene Mutation*	**Def.** a change in a gene, due to the base sequence of the DNA being altered. If it occurs in the formation of gametes it may be passed from one generation to the next. **Expan.** Its effects on the organism are usually harmful (Ex. Sickle cell Anaemia in humans) but occasionally may be beneficial. It can be caused by carcinogens or UV light.
Gene	**Def.** part of a chromosome that controls a single trait in an organism. It is located in the nucleus of cells and is made up of protein and DNA.
Gene Mutation*	**Def.** a change in the base sequence of the DNA in a gene. It is usually harmful. Ex. Sickle Cell Anaemia is caused by a gene mutation.
Genetic Engineering	**Def.** the manipulation of genetic material such as DNA for a practical use. Ex. The gene for the production of Insulin in humans can be inserted into bacteria. They can then produce large quantities of insulin that are identical to human insulin.
Genetics	**Def.** the study of the means by which characteristics are passed from parents to offspring.
Genotype*	**Def.** the genetic make-up of an individual, repeated in every somatic cell of the organism. Ex. Tt or TT.
Glomerular Filtrate*	**Def.** part of the blood that passes into the lumen of the Bowman's capsule by ultrafiltration. It does not contain blood cells or large blood proteins. **Expan.** It contains wastes such as urea, uric acid, excess salts and water. It also contains high threshold substances such as glucose and amino acids which must be reabsorbed back into the blood.
Glycolysis*	**Def.** the part of respiration that involves the incomplete chemical breakdown of glucose to pyruvic acid. A small amount of energy (ATP) is released. It occurs in the cytoplasm of the cell and oxygen is not used in this process.
Guttation	**Def.** the forcing of liquid water out through the leaves of plants. It is due to root pressure and occurs in conditions of high humidity.
Gymnosperm*	**Def.** cone-producing plants with needle shaped leaves. They are classified in phylum Spermatophyta. The ovule of its seeds is not enclosed by a carpel. Ex. Scots Pine.
Haemophilia	**Def.** a blood-clotting disorder in humans caused by a recessive gene. Its locus is on the X chromosome of the sex chromosomes. **Expan.** The gene that causes Haemophilia is said to be sex-linked or X-linked.
Haploid	**Def.** a cell (or nucleus) with half the full complement of chromosomes. Ex. sperm cell.
Hermaphrodite	**Def.** animals that possess both male and female sex organs. Ex. Fasciola (Liver fluke) and Lumbricus (Earthworm).
Heterotrophs	**Def.** organisms that cannot make their own food from simple inorganic substances. They must feed on organic matter in their environment.
Homologous Chromosomes*	**Def.** pairs of chromosomes containing genes that control the same traits. They come together in pairs (bivalents) during cell division. **Expan.** Homologous chromosomes separate at gamete formation so that only one of any pair can enter a single gamete.
Homologous Organs	**Def.** structures that have the same basic form in various animals but have different functions. Ex. bat wing for flying, whale fin for swimming.

Hormone*   **Def.** a generally slow-acting chemical messenger produced in minute quantities by an endocrine gland. It has a specific function and travels in the blood.

Immunity   **Def.** the resistance of an organism to disease.
Expan. It may be passive to prevent entry. Ex. skin, sweat and mucus. Active immunity is the struggle against the pathogen once it has entered the body with lymphocytes, granulocytes and antibodies.

Incomplete Dominance*   **Def.** when neither of a pair of alleles is dominant and both are expressed in the phenotype of the offspring. Ex. coat colour in cattle.
Expan. In cattle the R gene codes for a red coat and r codes for a white coat. An individual with RR has a red coat, rr has a white coat and Rr has a roan coat (a mixture of white and red).

Incomplete Metamorphosis   **Def.** the changes some insects go through in their life cycle. The stages are egg, nymph and adult. The nymph is structurally very similar to the adult. Ex. cockroach, locust.

Inoculation   **Def.** the transfer of micro-organisms to a nutrient agar plate using aseptic techniques.
Expan. An Inoculating Loop is used to transfer micro-organisms from a source to an agar plate.

Inspiratory* Reserve Volume   **Def.** the volume of air (about 2,500 cm^3) we can breathe in, over and above the tidal volume.

Insulin   **Def.** a hormone produced by the Islets of Langerhans in the pancreas. It reduces glucose levels in the blood.

Intercostal Muscles   **Def.** involved in breathing and located between the ribs. As we inhale they contract and lift the ribs. They relax to lower the ribs as we exhale.
Expan. Inhalation is active i.e. it requires energy. Exhalation is passive i.e. no energy is needed.

Krebs' Cycle   **Def.** the second stage of aerobic respiration. It occurs in the stroma of the mitochondria and involves the breakdown of Acetyl Coenzyme A, to form CO_2 and $NADH_2$.

Lateral Bud   **Def.** a bud located below the Terminal bud in woody Angiosperms. They produce lateral growth or twigs in the growing season.

Leaf Scar   **Def.** the scar remaining after leaf fall on the stem of a woody deciduous Angiosperm.

Legumes* (Leguminous)   **Def.** plants that have nodules in their roots where the nitrogen-fixing bacteria Rhizobium live in a symbiotic relationship. Ex. pea, clover.
Expan. they play a vital role in the nitrogen cycle by converting nitrogen gas (N_2) to nitrates (NO_3) which can then be absorbed by plant roots and converted to protein.

Lenticel*   **Def.** opening on the bark of woody Angiosperms that allows gaseous exchange to occur.

Light Stage (photosynthesis)   **Def.** a light-dependent stage of photosynthesis that occurs in the lamellae and grana of the chloroplast. It uses light energy to produce ATP, $NADPH_2$ and Oxygen.
Expan. It occurs in two forms, Cyclic Photophosphorylation and non-Cyclic Photophosphorylation.

Linkage*	**Def.** genes that control different traits (non-allelic) that have loci on the same chromosome are said to be linked. They do not sort independently at gamete formation.
Locus*	**Def.** is the position of a gene on a chromosome. Homologous chromosomes have allelic genes on the same loci.
Lymph Node	**Def.** swelling on lymph vessels, located mainly in the neck and groin that filter foreign bodies out of lymph. They are important in defence by producing lymphocytes and antibodies.
Lymph	**Def.** clear fluid that leaks from blood capillaries and enters lymph vessels. It is similar to plasma and contains white blood cells (Lymphocytes). Lymph has a function in defence.
Medulla Oblongata*	**Def.** an involuntary (not under conscious control) part of the hindbrain located above the spinal cord in mammals. It controls the rates of breathing and heartbeat. **Expan.** It is very sensitive to the CO_2 levels in the blood. As we exercise more respiration occurs, so the CO_2 in the blood increases. The medulla oblongata then stimulates the intercostal and diaphragm muscles to speed up and breathing occurs more quickly.
Meiosis*	**Def.** is a form of cell division where four cells are produced, each with half the full complement of chromosomes i.e. haploid or n. **Expan.** It is vital in the formation of gametes to halve the chromosome number. At fertilisation the correct full complement of chromosomes is restored to the offspring. In higher plants meiosis produces haploid spores which later form the haploid gametophyte stage of the plant's life cycle. Meiosis can lead to variation i.e. changes in the genotype of the offspring.
Mendel's First Law* **(Law of Segregation)**	The characteristics of organisms are controlled by pairs of genes (alleles) which separate at gamete formation. Only one of any pair can enter any single gamete. Ex. If a plant has the genotype Tt only one of the pair can enter a gamete, either T or t.
Mendel's Second Law (Law of Independent Assortment)*	When gametes are formed each member of a pair of alleles can combine with either member of another pair. **Expan.** If a plant has a genotype TtYy the T gene can enter a gamete with either Y or y. Similarly the t gene can enter a gamete with either Y or y. This means that if the genes are not linked equal numbers of the gametes TY, Ty, tY and ty would be expected. Mendel's second law does not hold true if genes are linked.
Meristem* **(Meristematic Tissue)**	**Def.** actively dividing (cells dividing by mitosis) plant tissues It is usually found in the root and shoot tips. Primary meristems lead to elongation and secondary meristems to widening or Secondary Thickening.
Mesoderm	**Def.** a middle germ layer of triploblastic metazoans, separating the ectoderm from the endoderm. It is produced during early development and gives rise to specific organs. **Expan.** In evolution as organisms grew larger they could no longer rely on simple diffusion to supply their inner cells with oxygen. A third germ layer, the mesoderm was developed that produced organs involved in gaseous exchange and transport. In higher animals these organs are the muscles, blood and blood vessels.

Metamorphosis*	**Def.** changes that occur in the form of an insect during its life cycle, from the egg to adult.
Mitosis*	**Def.** a form of cell division, where two cells are produced, identical to the parent cell. **Expan.** It is a means of preserving genotype from one generation of cells to the next.
Monohybrid Cross	**Def.** a genetic cross where only one characteristic is being observed. Ex. stem height.
Motor Neuron	**Def.** a nerve cell that transports messages from the central nervous system to an effector.
Multiple Alleles*	**Def.** When more than two alleles control a single trait. Ex. the trait blood group in humans is determined by three alleles, A, B and O.
Mutagen	**Def.** chemicals or forms of radiation that promote mutations. Ex. X-rays, nitrosamines.
Mutation	**Def.** a generally disadvantageous change in the base sequence of DNA that alters the genetic code. There are two types, gene and chromosome mutations. It can be caused by some chemicals and radiation.
Myelin Sheath	**Def.** an insulating layer around axons and dendrons secreted by Schwann cells. It speeds up the transmission of nerve impulses.
Natural Selection	**Def.** a theory of evolution by Charles Darwin that states: 'certain organisms with favourable characteristics that adapt them to their environment survive better and reproduce more.' i.e. survival of the fittest.
Natural Immunity	**Def.** the resistance of an organism to disease. **Expan.** It may be passive to prevent entry. Ex. skin, sweat and mucus. Active immunity is the struggle against the pathogen once it has entered the body with lymphocytes, granulocytes and antibodies.
Nephridium	**Def.** organ in the Earthworm (Lumbricus) that excretes urine. A pair of nephridia are present in almost all segments.
Nephron	**Def.** multicellular, tubular structure in the kidney. It functions in excretion forming urine, and in osmoregulation.
Nitrogen Cycle	**Def.** the changes that nitrogen and its compounds undergo in nature. **Expan.** It is a very important cycle as it provides nitrogen in a form (NO_3^-) that can be used by plants and then animals. Nitrogen is an essential component of proteins.
Nitrogen Fixation	**Def.** is the changing of atmospheric nitrogen (N_2) to nitrates (NO_3^-) by nitrogen-fixing bacteria. The nitrates can then be absorbed by the root hairs of plants and used to make proteins.
Noradrenaline	**Def.** a chemical transmitter that relays messages across synapses between nerve cells.
Nucleus	**Def.** a membrane-bound structure that contains DNA and a nucleolus. It controls all the activities in the cell. **Expan.** DNA in a cell at rest forms a mass of chromatin. When cells undergo cell division, the chromatin condenses to form chromosomes.
Organelles	**Def.** membrane-bound structures in cells that have specific functions. Ex. mitochondria, ribosomes, nucleus.
Osmoregulation*	**Def.** the control of the water/salt balance in the body.

Osmosis*	**Def.** the movement of water, from its region of high concentration (hypotonic) to its region of low concentration (hypertonic), across a semi-permeable membrane. It does not require energy.
Parasite*	**Def.** an organism that causes harm to a host by living off its materials for nourishment. Ex. flea, leech.
Parenchyma cells	**Def.** round thin-walled plant cells in plants that make and store food. Usually surrounded by air spaces, they are found in the cortex and pith of the stem and mesophyll of leaves.
Passive Transport	**Def.** the movement of a substance through a liquid or gas, with the diffusion gradient. It does not require energy. Ex. Osmosis or Diffusion.
Pasteurisation	**Def.** technique to preserve milk. Process involves heating to 72°C to inactivate most micro-organisms, then cooling quickly to below 10°C preventing heat spoilage.
Pathogen	**Def.** a disease-causing parasitic, micro-organism.
Pentadactyl Limb	**Def.** a five-digit limb common to many four-limbed vertebrates. **Expan.** This general structure, being common to many diverse animals, is used to support the theory of evolution.
Peristalsis	**Def.** the movement of food through the Alimentary Canal by the contractions of circular and longitudinal muscles.
Phloem*	**Def.** thin-walled living cells in higher plants, that transport food and hormones. They are found mainly in vascular bundles.
Photosynthesis	**Def.** the conversion of carbon dioxide and water to glucose and oxygen using sunlight energy and chlorophyll. **Expan.** A balanced equation of photosynthesis is: $$6CO_2 + 6H_2O \xrightarrow{\text{Sunlight Energy + Chlorophyll}} C_6H_{12}O_6 + 6O_2$$
Plasmolysis	**Def.** a process that occurs in plant cells when placed in a hypertonic environment. The cytoplasm and cell membrane separate from the cell wall due to water loss by osmosis.
Polar nuclei	**Def.** two haploid nuclei in the embryo sac, that fuse with a male gamete from pollen to form a triploid (3n) endosperm nucleus. **Expan.** The endosperm nucleus can develop to form the endosperm food store in the seed.
Polyploidy	**Def.** the gain of a whole set(s) of extra chromosomes in plants due to chromosome mutations. It usually leads to infertile gametes being produced. **Expan.** Many polyploid plants grow larger and more vigorously than normal plants and reproduce very well asexually. Farmers introduce this condition to increase crop yield.
Potometer	**Def.** a device used to measure the rate of transpiration in a woody shoot. It can be used to investigate the external conditions that affect the rate of transpiration. Ex. wind, temperature.
Predator*	**Def.** any animal that captures and feeds on another animal.
Prolactin	**Def.** hormone produced by the pituitary. It stimulates the mammary glands to produce milk.

Prophase **Def.** an early stage of cell division in both mitosis and meiosis where chromosomes become visible and make copies of themselves, forming pairs of sister chromatids joined at the centromere.

Protein **Def.** chain(s) of amino acids containing the elements Carbon, Hydrogen, Oxygen and Nitrogen. Meat, eggs, milk and nuts are all good sources of protein.
Expan. There are two main types of protein classified according to function.
1. Structural Ex.   keratin in hair and nails,
                     collagen in tendons and arteries.
2. Physiologically Active Ex. enzymes and hormones.

Recessive **Def.** the gene that is not expressed in the phenotype of an organism in the heterozygous condition.
Expan. If T is the gene for tall stem plant and t is a gene for a short stem an individual plant with the genotype Tt would have a tall stem. The t gene is recessive.

Recombinants **Def.** offspring with new combinations of genes formed on their chromosomes. The new combinations are due to linked genes crossing over during meiosis.
Expan. A cross between a fruit fly with a grey body and normal antennae (GgNn) and a fly with a black body and twisted antennae (ggnn) produced almost 50% with grey bodies and normal antennae and almost 50% with black body and twisted antennae. A small number of flies were produced with grey bodies and twisted antennae and black bodies and normal antennae. These are recombinants.

Reflex Action **Def.** a response to a stimulus that does not involve the brain. Ex. Knee jerk reaction.

Refractory Period **Def.** a compulsory period of rest for a nerve cell between the transmission of messages.

Residual Volume **Def.** the volume of air (about 1,500 cm^3) that remains in the lungs after all the air possible has been breathed out.

Respiration **Def.** the enzyme-controlled release of energy from food. It occurs in the cells of all organisms and the energy produced is stored chemically as ATP.

Rhizobium **Def.** a symbiotic bacteria, found in the nodules of leguminous plants. It carries out nitrogen fixation.

Rhizome* **Def.** a modified underground stem in the Fern and some flowering Plants that produces adventitious roots. It is a means of asexual reproduction.

Ribosome* **Def.** a cell organelle made of RNA that acts as a site for protein synthesis. It is located in the cytoplasm.

Ringing Experiments **Def.** used to provide evidence that translocation occurs in the phloem cells. They involve the removal of the bark and outer tissues (phloem) from a woody twig.

RNA (Ribonucleic acid) **Def.** a nucleic acid in the form of a single helix found mainly in the cytoplasm of the cell. It transports messages from DNA in the nucleus to ribosomes in the cytoplasm.

Saprophyte **Def.** an organism that feeds on the remains of dead organisms. Ex. Bread Mould (Rhizopus).

Scale Scars* **Def.** scars on a twig of a woody Angiosperm, showing the previous position of the terminal bud.

	Expan. The distance between any two sets of scale scars represents one year's growth on a twig.
Schwann Cells	**Def.** cells that secrete the myelin sheath around the Axons and dendrons of nerve cells.
Sclerenchyma Cells	**Def.** thick-walled cells located throughout the plant. They die at maturity and become lignified, their function is to provide support.
Secondary Thickening	**Def.** the lateral growth of perennial dicot. plant stems, providing strength and support. It occurs by a ring of cambium cells producing new xylem and phloem each year.
Sensory Neuron	**Def.** a nerve cell that transports messages from a sense organ to the central nervous system.
Sere*	**Def.** the stages of succession that lead to a climax community in a habitat. A Hydrosere is a sere that begins in water. A Xerosere is a sere that begins in dry conditions.
Setae	**Def.** extendable bristles on the surface of Annelids (Ex. Earthworm) used for movement.
Sex Chromosomes*	**Def.** a pair of chromosomes in mammals that determine the sex of the individual. There are two types: a large X and a smaller Y chromosome. XY = male, XX = female.
Sister Chromatids	**Def.** during prophase of cell division each chromosome forms an identical copy of itself and both are joined at the centromere. The two copies are sister chromatids.
Somatic Cell	**Def.** any cell in an organism not involved in reproduction. Ex. stomach or brain cell.
Species*	**Def.** a group of individuals that can interbreed successfully.
Spiracles*	**Def.** openings on the impermeable exoskeleton of Arthropods (insects), leading to tracheae. They facilitate gaseous exchange.
Spore	**Def. 1.** a haploid reproductive structure produced by the Sporophyte stage of higher plants. It develops to form the gametophyte. **2.** a resting stage of a fungus or bacteria that is resistant to adverse conditions. Under suitable conditions it germinates to form a new organism.
Sterilisation	**Def.** procedures used to destroy micro-organisms that could cause disease or spoilage.
Sweat Glands	**Def.** exocrine glands in the dermis of skin that secrete water and salts. They function in excretion and temperature control.
Symbiosis (Symbiotic)	**Def.** two different organisms existing together for the benefit of both. Ex. algae + fungus forming a lichen or, Rhizobium in the root nodules of clover.
Synapse	**Def.** space between the end of one nerve cell and the beginning of another. **Expan.** At this point a message is converted from an electrical to a chemical form that passes the message between the two cells.
Synaptic Knobs	**Def.** nerve cell endings that receive messages from the cell body. **Expan.** The message is changed from an electrical to a chemical form and secreted into a synapse.
Terminal (Apical) Bud*	**Def.** a bud at the tip of the stem of woody Angiosperms that produces auxin to control elongation of the stem. **Expan.** The terminal bud restricts the growth of lateral growth buds below it by producing large amounts of Auxin. This is known as Apical Dominance. If the

terminal bud is removed, elongation stops, the lateral buds grow much more quickly providing a thicker more bushy appearance.

Threshold (Level)*   **Def.** a level of stimulus below which a nerve cell will not conduct a message.

Thrombin*   **Def.** a blood enzyme, made in the liver that converts soluble fibrinogen to fibrin in the process of blood clotting.

Tidal Volume*   **Def.** the volume of air (about 500 cm^3) breathed in and out of the lungs while at rest.

Toxin   **Def.** a poison released by pathogenic micro-organisms (bacteria) into the body.

Transect*   **Def.** a procedure used to estimate plant types (qualitative survey) or plant numbers (quantitative survey) in a habitat.

Translocation   **Def.** the transport of food and hormones around a plant. In mature plants it occurs in the phloem vessels.

Expan. In seedlings translocation occurs mainly from the cotyledons to the root and shoot tips. In mature plants it occurs to provide food for developing buds and flowers.

Transpiration   **Def.** the loss of water vapour from the surface of a plant.

Transpiration Stream   **Def.** the movement of water from the soil into the root, up the xylem and out through the leaves of a plant.

Triplet Code   **Def.** a section of DNA or RNA that contains three nucleic acids, the type and sequence of which codes for a specific amino acid.

Triploblastic   **Def.** a metazoan that forms three germ layers, the ectoderm, mesoderm and endoderm, during early development. Ex. Liver Fluke (Fasciola).

Tropism   **Def.** the response of a plant to an external stimulus.

Expan. Tropisms position the plant most favourably in the environment. Ex. shoots grow towards light to provide maximum sunlight for leaves. Roots grow towards water and for anchorage.

Turgor (Turgid)   **Def.** the condition of plant cells in a hypotonic solution, when no more water can enter by osmosis.

Expan. Wall Pressure exerted by the cell wall prevents further entry of water.

Typhlosole*   **Def.** infolding of the alimentary canal of the Earthworm (Lumbricus), that increases the surface area for (a) absorption of digested food, and (b) the secretion of enzymes.

Ultrafiltration*   **Def.** filtration under pressure of the blood in the Bowman's capsule of the nephron to form the glomerular filtrate.

Vaccine*   **Def.** a suspension of weakened pathogens, injected into the body, to stimulate antibody production. It promotes greater resistance to disease.

Expan. On first exposure to a new pathogen, the body requires a number of days to recognise and produce specific antibodies to destroy it. During this time we suffer from the effects of the disease. On a second exposure to the same pathogen, the response is much faster and its effects are not developed.

Villus   **Def.** multiple finger-like structures in the ileum richly supplied with blood capillaries and lymph vessels. Their function is to increase surface area for absorption.

Virus   **Def.** an obligate parasite that consists of an outer protein coat surrounding either DNA or RNA.

	Expan. It can only reproduce inside a host cell (animal, plant or bacterial cell). It is very difficult to produce a vaccine against viral diseases as their structure is continually changing.
Visking Tubing	**Def.** artificial semi-permeable membrane used in diffusion and osmosis experiments.
Weathering*	**Def.** the physical and chemical breakdown of the inorganic part (stone) of soil by sun, wind, rainwater etc.
Xylem*	**Def.** thick-walled, lignified cells present in higher plants that function in water transport and support. Located mainly in vascular bundles of stems.
	Expan. There are two types: vessels and tracheids. Both are thick-walled and die when the plant matures.
Zoospores	**Def.** biflagellate, motile spores produced by the fungus Phytophthora (potato blight), during asexual reproduction.
Zygospore	**Def.** a diploid zygote surrounded by a thick resistant coat.
	Expan. It is produced after sexual reproduction in the alga Spirogyra and also the fungus Rhizopus.
Zygote	**Def.** a diploid nucleus formed by the fusion of two haploid gametes.

LEAVING CERTIFICATE EXAMINATION, 2004

BIOLOGY – ORDINARY LEVEL

2.00 to 5.00

Section A Answer any **five** questions from this section.
Each question carries 20 marks.
Write your answers in the spaces provided on the examination paper.

Section B Answer any **two** questions from this section.
Each question carries 30 marks.
Write your answers in the spaces provided on the examination paper.

Section C Answer any **four** questions from this section.
Each question carries 60 marks.
Write your answers in the answer book.

You should spend not more than 30 minutes on Section A and 30 minutes on Section B, leaving 120 minutes for Section C.

SECTION A

ANSWER ANY FIVE QUESTIONS.
Write your answers in the spaces provided.

1. Complete **four** of the following sentences by putting **one word** in the blank space.

    (a) The hepatic portal vein carries blood from the alimentary canal to the _Liver_.

    (b) A tendon joins _muscle_ to bone.

    (c) Phototropism is the growth response of a plant to _light_.

    (d) Hormones are secreted by _Endocrine_ glands.

    (e) Gas exchange between a leaf and the atmosphere takes place through the _stomata_.

2. Select the correct cell component from the following list and write it opposite its partner in column B.

ribosome, vacuole, chloroplast, cell membrane, mitochondrion

Column A	Column B
Contains chlorophyll	chloroplast
Site of protein formation	ribosome
Site of energy release	mito
Site of storage of water, salts and sugars	Vacuole
Allows osmosis to occur	Membrane

3. Indicate whether each of the following statements are true (T) or false (F) by drawing a circle around T or F.

Example: The pulmonary artery carries blood to the lungs — (T)   F

Mitosis is the division of a nucleus into two identical nuclei — (T)   F
A sperm contains the haploid number of chromosomes — (T)   F
Chromosomes are made of DNA and lipid — T   (F)
Organisms of the same species can usually produce fertile offspring — (T)   F
Aerobic respiration is the release of energy in the absence of oxygen — T   (F)
RNA is not found in ribosomes — T   (F)
Immobilised enzymes can act as catalysts — (T)   F

4. The diagram shows the structure of one type of joint.

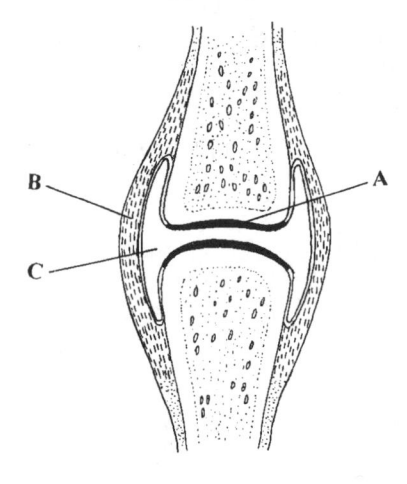

Name this type of joint. __Hinge__

Give **one** location in the human body of this type of joint. _____

Name the following parts

A _____

B _____

C _____

Name another type of joint found in the human body. _____

5. Fats are composed of fatty acids and _____

What name is given to fats that are liquid at room temperature? _____

State **two** functions of fats in the human body

(i) _____

(ii) _____

An example of a fat-soluble vitamin is _____.

A good source of this vitamin is _____.

A lack of this vitamin may lead to _____.

6. Answer the following questions in relation to the food web shown below.

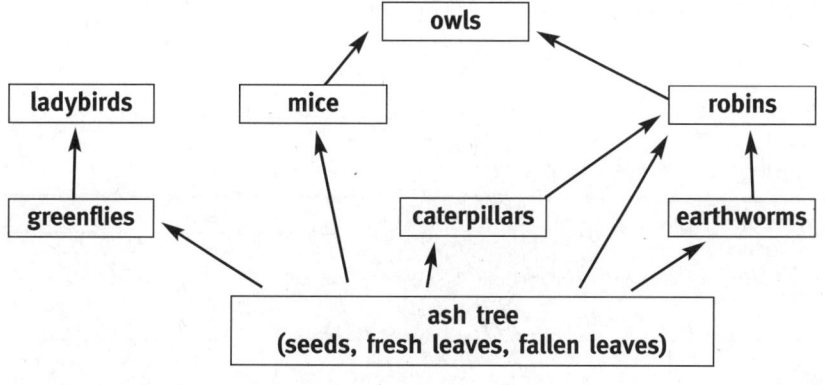

```
                    owls
           ↗         ↑    ↖
   ladybirds    mice      robins
       ↑         ↑       ↗    ↑
   greenflies  caterpillars  earthworms
       ↖        ↑        ↗
              ash tree
       (seeds, fresh leaves, fallen leaves)
```

Write out a food chain with **four** organisms in it. _____

_____

Name the primary producer in the web. _____

145

Name **two** secondary consumers in the web.

1 _____ 2 _____

Name **two** herbivores in the web.

1 _____ 2 _____

Name **one** omnivore in the web. _____

Name **one** carnivore in the web. _____

SECTION B

ANSWER ANY TWO QUESTIONS.
Write your answers in the spaces provided.

Part (a) carries 6 marks and part (b) carries 24 marks in each question in this section.

7. (a) Name the parts of the light microscope labelled A and B.

A _eye piece_

B _objective lens_

If the magnification of A is X 10 and the magnification of B is X 40, what magnification results when a slide is viewed using B? _X 400_

(b) Answer the following in relation to preparing a slide of stained plant cells and viewing them under the microscope.

(i) From what plant did you obtain the cells? _onion_

(ii) Describe how you obtained a thin piece of a sample of the cells.

• _peeled of thin film of plant tissue with foceps._

• _Cut the plant tissue with a blade_

What stain did you use for the cells on the slide? _____

iodine solution

Describe how you applied this stain. __using a dropper__

What did you do before placing the slide with the stained cells on the microscope platform? __put a cover slip over it at an angle so to trap no bubbles.__

State **two** features of these cells that indicate that they are typical plant cells.

1. __chloroplasts__
2. __cell wall__

8. (a) Name an ecosystem that you have studied. __Woodland/hedgerow__

Name **three** animals that are **normally** present in this ecosystem.

1. __fox__
2. __snail__
3. __caterpillar__

(b) Select **one** of the animals that you have named in (a) and answer the following questions in relation to it.

Which animal have you selected? __snail__

State **two** features that allowed you to identify the animal.

1. __no legs__
2. __shell__

Name an organism on which this animal normally feeds. __oak tree__

Explain how you attempted to find out how many of these animals were present in the ecosystem. __capture re-capture method__
• A number were

_____
_____
_____

Using the axes below draw a graph to show how you would expect the numbers of this animal to vary in the ecosystem in the course of a year.

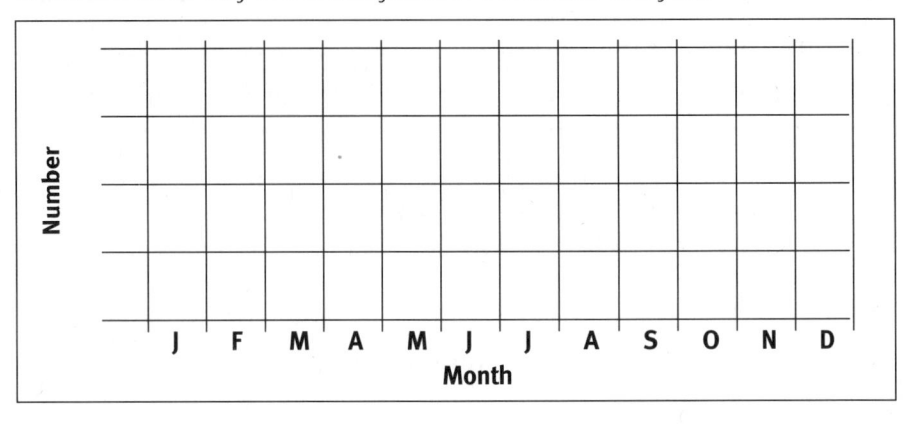

```
Number │
       │
       │
       │
       └──J─F─M─A─M─J─J─A─S─O─N─D──
                    Month
```

9. (a) Answer the following in relation to human breathing rate OR pulse rate.

State which of these you will refer to. _____

What is the average rate at rest? _____

State a possible effect of smoking on the resting rate. _____
_____

(b) How did you measure the resting rate? _____
_____
_____
_____

Describe how you investigated the effect of exercise on this rate.
_____
_____
_____
_____

Using the axes below draw a graph to show how rate is likely to vary as the exercise level increases.

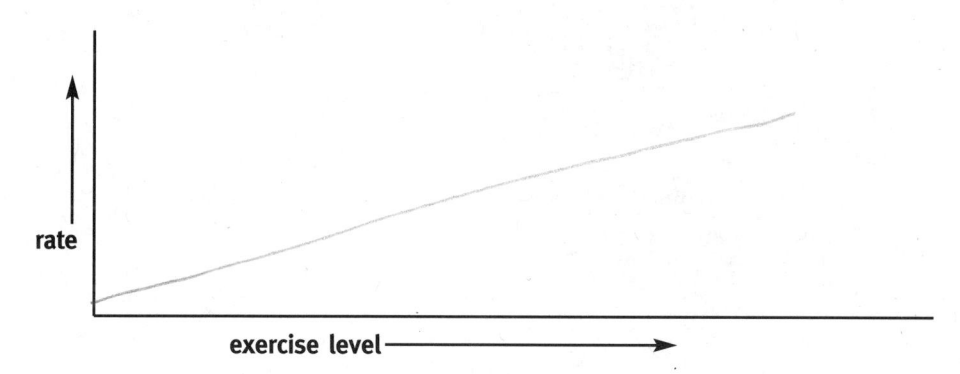

[Graph: rate vs exercise level, showing an increasing curve]

SECTION C

ANSWER ANY FOUR QUESTIONS.
Write your answers in the answer book.

solvent
nutrition
transport

10. (a) Water has many functions in the human body. State **three** of these functions. **(9)**

(b) (i) Name the chemical elements present in carbohydrates. *Carbon, Hydrogen, Oxygen*

(ii) Give an example of a carbohydrate that has a structural role. Where would you expect to find this carbohydrate in a living organism? *Cellulose – Cell wall*

(iii) State a role of carbohydrates other than a structural one. *energy storage*

(iv) Name a test that you would carry out to show the presence of a reducing sugar (e.g. glucose). *Bendedits solution, heat blue → brick red*

(v) Describe how you would carry out the test that you have named in (iv). **(24)**

(c) (i) Name a chemical element found in proteins that is **not** found in carbohydrates. *Nitrogen*

(ii) State **two** good sources of protein in the human diet. *meat*

(iii) Proteins are digested to simpler substances. What are these simpler substances called? *Amino Acids*

(iv) State **one** function of protein in the human body. *energy*

(v) Name a test for protein. *Biuret test*

(vi) Describe how you would carry out the test that you have named in (v). **(27)**

sodium hydroxide + copper sulfate
blue → purple.

11. (a) What are secondary sexual characteristics? Give an example of a human secondary sexual characteristic. **(9)**

(b) The diagram shows the reproductive system of the human male.

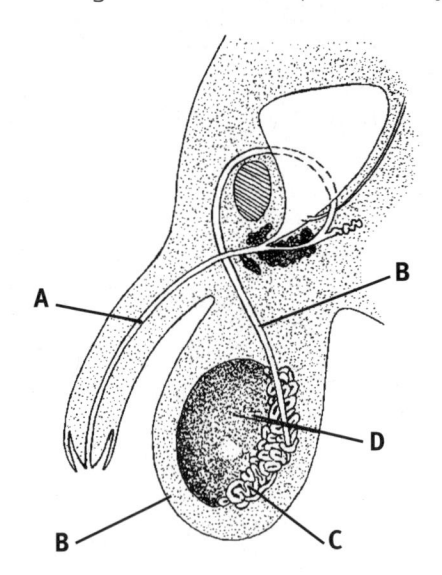

(i) Name the parts A, B, C, D, E.
(ii) Where are sperm produced? D — testis
(iii) What is the function of the prostate gland? produce fluid
(iv) State **one** way in which a sperm differs from an ovum (egg). has tail **(24)**

(c) (i) What is meant by infertility? State **one** cause of infertility in the human male.
(ii) Name **three** methods of contraception and, in each case, explain how the method prevents conception. **(27)**

12. (a) Explain the following terms that are used in genetics; dominance, genotype, phenotype. **(9)**

(b) In Aberdeen Angus cattle, the polled **(P)** condition (absence of horns) is dominant to the horned **(p)** condition. A heterozygous polled bull was crossed with a horned cow. Use the following layout in your answer book to find the possible genotypes and phenotypes of the calves that may result from this cross.

	Heterozygous polled bull	X	Horned cow
Genotypes of parents	_____		_____
Gametes	___ ___		___
Genotypes of calves	_____		_____
Phenotypes of calves	_____		_____

(27)

(c) (i) What is meant by DNA profiling?
 (ii) Describe briefly how DNA profiling is carried out.
 (iii) Give **two** uses of DNA profiling. **(24)**

13. (a) What is metabolism? Describe briefly the part played by enzymes in metabolism. **(9)**
 (b) The following equation summarises the process of photosynthesis.

$$\text{Gas A + Water} \xrightarrow[\text{Chlorophyll}]{\text{Energy}} \text{Glucose + Gas B}$$

 (i) Name Gas A.
 (ii) Name Gas B.
 (iii) Name the energy source.
 (iv) Plants obtain Gas A from the air. Name **two** processes that release this gas into the air.
 (v) Suggest **two** possible fates for Gas B, following its production in the plant.
 (vi) Where in a leaf would you expect to find cells with most chlorophyll?
 (vii) What term is used to describe the nutrition of plants? **(27)**

 (c) The apparatus shown below may be used to investigate the effect of an environmental factor on the rate of photosynthesis.
 (i) Name X and Y.
 (ii) How would you measure the rate of photosynthesis?
 (iii) Name an environmental factor that you would vary in this experiment.
 (iv) Explain how you would vary the factor that you have named in (iii).
 (v) Other environmental factors should be kept constant during the experiment. Name **one** of these factors. **(24)**

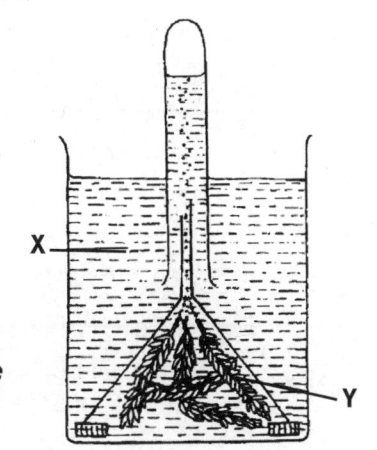

14. Answer **any two** of (a), (b), (c). (30, 30)

(a) (i) State a function of each of the following parts of a flower:
1. petal   2. sepal   3. anther.

(ii) Explain what is meant by pollination. What is the difference between self-pollination and cross-pollination?

(iii) Name **two** ways in which cross-pollination happens.

(iv) Suggest why cross-pollination is preferable to self-pollination.

(b) (i) Name a part of a flower from which a fruit develops.

(ii) In each of the following cases give **one** example of a plant that uses the stated method of seed dispersal:
1. wind
2. animal

(iii) Why is it important for plants to disperse their seeds?

(iv) What is meant by the dormancy of seeds?

(v) Suggest an advantage of dormancy of seeds to a plant.

(c) (i) What is meant by germination?

(ii) List **three** factors that are essential for germination.

(iii) In the case of **one** of the factors that you have named in (ii), explain how it affects germination.

(iv) Describe an experiment to demonstrate that the factors you have named in (ii) are essential for germination. Include a diagram of the apparatus in your answer.

15. Answer **any two** of (a), (b), (c). (30, 30)

(a) The diagram shows the structure of the human ear.

(i) Name the parts A, B, C, D, E, F.

(ii) What is connected to the ear by D?

(iii) Which is present in G, gas or liquid?

(iv) State the function of E.

(v) State the function of F.

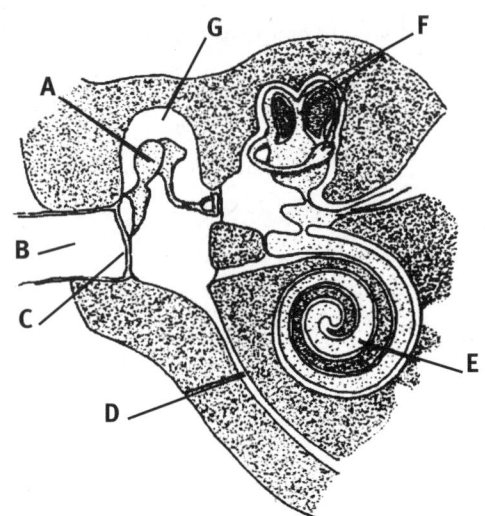

(b) (i) What is a hormone?
 (ii) Draw an outline diagram of the human body and indicate on it the location of the following hormone-producing glands by using the following letters:
 W   Pituitary
 X   Thyroid
 Y   Pancreas (Islets of Langerhans)
 Z   Adrenals
 (iii) In the case of **one** of the hormone-producing glands that you have located in your diagram, state:
  1. the gland and a hormone that it produces.
  2. a function of this hormone.
  3. a deficiency symptom of this hormone.
 (iv) State **one** way in which hormone action differs from nerve action.

(c) Diagrams A and B are of plant vascular tissues.

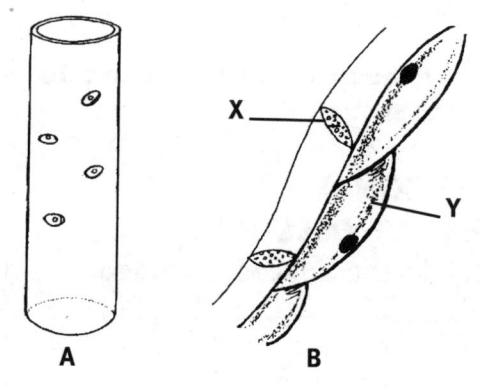

 (i) Identify A and B.
 (ii) What is meant by a vascular tissue?
 (iii) Name X and Y.
 (iv) State a function of A.
 (v) State a function of B.
 (vi) Where would you expect to find A and B in a leaf?
 (vii) Name **one** substance found in the walls of A but not found in the walls of B.

LEAVING CERTIFICATE EXAMINATION, 2004

BIOLOGY – HIGHER LEVEL

2.00 to 5.00

Section A Answer any **five** questions from this section.
Each question carries 20 marks.
Write your answers in the spaces provided on the examination paper.

Section B Answer any **two** questions from this section.
Each question carries 30 marks.
Write your answers in the spaces provided on the examination paper.

Section C Answer any **four** questions from this section.
Each question carries 60 marks.
Write your answers in the answer book.

You should spend not more than 30 minutes on Section A and 30 minutes on Section B, leaving 120 minutes for Section C.

SECTION A
ANSWER ANY <u>FIVE</u> QUESTIONS.
Write your answers in the spaces provided.

1. Answer **any five** of the following.
   (a) Name an autotrophic organism. _Grass_
   (b) Give an example of a catabolic reaction. _Respiration_
   (c) The conversion of atmospheric nitrogen to nitrates by bacteria is called _nitrification_
   (d) What is the ratio of hydrogen atoms to oxygen atoms in a carbohydrate? _2:1_
   (e) A relationship between two organisms in which both benefit is called _mutualistic_.
   (f) An example of a protein that has a structural role is _myosin_.

2. The diagram shows the distribution of heights in a group of men between the ages of 18 and 23.

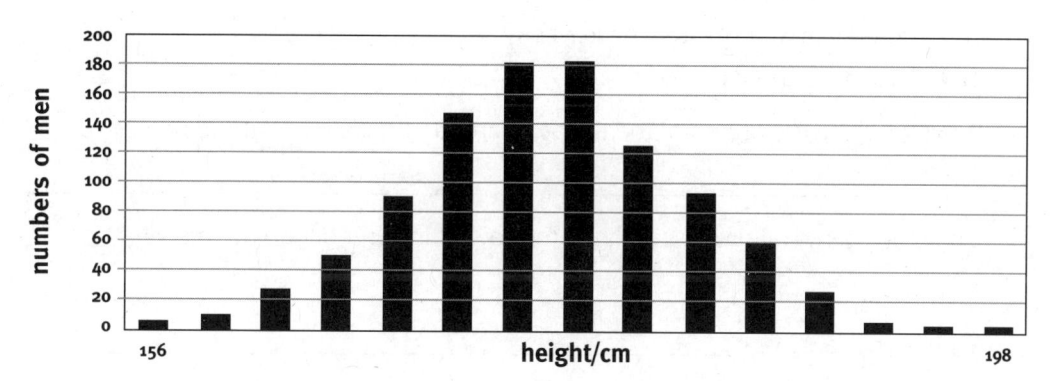

[Bar chart: numbers of men (y-axis, 0–200) vs height/cm (x-axis, 156 to 198)]

What term is used by biologists to describe differences within a population with respect to features such as height? _____

State **two** factors that could be responsible for the differences shown.

1. _____

2. _____

Would you expect a similar distribution if the students were weighed instead of being measured for height? _____

_____

Explain your answer. _____

_____

What is a mutation? _____

State **one** cause of mutation. _____

Give an example of a condition, found in the human population, that results from a mutation. _____

_____

3. In tomato plants the allele responsible for purple stem **(P)** is dominant to that for green stem **(p)** and the allele for cut leaf **(C)** is dominant to the allele for potato type leaf **(c)**. A plant with a purple stem and cut leaves was crossed with a plant with a green stem and potato type leaves. A total of 448 seeds was obtained. When the seeds were germinated four types of progeny resulted and they had the following phenotypes:

110 purple stem and cut leaves
115 green stem and potato type leaves
114 purple stem and potato type leaves
109 green stem and cut leaves

What were the genotypes of the tomato plants that gave rise to these progeny? ____

_____

Do the progeny of this cross illustrate the Law of Independent Assortment? _____

_____

Explain your answer. _____

_____

_____

_____

4. (a) The diagram shows part of the under surface of a leaf as seen through the microscope. A is an aperture. B and C are cells.

© Eric Grave/Science Photo Library

Name A, B, C.

A _____ B _____ C _____

What is the function of A? _____

Name a factor that influences the diameter of A. _____

Name the apertures in stems that are equivalent to A. _____

(b) In some species of flowering plants the leaves are modified for the storage of food.

Name a plant in which the leaves are modified for food storage. _____

Name a carbohydrate that you would expect to find in the modified leaves of the plant that you named above. _____

Name a type of modified stem that functions in food storage. _____

5. (a) What is meant by pollution? _____

Give an example of a human activity that results in the pollution of air or water. _____

Suggest a means of counteracting this pollution. _____

(b) Explain conservation in relation to wild plants and animals. _____

Suggest **two** reasons for conserving wild species.

(i) _____

(ii) _____

State **one** conservation practice from agriculture **or** fisheries **or** forestry. _____

6. Answer the following questions in relation to the human alimentary canal.

What is peristalsis? _____

State **one** reason why a low pH is important in the stomach. _____

Why is fibre important? _____

Name an enzyme that is involved in the digestion of fat. _____

What are the products of fat digestion? _____

What is the role of bile in fat digestion? _____

State a role of beneficial bacteria in the alimentary canal. _____

SECTION B

ANSWER ANY TWO QUESTIONS.
Write your answers in the spaces provided.

Part (a) carries 6 marks and part (b) carries 24 marks in each question in this section.

7. (a) Yeast cells produce ethanol (alcohol) in a process called fermentation.

Is this process affected by temperature? _____

Explain your answer. _____

_____

_____

(b) Answer the following in relation to an experiment to prepare and show the presence of ethanol using yeast.

Draw a labelled diagram of the apparatus that you used.

Name a substance that yeast can use to make ethanol. _____

What substance, other than ethanol, is produced during fermentation? _____

Describe the control that you used in this experiment. _____

_____

Explain the purpose of a control in a scientific experiment._____

_____

_____

How did you know when the fermentation was finished? _____

_____

_____

Why were solutions of potassium iodide and sodium hypochlorite added to the reaction vessels after a certain period of time? _____

_____

Name a substance produced during aerobic respiration that is not produced during fermentation. _____

_____

8. (a) Observation of a transverse section of a dicotyledonous stem reveals vascular and other tissues. Name **two** of the tissues that are not vascular tissues.

1. _____   2. _____

(b) Answer the following questions in relation to the preparation of a microscope slide of a transverse section of a dicotyledonous stem.

State **one** reason why you used an herbaceous stem rather than a woody one.

_____

_____

Explain how you cut the section. _____

_____

_____

_____

Why is it desirable to cut the section as thinly as possible?

Draw a diagram of the section as seen under the microscope. Label the vascular tissues that can be seen.

State **one** precise function of each of the vascular tissues labelled in your diagram.

_____

_____

_____

_____

9. (a) (i) Cardiac muscle may be described as a <u>contractile</u> tissue. Explain the meaning of the underlined term. _____

_____

    (ii) Which chamber of the heart has the greatest amount of muscle in its wall?

_____

(b) Describe how you dissected a mammalian heart in order to investigate the internal structure of atria and ventricles.

_____

_____

_____

_____

_____

_____

_____

Draw a labelled diagram of your dissection to show the location and structure of the bicuspid and tricuspid valves.

State the procedure that you followed to expose a semilunar valve.

_____

_____

_____

_____

What is the function of a semilunar valve?

_____

Where in your dissection did you find the origin of the coronary artery?

_____

SECTION C

ANSWER ANY FOUR QUESTIONS.
Write your answers in the answer book.

10. (a) Explain the following terms that are used in ecology: biosphere, habitat, niche. **(9)**

(b) In ecological studies it is found that the distribution of organisms is influenced by <u>abiotic</u> and <u>biotic</u> factors.
  - (i) Distinguish between the underlined terms.
  - (ii) Name an ecosystem that you have investigated and give an example of an abiotic factor that influences the distribution of a named plant in the ecosystem.
  - (iii) In the case of your named ecosystem give an example of a biotic factor that influences the distribution of a named animal.
  - (iv) What is meant by a pyramid of numbers? Construct a pyramid of numbers from organisms in the ecosystem that you have studied.
  - (v) What term is used by ecologists to describe the organisms that form the base of the pyramid? **(24)**

(c) Lemmings are small rodents that are widespread in northern latitudes. The graph shows the fluctuations in lemming numbers in northern Manitoba between 1929 and 1943.

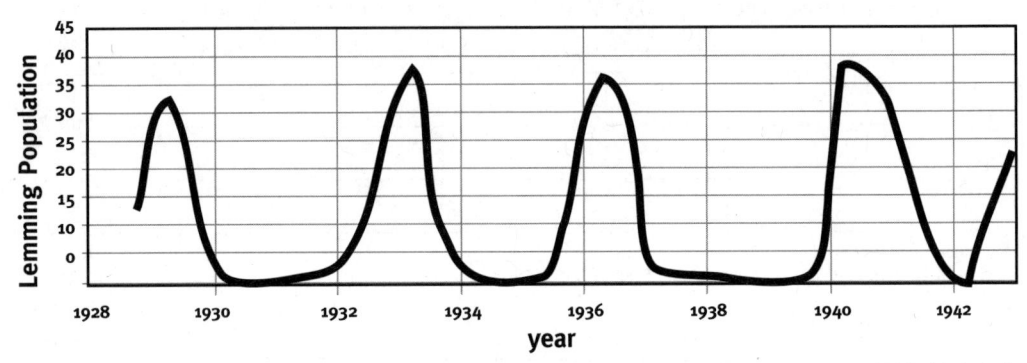

[Adapted from J.P. Finerty (1980). *The Population Ecology of Cycles in Small Mammals*. Yale University Press, New Haven].

- (i) The graph indicates that population peaks occur at fairly regular intervals. What is the approximate average time between these peaks?
- (ii) What is the mean maximum population density (numbers per hectare) for the period covered by the graph?
- (iii) What is a predator? The Arctic fox is a predator of the lemming. Copy the graph into your answer book and draw on it a graph to show how you would expect the population of the Arctic fox to have varied in northern Manitoba during the period 1929–1943.
- (iv) Suggest **two** factors other than predation that might account for the declines in lemmings shown in the graph.
- (v) Suggest **two** factors that may have been responsible for the fairly regular increase in lemming numbers shown in the graph. **(27)**

11. (a) ATP is an abbreviation. What does it stand for? Explain briefly the role of ATP in the energy exchanges of a cell. **(9)**

(b) (i) The first stage of photosynthesis is commonly known as the light-dependent stage. It involves the energising of electrons and their subsequent passage along two possible pathways. Give an account of what happens on each of these pathways.

(ii) What is the fate of each of the products of the light-dependent stage? **(27)**

(c) The effect of changing light intensity or carbon dioxide concentration on the rate of photosynthesis may be investigated by using the pond weed **Elodea**. Answer the following in relation to this investigation.

- (i) Why is a water plant rather than a land plant used in this experiment?
- (ii) How is the temperature kept constant in this experiment?

(iii) If pond water is used in the experiment, it is likely to contain dissolved carbon dioxide. Suggest two possible sources of carbon dioxide in pond water.

(iv) Explain how light intensity or carbon dioxide concentration may be varied.

(v) Each time light intensity or carbon dioxide concentration is varied a precaution is necessary. What is this precaution and why is it necessary? **(24)**

12. (a) What is homeostasis? State the role of the kidneys in homeostasis. **(9)**

(b) (i) Draw a labelled diagram of a nephron. Include blood vessels in your diagram.

(ii) Filtration and reabsorption are vital processes that take place in the nephron. Describe how each of these processes occurs. **(27)**

(c) Answer the following questions in relation to human body temperature.

(i) What is the source of the heat that allows the body to maintain a constant internal temperature?

(ii) State **two** ways in which the body is insulated against loss of heat.

(iii) Describe the ways in which the body responds when its internal temperature rises above the normal level.

(iv) Describe briefly the hormonal and nervous responses that occur when internal body temperature drops. **(24)**

13. (a) Copy the diagram into your answer book and then complete it to show the complementary base pairs of the DNA molecule. Label all parts not already labelled. **(9)**

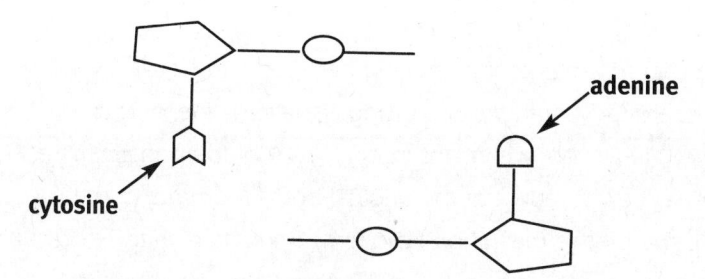

(b) The genetic code incorporated into the DNA molecule finds its expression in part of the formation of protein. This formation requires the involvement of a number of RNA molecules. List these RNA molecules and briefly describe the role of each of them. **(24)**

(c) Read the following passage and answer the questions that follow:

Dolly, the most famous sheep in the world, was cloned in the Roslin Institute in Scotland in 1996. When this was announced in February 1997 it caused a sensation, because until then many scientists thought that such cloning was impossible.

Such cloning is the production of one or more animals that are genetically identical to an existing animal. This cloning technique is based on the fact that, with the exception of the sperm and the egg, every cell in the body contains in its DNA all of the genetic material needed to make an exact replica of the original body. During the normal development process from embryo to fully-fledged animal, all of the cells in the body are differentiated to perform specific physiological functions. Before Dolly, the majority view was that such differentiated cells could not be reprogrammed to be able to behave as fertilised eggs.

Dolly was produced by a process known as 'adult DNA cloning', which produces a duplicate of an existing animal. The technique is also known as 'cell nuclear replacement'. During adult DNA cloning, the DNA is sucked out from a normal unfertilised egg cell, using a device that acts somewhat like a miniature vacuum cleaner. DNA that has already been removed from a cell of the adult to be copied is then inserted in place of the original DNA. Following this stage, the cell containing the inserted DNA is implanted in the womb of an animal of the same species, and gestation may begin.

To make Dolly, a cell was taken from the mammary tissue of a six-year-old sheep. Its DNA was added to a sheep ovum (egg) from which the nucleus had been removed. This artificially fertilised cell was then stimulated with an electric pulse and implanted in a ewe.

(Adapted from www.biotechinfo.ie)

(i) What is the difference between a nucleus of an egg cell and that of a somatic (body) cell of an animal?
(ii) Suggest an advantage of producing genetically identical animals.
(iii) Suggest a disadvantage of producing genetically identical animals.
(iv) 'Every cell in the body contains in its DNA all of the genetic material needed to make an exact replica of the original body'. Comment on this statement.
(v) What is the precise meaning of the term 'implanted' in the extract above?
(vi) Suggest a purpose for stimulating the fused egg with an electric pulse.
(vii) What do you think is meant by the phrase 'artificially fertilised cell'? **(27)**

14. Answer **any two** of (a), (b), (c). (30, 30)

(a) The diagram shows a vertical section through a carpel.
  (i) Name A, B, C, D, E.
  (ii) What happens to the two nuclei labelled D?
  (iii) In the case of B and E state what may happen to each of them after fertilisation.
  (iv) Copy the diagram into your answer book and add a pollen tube that has completed its growth. Label the nuclei in the pollen tube.

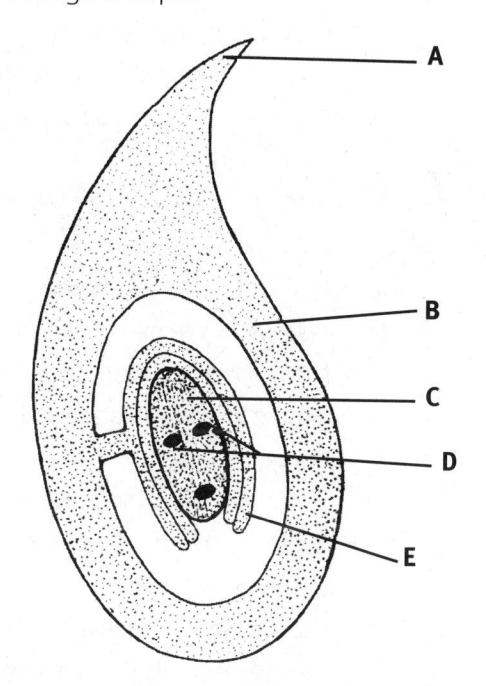

(b) (i) Draw a labelled diagram of the reproductive system of the human female.
  (ii) What is fertilisation? Indicate where fertilisation normally occurs on your diagram.
  (iii) State **one** cause of infertility in the female and **one** cause of infertility in the male.
  (iv) What is meant by **in vitro** fertilisation? What is done with the products of **in vitro** fertilisation?

(c) Answer the following questions from your knowledge of human embryology.
  (i) What is a germ layer? List the **three** germ layers.
  (ii) Relate each of the germ layers that you have listed in (i) to an organ or system in the adult body.
  (iii) From what structures does the placenta develop? State **three** functions of the placenta.
  (iv) Name a hormone associated with the maintenance of the placenta.
  (v) Describe the amnion and state its role.

15. Answer **any two** of (a), (b), (c). (30, 30)

(a) (i) Draw and label sufficient of two neurons to show a synaptic cleft.
 (ii) Describe the sequence of events that allows an impulse to be transmitted across a synapse from one neuron to the next.
 (iii) Suggest a possible role for a drug in relation to the events that you have outlined in (ii).

(b) (i) What is an auxin? State a site of auxin secretion. How may the action of an auxin be considered similar to the action of a hormone in the human body?
 (ii) Define tropism. List **three** types of tropism.
 (iii) Relate the role of an auxin to one of the tropisms that you have listed in (ii).

(c) (i) Draw a labelled diagram to show the structure of **Rhizopus**. State **one** feature in your diagram that indicates the **Rhizopus** belongs to the kingdom Fungi.
 (ii) Sexual reproduction in **Rhizopus** leads to the formation of a zygospore. Show, by means of labelled diagrams, the stages involved in the production of the zygospore.
 (iii) Explain what happens when the zygospore reaches a location at which conditions for its germination are suitable.

MARKING SCHEME

LEAVING CERTIFICATE EXAMINATION, 2004

BIOLOGY – ORDINARY LEVEL

SECTION A

Answer any five questions.

1. any four   2(8)+2(2)

   (a)   liver

   (b)   muscle

   (c)   light or source

   (d)   endocrine or ductless glands or name of gland

   (e)   stomata or dermal tissue or named tissue

2.   2(7) + 3(2)

Column A	Column B
a. Contains chlorophyll	chloroplast
b. Site of protein formation	ribosome
c. Site of energy release	mitochondrion
d. Site of storage of water, salts and sugars	vacuole
e. Allows osmosis to occur	cell membrane

3.   2(5) + 5(2)

   a.   Mitosis .... T

   b.   A sperm .... T

   c.   Chromosomes .... F

   d.   Organisms .... T

   e.   Aerobic respiration .... F

   f.   RNA .... F

   g.   Immobilised enzymes .... T

4. 5 + 5(3)

(i) articulating joint (allow hinge joint) or explained example
(do not allow location i.e. knee)

(ii) location of <u>any</u> articulating joint (if type of articulating joint specified in first answer then location must match)

(iii) A = cartilage
B = ligament or capsule
C = synovial or fluid

(iv) fixed joint or non-articulating joint
or any named joint not mentioned above

5. 2(5) + 5(2)

a. glycerol

b. oil

c. **two** functions – insulation / energy / storage / cell membrane / myelin sheath / medium for vitamins / protection / structural **any two**

d. vitamin A / vitamin D / vitamin E / vitamin K **any one**

e. source
[vitamin A – milk / butter / egg / fish oil / carrot / etc.
vitamin D – sunlight (on skin) / fish oil / butter / margarine /
vitamin E – egg / green vegetables / wheat germ /
vitamin K – fish oil / spinach / bacteria in gut]

Or any other correct sources

f. deficiency
[vitamin A – night blindness / hardening and thickening of skin / kidney stones
vitamin D – rickets
vitamin E – infertility (in rats)
vitamin K – lack of prothrombin / bleeding / slow clotting]

Or any other correct sources

NOTE: Incorrect vitamin = 0
Correct source of incorrect vitamin = OK

6. 6, 3, 0 + 7(2)

a. Ash tree → caterpillars → robins → owls
or
Ash tree → earthworms → robins → owls
(Any one error, then only allow 3 marks – two or more errors = 0)

b. ash tree

	c.	ladybirds / robins / owls	**any two**
	d.	greenflies / mice / caterpillars / earthworms	**any two**
	e.	robin	
	f.	ladybird / owl	**any one**

SECTION B

Answer any two questions.

7. (a) A = eye piece   B = objective or lens or high power
(allow lens for A or B but not for both)
X 400   3(2)

(b) (i) name of plant   3

(ii) description – peel off thin film of plant tissue with forceps / cut thin section of plant tissue with blade (or microtome) or any other correct method   i.e. How = 3 plus instrument = 3   2(3)

(iii) name of stain   3

(iv) application of stain – use dropper to place stain on tissue on slide <u>or</u> place tissue in stain or any other correct method.   3

(v) put on cover slip <u>or</u> remove excess stain   **any one**   3

(vi) cell wall / chloroplasts or chlorophyll / (large) vacuoles / (starch) granules / leucoplasts / chromoplasts / shape   **any two**   2(3)

8. (a) name of ecosystem   3

three animals   3(1)

(b) name of animal (mark already awarded above)   0

two features including generic name of feature e.g. No. of legs
(allow marks for 'other' animal i.e. not from the 3 named earlier but from same ecosystem, features   2(3)

name of organism   3

<u>quantitative estimate</u> – any appropriate description

Name of method ⎫
Description   ⎬   6 + 3

Graph (decrease / increase)   2(3)

169

9.	(a)	i.	State which one (No mark – repeat of quest)	**0**
		ii.	Average rate at rest (Pulse 65 to 79 bpm or Breathing 11 to 21 bpm)	**3**
		iii.	raises rate	**3**
	(b)	i.	<u>measure of resting rate:</u> use pulse monitor / read result in bpm <u>or</u> use of finger or wrist (radial pulse) / use timer or calculate in bpm observe / count / repeat / average / record	**2(3)**
		ii.	<u>investigation:</u> (measure) resting rate / description of exercise / measure rate during (or immediately after) exercise / repeat / compare or state result / record **any three** **6 + 2(3)**	
		iii.	<u>graph</u> (Showing increase – starting at origin is OK)	**6**

SECTION C

Answer any four questions.

10.	(a)		solvent / transport / structural or other correct function including thirst quenching	**any three**	**3(3)**
	(b)	(i)	carbon/ hydrogen/ oxygen (or symbols) (Only take first 3 of a list)		**3(1)**
		(ii)	cellulose or other correct answer	**any one**	**3**
			cell wall or other correct answer (location must correspond with carbohydrate)	**any one**	**3**
		(iii)	energy store or other correct answer	**any one**	**3**
		(iv)	Benedict's / Fehling's	**any one**	**3**
		(v)	dissolve sample in water <u>or</u> put in test tube / add reagent / heat / don't boil / observe change or state result (brick-red-orange precipitate)	**any three**	**3(3)**
			[If reagent is named in (v) but not in (iv) then allow 3 marks in both cases]		
	(c)	(i)	nitrogen (sulphur / phosphorus)	**any one**	**3**
		(ii)	fish / meat / egg / milk / other correct dairy products / pulses	**any two**	**2(3)**
		(iii)	amino acids / peptides	**any one**	**3**
		(iv)	structural (growth, repair, muscle, hair, nails) <u>or</u> metabolic (enzymes) <u>or</u> immunity (antibodies)	**any one**	**3**
		(v)	biuret test <u>or</u> named chemicals <u>or</u> other correct test		**3**

		(vi)	add biuret reagent (or sodium hydroxide and copper sulfate) / to sample / heat or shake		
		(vii)	observe or record colour change (purple-violet)	**any three**	3(3)
			[If reagent is named in (v) but not in (iv) then allow 3 marks in both cases]		

11. (a) definition – features developing at puberty or features for sexual attraction. **3**

example **6**

(b) (i) A = urethra, B = scrotum, C = epididymis, D = testis, E = vas deferens (sperm duct) **5(3)**

(ii) testis (or D or Seminiferous tubule) **3**

(iii) (seminal) fluid or nutrition (of sperm) **3**

(iv) is motile or has a tail or correct comment on shape or size or very little cytoplasm or may contain 'Y' chromosome or has more mitochondria. **any one** **3**

(c) (i) inability to produce (or release) gametes (or eggs or sperm) or inability to fertilise gamete (or egg) or inability to conceive (or induce conception) or inability to reproduce **any one** **6**

low sperm count or low sperm motility or hormonal or other correct cause **any one** **3**

(ii) name of method **any three** **3(3)**

method of prevention **any three** **3(3)**

[mechanical or example – prevents contact between sperm and egg
surgical or example – prevents contact between sperm and egg
chemical or example – prevents ovulation or hormone levels changed
natural – (safe period) – intercourse takes place avoiding ovulation]

12. (a) dominance – one allele masking the expression of its partner **3**

genotype – all the genes of an individual or genetic makeup or genome or example e.g. Tt **3**

phenotype – the expression of a genotype (the appearance or the characteristic(s) of an organism) **3**

(b)

genotypes of parents	**Pp**	**pp**
gametes	**P p**	**p**
genotypes of calves	**Pp**	**pp**
phenotypes of calves	**polled**	**horned**

(NOTE: This may be done in the Question Book) **9(3)**

(c) (i) (to look at) an organism's pattern of DNA fragments or genetic fingerprinting or (preparing) a pattern of DNA fragments **6**

171

(ii) cells are broken down / how cells are broken down / DNA is released / DNA is cut into fragments / by (restriction) enzymes / the fragments are separated / on the basis of their size **any four** 4(3)

(iii) forensic / paternity / medical or examples **any two** 2(3)

13. (a) metabolism – (chemical) reactions taking place in a cell or in an organism 3

enzymes are catalysts / reactions in cells controlled by enzymes <u>or</u> enzymes affect (initiate, speed up) chemical reactions 2(3)

(b) (i) carbon dioxide or CO_2 3

(ii) oxygen or O_2 3

(iii) stated source or light 3

(iv) respiration or breathing / combustion 2(3)

(v) used in respiration or inhaled / released (into environment) 2(3)

(vi) near upper surface or other correct answer 3

(vii) autotrophic (photosynthesis) 3

(c) (i) X = water Y = pondweed or aquatic plant – do not allow 'plant' on its own. 2(3)

(ii) number of bubbles or volume / in a fixed time 2(3)

(iii) carbon dioxide or light or other factor **any one** 3

(iv) addition of sodium hydrogen carbonate <u>or</u> changing distance of light source (must correspond to (iii)) **any one** 6

(v) light <u>or</u> carbon dioxide <u>or</u> temperature (not mentioned in (iii)) 3

14. Answer **any two** of (a), (b), (c). (30, 30)

(a) (i) 1. attraction of insects or feature of <u>or</u> platform for insects to land on **any one** 3

2. protection (of flower)(bud) <u>or</u> photosynthesis **any one** 3

3. (production, storage, use of) pollen 3

(ii) transfer of pollen / to carpel (stigma) or to female 2(3)

self pollination – occurs on same plant (or flower) 3

cross pollination – occurs between plants 3

(iii) wind / animal **any two** 2(3)

(iv) cross pollination increases variation <u>or</u> reduces chance of genetic problems. 3

(b) (i) carpel / ovary / style / receptacle **any one** 3

(ii) wind dispersal e.g. dandelion / sycamore **any one** 3

animal dispersal e.g. blackberry / burdock **any one** 3

		(iii)	colonise new areas / reduce competition / survival of species	**any two** 6 + 3
		(iv)	period of very low metabolism <u>or</u> period before germination <u>or</u> period during which germination will not occur.	**any one** 6
		(v)	to prevent germination in unfavourable conditions <u>or</u> has longer period available for dispersal <u>or</u> (evolution has guaranteed) optimal germination conditions.	**any one** 6
(c)	(i)		(resumption of) growth of seed <u>or</u> explained	**any one** 3
	(ii)		suitable temperature / oxygen / water	3(3)
	(iii)		<u>oxygen</u> – needed to respire <u>or</u> needed for energy <u>water</u> – needed as medium for reactions <u>or</u> needed as solvent for food store <u>or</u> needed for formation of new tissue <u>or</u> needed for splitting testa <u>or</u> needed for absorbing minerals. <u>suitable temperature</u> – optimal temp. for enzymes	**any one** 3
	(iv)		diagram (showing vessel, seeds & cotton wool (at least one of which must be labelled) (Any one missing only allow 3 marks – more missing = 0)	6, 3, 0
			seeds / experiment or one factor missing / explain how one factor was removed / control <u>or</u> all three factors present / identical conditions / leave for period / observe <u>or</u> state result	**any three** 3(3)

15. Answer **any two** of (a), (b), (c). (30, 30)

    (a) 6(3)

		(i)	A = malleus (hammer) (allow bone or ossicle) B = auditory canal <u>or</u> outer ear C = tympanum (ear drum)(Tympanic membrane) D = Eustachian tube E = cochlea F = semicircular canals	
		(ii)	pharynx (throat)	3
		(iii)	gas	3
		(iv)	hearing	3
		(v)	balance	3
	(b)	(i)	a chemical / messenger / secreted by a ductless gland / transported in the blood / to a target area / causing a response	**any two** 2(3)
		(ii)	diagram with correctly positioned labels (word or letter)	4(3)
		(iii)	1. **Name or letter of gland repeated**	0
			Hormone name	3
			2. **function**	3
			3. **deficiency symptom**	3

	(iv)	hormone vs nerve		
		slower to act or more sustained or chemical (cf. ionic or electrical)		
		(comments taken to refer to hormone)	**any one**	3
(c)	(i)	A = xylem or vessel B = phloem		2(3)
	(ii)	transports substances		6
	(iii)	X = sieve plate (allow sieve tube)		3
		Y = companion cell or cytoplasm		3
	(iv)	transport of water or minerals or support		3
	(v)	transport of food		3
	(vi)	vein or mid rib or bundle		3
	(vii)	lignin		3

MARKING SCHEME

LEAVING CERTIFICATE EXAMINATION, 2004

BIOLOGY – HIGHER LEVEL

SECTION A

Answer any five questions.

Q 1. 2(7) + 3(2)

(i.e. 7 marks for the first 2 correct points and 2 marks for each subsequent correct point)

(a) Any <u>named</u> plant **or** <u>named</u> photosynthetic bacteria **or** cyanobacteria [**allow** grass, seaweed, fern, moss]

(b) Respiration **or** digestion **or** deamination **or** any correctly described reaction e.g. protein → amino acids **or** equation

(c) (nitrogen) fixation

(d) 2:1 [allow if correctly shown in formula e.g. $C_6H_{12}O_6$]

(e) Mutualism **or** symbiosis

(f) Keratin **or** myosin **or** elastin **or** collagen **or** other correct example [**allow** fibrin]

Q 2. 2(4) + 6(2)

(i.e. 4 marks for the first 2 correct points and 2 marks for each subsequent correct point)

- Variation
- Genetic **or** examples / environment or examples / age / [NOTE – environment + food = 1 point] **any two points**
- Yes **or** No **or** implied in text (on this line)

Explanation:

- Weight is also determined by genetic **or** environmental factors [**for 'yes' above**] **or** valid reason e.g. reference to eating habits or exercise [**if 'no' given above**]

[Note: reason must match the Yes/No above]

- Change in genetic makeup (or in DNA, in gene, in chromosome, etc.)
- Radiation **or** chemical **or** viruses **or** carcinogens **or** named example of any one of these [**allow smoking**]

- Down's syndrome **or** other correct condition e.g. cancer or stripe in eye colour
  [**any spontaneous change – one incorrect does not cancel**]

Q 3.

PpCc	ppcc	4 + 4
Yes [**or implied in statement**]		4
Parentals and non-parentals (i.e. all possible phenotypes) **or** each allele can combine with either of the other pair /		4
in 1:1:1:1: ratio (or in equal numbers or some indication of this)		4

Q 4. 4 + 8(2)

(i.e. 4 marks for the first correct point and 2 marks for each subsequent correct point)

(a) **A** = stoma

B = guard cell

C = (epi)dermal cell

To allow movement (exchange) of gas (or air or water vapour) **or** transpiration

CO_2 (allow light **or** potassium ions **or** water)

Lenticels **or** stomata

(b) Onion **or** tulip **or** daffodil **or** cabbage **or** other correctly named plant

Starch **or** sucrose **or** cellulose **or** fructose **or** glucose [**not 'sugar'**]

Rhizome **or** corm **or** tuber [**allow stolon**]

Q 5. (a) 2(5) + 5(2)

- Any harmful (undesirable) (addition to) the environment (or named ecosystem)
- Any correct example of human activity
- Counteracting method (must relate to example given above) [**allow 'clean up'**]
- **Explain conservation:** Retention of viable populations (e.g. stopping extinction) **or** their habitats **or** comment on management **or** any one explained [allow '**wise use of environment**']

  (i) and **(ii) NB <u>any two reasons for conservation</u>** aesthetic / recreational / food supplies / possible sources of drugs / source of other materials / species' right to existence / prevent extinction / biodiversity **or** balance / **or** any 2 correct examples

  [Note: group term + example = 1 point; 2 examples = 2 points]
- **One conservation practice:**

Control of fertiliser usage **or** control of mesh size **or** plant trees **or** any valid example explained

Q 6. **2(5) + 5(2)**

Muscular activity **or** description e.g. contractions to move food [**allow 'movement of food'**]

Kills germs **or** optimal pH for enzymes **or** hydrolysis of starch **or** other correct reason

Peristalsis **or** explained (e.g. bulk for movement) [**accept reference to constipation or bowel cancer**]

Lipase

Fatty acids **or** glycerol

Emulsification (must imply smaller globules produced) **or** pH effect **or** explained

Production of vitamins **or** inhibition of pathogens **or** (aids) digestion **or** example

SECTION B

Answer any two (2) questions.

Q7. (a) Yes 3

(Rate of) enzyme reaction (affected by temperature) 3

(b) Diagram 3, 0

[**must include evidence of anaerobic conditions and two correct labels for 3 marks**]

- Sugar **or** named sugar **or** starch 3
- Carbon dioxide **or** any product of glycolysis 3
- Yeast absent (or dead) in same set up 3
- Comparison **or** purpose described 3
- No more gas given off (no more bubbles) 3
- ***NB –** To test for alcohol – **All candidates who attempt Q** 3
- Water (allow other correct product from Kreb's cycle) 3

Q 8.(a) dermal / ground / meristematic **any two** **2(3)**

[allow correctly named tissue e.g. cambium]

(b) Why:

Easier to cut (thin) sections **or** relevant comment on tissue arrangement (e.g. easier to see vascular bundles) 3

Method described:

Cut thin / named instrument e.g. blade, microtome, scalpel / between nodes / named support e.g. pith, carrot, wax / at right angle (across) / any safety procedure stated / **any two** **2(3)**

To ensure light can pass through **or** to see (cells) clearly 3

Diagram		**3, 0**

[Diagram – **section with vascular bundles in ring (4) or at least one bundle divided**]

Labels: xylem and phloem in correct position	**labels**	3
Functions:		
Phloem:– transport of food (or minerals or auxins)		3
Xylem:– transport of water **or** minerals		3

Q 9.(a) (i) it can shorten or contract   3

        (ii) left ventricle   3

   (b) Dissection:

Identify sides (or front/back) / <u>how identified</u> / ventral side uppermost / on board **or** dish / named cutting instrument / described (location of) cut / any safety procedure stated e.g. gloves, goggles, white coat   **any three**   3(3)

Diagram   **3, 0**

[4 chambers + indication of 2 valves]
labels (bicuspid and tricuspid valves in correct position)   3

Expose semilunar valve:
Cut aorta **or** cut pulmonary artery   3

Function semilunar valve:
Stops back flow of blood (into ventricle or from artery)   3

Origin of coronary artery:
aorta **or** near semilunar valve   3

SECTION C

Answer any four questions.

Q 10. (a) Biosphere: Parts of the earth that support life   3

        Habitat: Place where organism(s) live(s)   3

        Niche: Role of organism (in an ecosystem) **or** explained e.g. 'how it fits'   3

   (b) (i) Abiotic factors are non-living **and** biotic factors are living   3

        (ii) Example of abiotic factor <u>named</u> or group e.g. climatic   3

            Named plant   3

        (iii) Example of biotic factor <u>named</u>   3

            Named animal   3

[If ecosystem not named or incorrectly named can only get **either** animal **or** plant mark, NOT both]

(iv) Pyramid of numbers:

Shows numbers of different organisms in a food chain (**or** in trophic levels **or** named trophic levels)   **3**

Pyramid   **3**

(v) Producers **or** autotrophs   **3**

(c) (i) 3.5 – 4.5 years   **3**

(ii) 33 – 39   **3**

(iii) Predator: an animal (or organism) that <u>eats</u> another animal   **3**

Graph: showing lower numbers **and** out of phase   **3 + 3**

(iv) Why decline: food shortage / disease / migration / correct climatic change **or** example / decrease in reproductive rate / other correct reason e.g. lack of space, competition, **or** human activity e.g. trapping, poisoning etc   <u>**any two**</u>   **2(3)**

(v) Why increase: (increased) food supply / decline in predator numbers / increase in reproductive rate / correct climatic change **or** example / migration / other correct example e.g. more space   <u>**any two**</u>   **2(3)**

Q 11. (a) Adenosine triphosphate   **3**

Role: P – P bond / holds or stores (energy) / passes on **or** releases (energy) **or** ATP ⟶ ADP + P / + energy (<u>or</u> the reverse reaction)   <u>**any two**</u>   **2(3)**

(b) (i) Pathway 1.

Light energising electrons **or** light into chlorophyll / (e^-) from chlorophyll / ATP formed / (e^-) returned to chlorophyll

Pathway 2.

(e^-) to NADP / photolysis (or H_2O split) / H+ (protons) to NADP / NADPH formed / ATP formed / O_2 formed / different electrons / (e^-) back to chlorophyll   **6(3)**

[maximum 4 points from either pathway]

(ii)

Product	Fate
ATP	for dark phase **or** explained or any metabolic reaction
NADPH	for dark phase **or** explained
O_2	respired or released (into atmosphere)

<u>**any three**</u>   **3(3)**

(c) (i) Why Elodea?: ease of measurement of rate **or** explained   **3**

(ii) How temp constant: water bath **or** described   **3**

(iii) Sources of CO_2: animal respiration / plant respiration / from air / bacterial respiration **or** decomposition   **2(3)**

[Note: respiration alone = 1 point]

    (iv) How varied: lamp / different distances (**or** different wattage) **OR** sodium hydrogen carbonate / different amounts   **3 + 3**

    (v) Precaution at each change:
        Allow time (before counting bubbles)   **3**
    Reason:
        Plant adjusting **or** equilibration **or** explained   **3**

Q 12. (a) Maintaining (a constant) internal environment **or** described   **3**
    Role of kidneys: Maintaining salt balance **or** explained /   **3**
    Maintaining water balance **or** explained /   **3**
    [Note: <u>Osmoregulation</u> = 2 points]

  (b) (i) **Diagram** of nephron   **3, 0**
       Diagram of blood supply   **3, 0**
       labels   **3(1)**

    (ii) Filtration:
    Blood in arteriole / under pressure / plasma (accept blood) **or** small molecules **or** named from (**or** in) glomerulus / in **or** into (Bowman's) capsule / large molecules **or** named **or** cells **or** named cells cannot pass   **any three**   **3(3)**

    Reabsorption:
    Substance (or named) from (**or** in) tubule (or named part or from filtrate) / into blood / active transport / diffusion / osmosis / mention of hormonal control
                any three   **3(3)**

  (c) (i) Source: respiration **or** named site e.g. muscle, liver, kidney, brain **or** named food e.g. carbohydrate or named   **3**

    (ii) Two methods of insulation: fat (adipose tissue) / trapped) air **or** hair   **2(3)**

    (iii) When temp high: vasodilation (or explained) / (secretion of) sweat / hairs lie flat **or** less air trapped   **any two**   **2(3)**

    (iv) Response when temp drops: receptor (or detection) / receptor in skin / receptor in medulla **or** brain / shiver / generates heat / hairs stand up or goose bumps / air trapped / vasoconstriction (or explained) / increased metabolic rate or increased respiration / any relevant comment on named hormone e.g. thyroxine increases metabolic rate or increases respiration
                any three   **3(3)**

Q 13. (a) Completed **diagram** showing two additional sugar molecules and two more bases
    <u>**diagram completed correctly**</u> **or** shapes of bases **or** show bonding   **3, 0**
    new bases named and matched   **3, 0**
    deoxyribose or phosphate labelled   **3, 0**

(b) mRNA (messenger RNA) **3**
rRNA (ribosomal RNA) **3**
tRNA (transfer RNA) **3**

Functions:

mRNA: mRNA formed to match DNA (or transcription or explained) / leaves nucleus **or** into cytoplasm / (carries instructions) to ribosomes **or** for translation

rRNA: rRNA binds (holds) mRNA in place / for translation (**or** explained) / structure of ribosome

tRNA: tRNA carries an amino acid / complementary to mRNA / to ribosomes

<u>**any five functions**</u> **5(3)**

[must be at least one point from each RNA type]

(c) (i) Difference: egg cell is haploid **or** somatic cell is diploid **or** quote from passages lines **6 and 7** **3**

(ii) Advantage: any valid example e.g. same wool quality **3**

(iii) Disadvantage: any valid example e.g. lack of variation **or** consequence e.g. prone to disease **3**

(iv) Comment: valid / mitosis yields genetically identical nuclei / not all genes switched on / genetic potential to produce new organism or explained / comment on significance e.g. forensics

[If 'not valid' stated for one point, second point got from a reason why not e.g. not sex cells]

<u>**any two**</u> **2(3)**

(v) Implanted: attached (embedded) [**allow inserted, placed or put**] to the endometrium [**allow uterus or womb**] **or** explained **3**

(vi) Why electric pulse: any reasonable suggestion e.g. to initiate cell division, keep alive, boost viability, energise. **3**

(vii) Artificially fertilised: (diploid) nucleus / into ovum without nucleus / rather than from <u>fusion</u> of haploid nuclei (**or** gametes)

[These 2 points will be got by quoting from last paragraph]

<u>**any two**</u> **2(3)**

Q 14. (a) Answer <u>any two</u> of (a), (b), (c). **(30, 30)**

(i) **A** = stigma **or** style **2**
B = ovary **2**
C = embryo sac (**allow nucellus**) **2**
D = polar nuclei **2**
E = ovule (allow integuments) **2**

(ii) **What happens to D:**
Fuse / form diploid (or primary endosperm) / (then fusion) to triploid **or** fertilisation / endosperm nucleus   2(3)

(iii) **E** becomes the seed **or** testa   2
B becomes the fruit   2

(iv) **Diagram**   6, 3, 0
2 named nuclei labels   2(2)

(b) (i) **Diagram female:**   6, 3, 0
labels   3(2)

(ii) **Fertilisation:** <u>fusion</u> of gametes   3
Indicate on diagram: location indicated correctly on diagram   3

(iii) **Female infertility:** any named pathological condition e.g. hormonal **or** blockage **or** failure to ovulate   3
Male infertility: low sperm count or reason for / named pathological condition / hormonal   3

(iv) **In vitro:** fertilisation outside the body **or** description   3
Fate: implanted in a womb **or** stored for future use **or** destroyed   3

(c) (i) **Germ layer:**
Layer of cells / in the blastula (embryo) / (potential to) give rise to (specific) tissues (or organs)   **any two**   2(2)
Name 3 germ layers: ectoderm   2
endoderm   2
mesoderm   2

(ii) **Fate of 3 germ layers:**
ectoderm – skin **or** nails **or** hair **or** nervous system   2
endoderm – (inner lining of) gut **or** named part of **or** liver **or** pancreas   2
mesoderm – muscles **or** skeleton **or** excretory system **or** respiratory system **or** circulatory system (or blood)   2

(iii) **Placenta origin:** uterine tissue **and** embryonic tissue
[allow from mother **and** baby]   2
3 Functions:
produces hormones (or named) / allows passage of food (or named) / and oxygen / antibodies / waste (or named) / acts as a barrier **or** explained
    any three   3 (2)

(iv) Progesterone   2

(v) **Amnion:** sac or membrane 2
holds **or** produces fluid **or** protects embryo (or foetus) 2

Q 15. Answer any <u>two</u> of (a), (b), (c). (30, 30)
(a) (i) **Diagram of synaptic cleft:** 6, 3, 0
3 labels 3(2)
(ii) **Transmission of impulse:** arrival of impulse / synaptic bulbs (or vesicles) / (secretes) transmitter (substance) / passage of neurotransmitter / impulse starts in next neuron / neurotransmitter broken down / by enzymes
<u>any five</u> 5(3)
(iii) **A drug** may be used to inhibit **or** enhance transmission of impulse **or** similar comment
[any reasonable suggestion] 3

(b) (i) **Auxin:** a (growth) regulator in <u>plants</u> 3
Site: tip of shoot **or** buds **or** meristem / developing leaves **or** seeds **or** other correct location 3
Action similar to hormone:
Made in one place / transported to other part / causes response / slow acting /long lasting **any two** 2(3)
(ii) **Tropism:** <u>growth</u> response (of plant to a stimulus) 3
Types of tropisms:
thigmotropism / phototropism / geotropism (gravitropism) / hydrotropism / chemotropism **any three** 3(3)
(iii) **Role of auxin:** unequal distribution / caused by light **or** gravity / unequal growth / results in bending **or** direction
<u>any two</u> 2(3)

(c) (i) **Rhizopus diagram** 6, 3, 0
3 labels 3(1)
Why a fungus: stolon **or** rhizoids **or** mycelium **or** hyphae **or** sporangium **or** spores <u>any one</u> 3
(ii) **Diagram sexual reproduction:** 6, 3, 0
(series of diagrams **or** 3 stages in one diagram)
3 labels 3(1)
(iii) **Fate of zygospore:**
meiosis / hypha grows / sporangium (produces) / (asexual) spores / released / spores germinate <u>any three</u> 3(3)

Coimisiún na Scrúduithe Stáit
State Examinations Commission

LEAVING CERTIFICATE EXAMINATION, 2005

BIOLOGY – ORDINARY LEVEL

Tuesday, 14 June – Afternoon – 2.00 to 5.00

Section A Answer any **five** questions from this section.
Each question carries 20 marks.
Write your answers in the spaces provided on **this examination paper.**

Section B Answer any **two** questions from this section.
Each question carries 30 marks.
Write your answers in the spaces provided on **this examination paper.**

Section C Answer any **four** questions from this section.
Each question carries 60 marks.
Write your answers in the **answer book.**

You should spend not more than 30 minutes on Section A and 30 minutes on Section B, leaving 120 minutes for Section C.

SECTION A

ANSWER ANY FIVE QUESTIONS.
Write your answers in the spaces provided.

1. Explain **four** of the following terms that are used in ecology.

(a) Biosphere _____

_____

(b) Habitat _____

_____

(c) Consumer _____

_____

(d) Producer _____

_____

(e) Niche _____

_____

2. Use ticks (✓) to show if the named structure is present in an animal cell, in a plant cell or in a plant cell. The first has been completed as an example.

Structure	Cytoplasm	Cell Wall	Chloroplast	Nucleus	Vacuole
Animal Cell	✓				
Plant Cell	✓				

3. The diagram shows the external structure of a stamen.

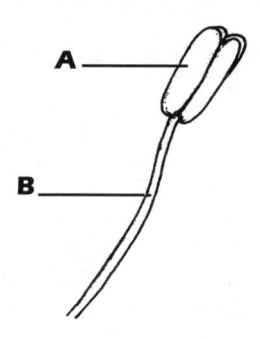

(a) Name A and B.

A _____ B _____

(b) Where is pollen produced, in A or in B? _____

(c) To which part of a flower is pollen carried? _____

(d) What is meant by cross-pollination? _____

(e) Name two methods of cross-pollination.

1. _____

2. _____

4. The diagram shows a stage of mitosis.

(a) Name A and B.

A _____

B _____

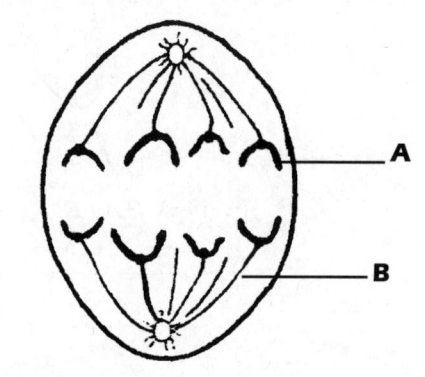

(b) What is happening during this stage of mitosis? _____

_____

(c) How many cells are formed when a cell divides by mitosis? _____

_____

(d) For what purpose do single-celled organisms use mitosis? _____

_____

5. The table below includes some common elements found in food. Complete the table by putting a tick (✓) in the box if an element is present and a cross (✗) if an element is absent. Two boxes have been completed as examples.

	Carbohydrate	Protein	Fat
Oxygen	✓		
Nitrogen	✗		
Hydrogen			
Carbon			

6. (a) The diagram shows the structure of **Amoeba**.

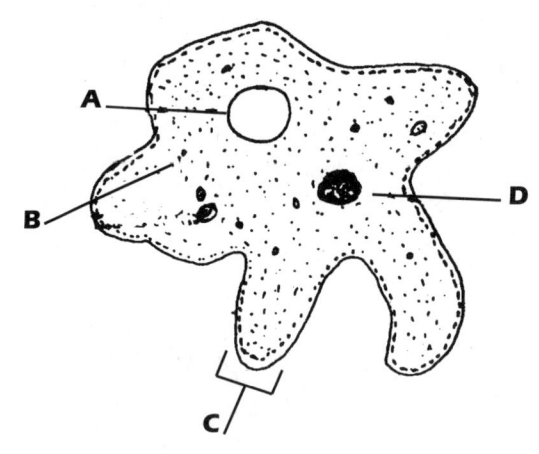

(i) Name A, B, C, D.

A _____ B _____

C _____ D _____

(ii) To which kingdom does **Amoeba** belong? _____

(b) The diagram shows the structure of a typical bacterium.

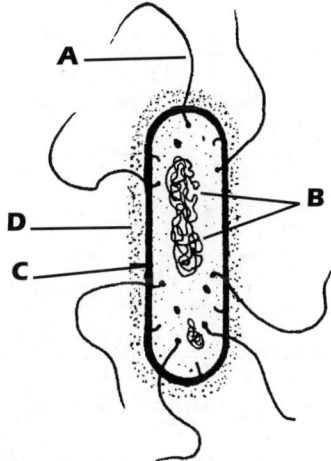

(i) Name A, B, C, D.

A _____   B _____

C _____   D _____

(ii) To which kingdom do bacteria belong? _____

SECTION B

ANSWER ANY TWO QUESTIONS.
Write your answers in the spaces provided.

Part (a) carries 6 marks and part (b) carries 24 marks in each question in this section.

7. (a) (i) What is osmosis? _____
   _____

   (ii) What is a selectively permeable (semi-permeable) membrane?
   _____

   (b) (i) Draw a labelled diagram of the apparatus that you used to demonstrate osmosis.

(ii) Describe how you carried out the experiment to demonstrate osmosis.

_____

(iii) How were you able to tell that osmosis had taken place?

_____

8. (a) (i) What is an enzyme? _____

(ii) Comment on the shape of enzyme molecules. _____

(b) Answer the following questions in relation to an experiment that you carried out to investigate the effect of temperature on enzyme activity.

(i) What enzyme did you use? _____

(ii) What substrate did you use? _____

(iii) Draw a labelled diagram of the apparatus that you used.

(iv) How did you know that the enzyme had completed its activity?

_____

(v) How did you vary the temperature in your experiment?

_____

_____

(vi) Draw an outline graph of the results that you obtained.

rate | temperature

9. (a) (i) What is meant by the germination of a seed? _____

_____

(ii) State **one** reason why water is needed for germination. _____

_____

(b) Answer the following questions in relation to an experiment that you carried out to investigate the effects of water, oxygen and temperature on germination.

(i) Draw a labelled diagram of the apparatus that you used.

(ii) Describe how you carried out the experiment. _____

_____

_____

_____

_____

_____

_____

(iii) Describe the results of this experiment, including the result of the control.

SECTION C

ANSWER ANY FOUR QUESTIONS.
Write your answers in the answer book.

10. (a) (i) What is an ecosystem?

(ii) Name **two** ecosystems found in Ireland. **(9)**

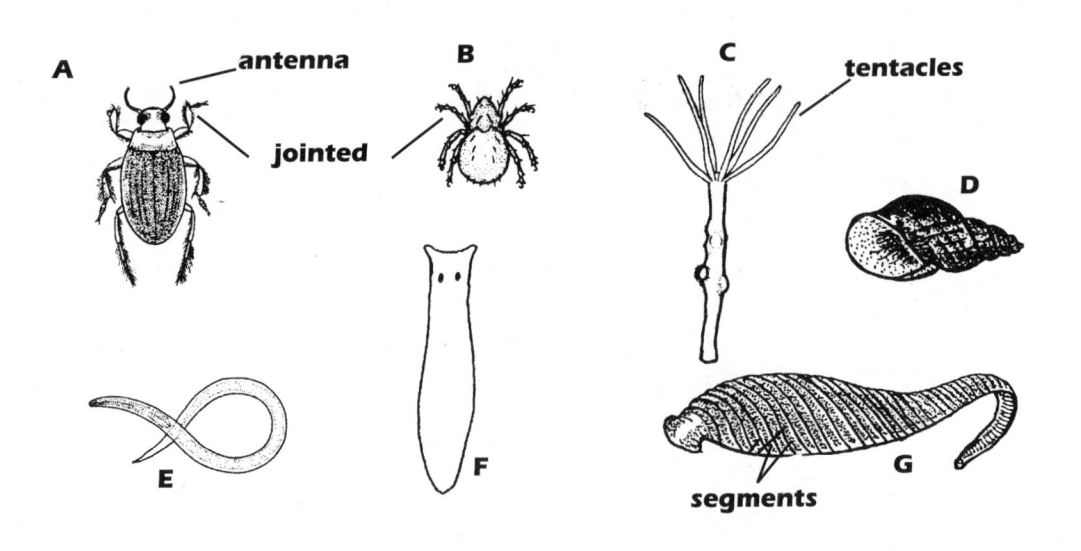

A — antenna, jointed
B
C — tentacles
D
E
F
G — segments

(b) Animals A, B, C, D, E, F, G were found in a small lake. They are not drawn to the same scale. Use the following key to identify each of these animals. Write down each letter and the animal it represents in your answer book. **(21)**

1. Jointed legs present 2
   Jointed legs absent 3

2. **Three** pairs of jointed legs ....Diving beetle
   Four pairs of jointed legs..Water mite

3. Body divided into segments ....Leech
   Body not divided into segments 4

4. Shell present ....Pond snail
   Shell absent 5

5. Ring of tentacles around the mouth ....**Hydra**
   No tentacles 6

6. Flat body with eye spots ....Planarian
   Round body with pointed ends ....Nematode

(c) (i) What is meant by pollution?
  (ii) Describe a human activity that may result in pollution. Suggest a way in which this pollution could be prevented.
  (iii) What do you understand by the term conservation?
  (iv) Suggest **three** reasons for conserving wild animals and plants. **(30)**

11. (a) (i) Complete the following equation, which is a summary of photosynthesis.
    $6CO_2 + 6H_2O + light + chlorophyll \longrightarrow$
  (ii) Where in the cells of a leaf is chlorophyll found? **(9)**

(b) (i) Light energy trapped by chlorophyll is used to split water. List **three** products that result when water is split.
  (ii) Describe what happens to each of the **three** products that you have listed in (i).
  (iii) Carbon dioxide is essential for photosynthesis. Where does it enter the leaf?
  (iv) From your knowledge of photosynthesis suggest a way to increase the yield of plants such as lettuces in a greenhouse. **(24)**

(c) (i) Some of the carbohydrates produced in photosynthesis are used in respiration. What is respiration?
(ii) Suggest **one** reason why living organisms need to respire.
(iii) What is aerobic respiration?
(iv) Respiration can also be anaerobic. Which of the two types of respiration releases more energy?
(v) Anaerobic respiration by micro-organisms is called fermentation. Give **one** example of industrial fermentation, including the type of micro-organism and the substance produced. **(27)**

12. (a) (i) Name the major blood vessels that carry blood
1. from the heart to the lungs
2. from the lungs to the heart.
(ii) What gas is released from the blood when it reaches the lungs? **(9)**

(b) The diagram shows part of the human breathing system.

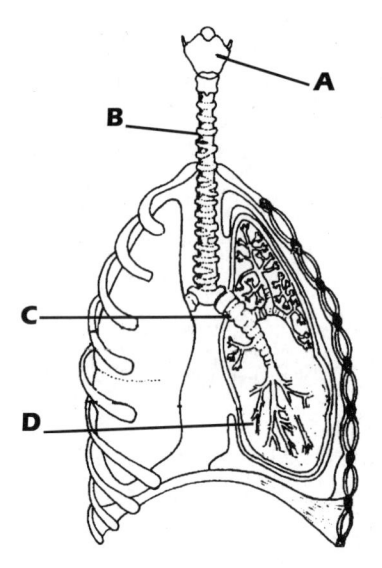

(i) Name A, B, C, D.
(ii) D ends in a small sac. What is the name of this sac?
(iii) What is the function of A?
(iv) B contains rings of cartilage. Suggest a function of this cartilage.
(v) Where is the epiglottis? What is its function? **(27)**

(c) (i) Name the muscles that are used in breathing.
 (ii) Breathing causes pressure changes in the thoracic cavity. Describe briefly how these pressure changes are brought about.
 (iii) Name a breathing disorder. Give a possible cause of this disorder and suggest a means of prevention **or** treatment. **(24)**

13. (a) For each of the following parents give the genotypes of all the possible gametes that it can produce.
 (i) Parent Aa.
 (ii) Parent AaBb. **(9)**

(b) (i) Name the four bases that are found in DNA.
 (ii) These bases form a triplet code. What is meant by a triplet code?
 (iii) The triplet code is transcribed into mRNA. What does this statement mean?
 (iv) To which structures in the cell does mRNA carry the code? **(24)**

(c) (i) What is evolution?
 (ii) What is natural selection?
 (iii) Name **one** of the scientists who developed the theory of natural selection.
 (iv) Give a brief account of the evidence for evolution from **one** named source. **(27)**

14. Answer any **two** of (a), (b), (c). **(30, 30)**

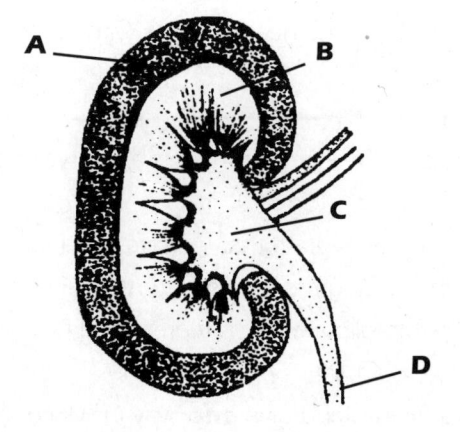

(a) The diagram shows a section through a human kidney.
 (i) Name A, B, C, D.
 (ii) To what structure does D connect the kidney?

193

(iii) Filtration is an essential process in the formation of urine. In what part of the kidney does it take place?
(iv) Reabsorption of useful substances takes place in the kidney. In what part does this occur?
(v) Name an excretory substance present in urine.
(vi) Name an excretory organ in the human body other than the kidney. Name a substance, other than the one you have named in (v), excreted by this organ.

(b) (i) Draw a large labelled diagram of the reproductive system of the human female.
(ii) Indicate on your diagram where each of the following events takes place: fertilisation, implantation.
(iii) What is the menstrual cycle? Outline the main events of the menstrual cycle.

(c) Answer the following questions in relation to blood vessels in the human body.
(i) Valves are present in veins. What is their function?
(ii) Why are valves not needed in arteries?
(iii) Which has the bigger lumen (cavity), an artery or a vein?
(iv) The wall of capillaries is only one cell thick. How is this related to their function?
(v) How does a portal vein differ from other veins?
(vi) Name the following blood vessels:
   1. the vessels that carry blood from the aorta to the kidneys
   2. the vessels that supply the heart's muscle with blood.

15. Answer any **two** of (a), (b), (c). (30, 30)
(a) (i) Which of the two diagrams 1 or 2 represents a transverse section of a young root?
(ii) State **two** features of the diagram that indicate it is a root.
(iii) The letters A, B, C in the diagram represent three different tissue types. State which tissue type in the following list is represented by each letter: ground tissue, vascular tissue, dermal tissue.
(iv) Name **two** vascular tissues and give **one** way in which they differ.
(v) State a function of ground tissue.

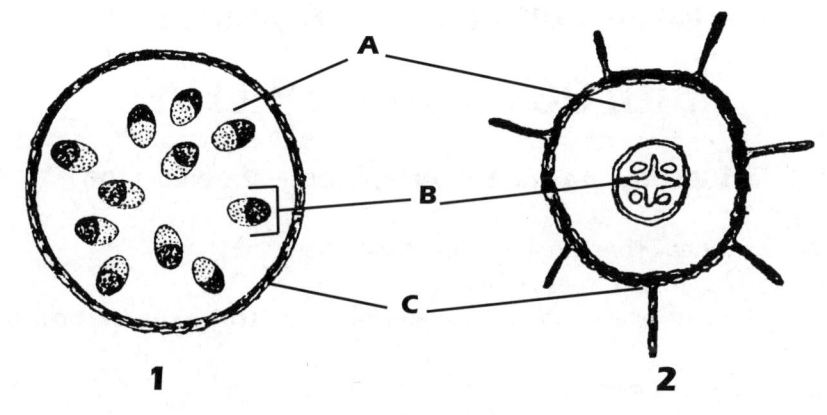

(b) (i) What is vegetative propagation?
 (ii) Give **one** example of vegetative propagation and state whether it involves a stem, a root, a leaf or a bud.
 (iii) How does vegetative propagation differ from reproduction by seed?
 (iv) Artificial propagation is widely used in horticulture. Give **two** examples of artificial propagation.
 (v) Suggest **one** advantage and **one** disadvantage of artificial propagation.

(c) The diagram shows part of the mycelium of **Rhizopus**.

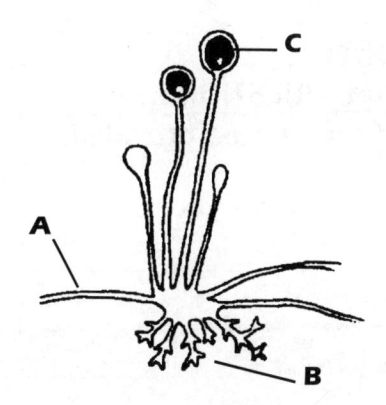

 (i) Identify A, B, C.
 (ii) State a function of B.
 (iii) State a function of C.
 (iv) What term is used to describe the nutrition of **Rhizopus**? Explain the importance of this type of nutrition in nature.
 (v) To what kingdom does **Rhizopus** belong?
 (vi) Name another organism that you have studied in your biology course that belongs to the same kingdom as **Rhizopus**.

LEAVING CERTIFICATE EXAMINATION, 2005

BIOLOGY – HIGHER LEVEL

Tuesday, 14 June – Afternoon – 2.00 to 5.00

Section A Answer any **five** questions from this section.
Each question carries 20 marks.
Write your answers in the spaces provided on **this examination paper.**

Section B Answer any **two** questions from this section.
Each question carries 30 marks.
Write your answers in the spaces provided on **this examination paper.**

Section C Answer any **four** questions from this section.
Each question carries 60 marks.
Write your answers in the **answer book.**

You should spend not more than 30 minutes on Section A and 30 minutes on Section B, leaving 120 minutes for Section C.

SECTION A
ANSWER ANY <u>FIVE</u> QUESTIONS.
Write your answers in the spaces provided.

1. Answer **five** of the following by writing a word in the space provided.

   (a) Cellulose is an example of a structural _____.

   (b) Vitamins are either water-soluble or _____-soluble.

   (c) Fats are composed of oxygen, hydrogen and _____.

   (d) When an iodine solution is added to a food sample and remains red-brown in colour, _____ is absent.

   (e) When two monosaccharides unite they form a _____.

   (f) Removal from the body of the waste products of metabolism is called _____.

2. Explain each of the following terms in relation to the scientific method.

(a) Hypothesis _____

_____

(b) Control _____

_____

(c) Data _____

_____

(d) Replicate _____

_____

(e) Theory _____

_____

3. Indicate whether the following are true (T) or false (F) by drawing a circle around T or F.

(a)	Urea is formed in the kidneys.	T	F
(b)	Motor neurons conduct impulses towards the central nervous system.	T	F
(c)	Endocrine glands secrete hormones.	T	F
(d)	Tendons join muscles to bones.	T	F
(e)	The sino-atrial node (pacemaker) is located on the right side of the heart.	T	F
(f)	A nucleus is absent from human red blood cells.	T	F
(g)	Light is essential for the germination of seeds.	T	F
(h)	Lenticels serve the same function as stomata.	T	F
(i)	Parallel leaf veins are characteristic of monocotyledonous plants.	T	F
(j)	Endosperm is a food reserve in some seeds.	T	F

4. The following graph shows how the rate of photosynthesis varied when a plant was subjected to varying levels of light intensity **or** carbon dioxide concentration.

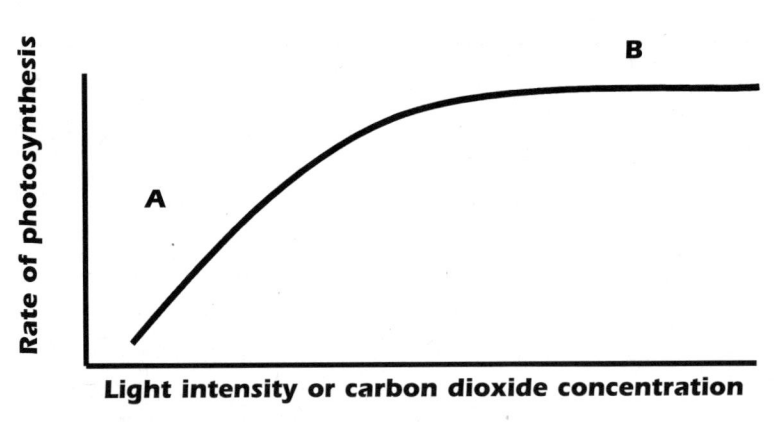

(a) What is happening at A? _____

(b) What is happening at B? _____

(c) Suggest a reason for your answer in (b). _____

_____

(d) Where in a cell does photosynthesis take place? _____

(e) Give **two** sources of the carbon dioxide that is found in the atmosphere.

(i) _____

(ii) _____

(f) Suggest **one** way in which the rate of photosynthesis of plants in a greenhouse could be increased. _____

_____

5. (a) In the space below draw a diagram of a nucleus during metaphase of mitosis where 2n = 6. Label the spindle and a centromere in your diagram.

(b) State a function of mitosis in a single-celled organism. _____

_____

(c) State a function of mitosis in a multicellular organism. _____

_____

(d) State one way in which mitosis differs from meiosis. _____

_____

(e) When the normal control of mitosis in a cell is lost, cancer may result. Suggest **two** possible causes of cancer.

1. _____

2. _____

6. The diagram shows part of a section of the human small intestine.

(a) Name A, B, C.

A _____

B _____

C _____

(b) State **two** ways in which A is adapted for the absorption of soluble foods.

1. _____

2. _____

(c) Name a process by which soluble foods are absorbed into the blood from the small intestine.

_____

(d) What type of food is mainly absorbed into B?

_____

SECTION B

ANSWER ANY TWO QUESTIONS.
Write your answers in the spaces provided.

Part (a) carries 6 marks and part (b) carries 24 marks in each question in this section.

7. (a) Immobilised enzymes are sometimes used in bioreactors.

   (i) What is a bioreactor? _____

   (ii) State **one** advantage of using an immobilised enzyme in a bioreactor.

   _____

   (b) Answer the following questions in relation to an experiment that you carried out to immobilise an enzyme and use that immobilised enzyme.

   (i) Name the enzyme that you used. _____
   (ii) Draw a labelled diagram of the apparatus that you used to immobilise the enzyme.
   (iii) Describe how you used this apparatus to immobilise the enzyme. In your answer name the solutions that you used and explain their purpose.

   _____

   (iv) Describe briefly how you used the immobilised enzyme.

   _____

8. (a) Explain each of the following terms in relation to DNA.

(i) Replication _____

_____

(ii) Transcription _____

_____

(b) As part of your practical activities you extracted DNA from a plant tissue. Answer the following questions in relation to this experiment.

(i) What plant did you use? _____

(ii) It is usual to chop the tissue and place it in a blender. Suggest a reason for this. _____

_____

_____

_____

(iii) For how long should the blender be allowed to run? _____

_____

(iv) Washing-up liquid is normally used in this experiment. What is its function?

_____

_____

_____

_____

(v) Sodium chloride (salt) is also used. Explain why. _____

_____

_____

_____

(vi) What is a protease enzyme? _____

(vii) Why is a protease enzyme used in this experiment? _____

_____

_____

_____

(viii) The final separation of the DNA involves the use of alcohol (ethanol). Under what condition is the alcohol used? _____

_____

9. (a) (i) Yeasts are eukaryotic organisms. What does this mean? _____

_____

(ii) To which kingdom do yeasts belong? _____

(b) Answer the following questions in relation to an experiment that you carried out to investigate the growth of leaf yeast.

(i) From which plant did you collect the leaf sample? _____

(ii) Describe how you collected the leaf sample. _____

_____

_____

_____

(iii) What did you do with the leaves when you returned to the laboratory?

_____

_____

_____

_____

(iv) Nutrient agar plates are used in this experiment. What are nutrient agar plates and what is their purpose? _____

_____

_____

_____

_____

(v) What did you observe in the agar plates at the end of the experiment?

_____

_____

_____

_____

(vi) Having finished the experiment, what did you do with the agar plates?

_____

_____

_____

SECTION C

ANSWER ANY FOUR QUESTIONS.
Write your answers in the answer book.

10. (a) (i) What is meant by genetic engineering?
     (ii) State **two** applications of genetic engineering, **one** involving a micro-organism and **one** involving a plant. **(9)**

  (b) Cystic fibrosis is a serious condition that affects the lungs and digestive system. The condition results from the inheritance of a single pair of <u>recessive</u> <u>alleles</u>.
    (i) Explain each of the underlined terms.
    (ii) Suggest why a person with a heterozygous allele pair does not suffer from the condition.
    (iii) If both parents are heterozygous what is the percentage chance that one of their children may inherit the condition? Explain how you obtained your answer.
    (iv) What is meant by genetic screening?
    (v) Parents who are suspected of being carriers of disease-causing alleles may be advised to consider a genetic test. Suggest a role for such a test after **in-vitro** fertilisation. **(27)**

  (c) (i) Define the following terms as used in genetics: linkage, sex linkage.
    (ii) Explain why linked genes do not assort independently.
    (iii) Red-green colour blindness is a sex (X)-linked condition. Normal red-green vision results from the possession of a dominant allele (**C**). In each of the following cases give the genotypes of the mother and of the father.
       1. A family in which one daughter is red-green colour blind and one daughter has normal colour vision.
       2. A family in which all the sons are red-green colour blind and all the daughters are carriers (heterozygous). **(24)**

11. (a) (i) Distinguish between aerobic and anaerobic respiration.
     (ii) Write a balanced equation to summarise aerobic respiration. **(9)**

(b) Answer the following questions in relation to the first stage of respiration.
   (i) Where in the cell does this stage occur?
   (ii) During this stage a small amount of energy is released. Explain the role of ADP in relation to this released energy.
   (iii) What is the final product of this stage under aerobic conditions?
   (iv) If conditions in the cell remain aerobic the product you have named in (iii) is used for the second stage of respiration. Where does this second stage take place?
   (v) If conditions in a human cell (e.g. muscle) become anaerobic the product named in (iii) is converted to another substance. Name this other substance.
   (vi) When the substance named in (v) builds up in the blood, a person is said to be in oxygen debt. This debt must eventually be paid. Suggest how the debt is paid. **(24)**

(c) If yeast cells are kept in anaerobic conditions alcohol (ethanol) and another substance are produced.
   (i) Describe, with the aid of a diagram, how you would keep yeast under anaerobic conditions in the laboratory.
   (ii) Name a carbohydrate that you would supply to the yeast as an energy source.
   (iii) Give an account of a chemical test to demonstrate that alcohol (ethanol) has been produced. Include the initial colour and final colour of the test.
   (iv) What is the other substance produced under anaerobic conditions?
   (v) Alcohol (ethanol) production is an example of fermentation. How would you know when fermentation has ceased?
   (vi) Why does fermentation eventually cease? **(27)**

12. (a) (i) What does an ecologist mean by competition?
   (ii) Competition is generally more intense between members of the same species than between members of different species. Comment on the validity of this statement. **(9)**

(b) Read the following extract and then answer the questions below.
'A migratory flight involves preparation. The initial stimulus for spring migration among birds wintering in European latitudes comes from the increase in day length past an initial threshold. Physiological changes encourage the deposition

of fat, particularly beneath the skin (subcutaneous) and inside the abdomen (visceral). Fat is the vital fuel used by migrating birds, which often have to cross long stretches of sea or perhaps desert where feeding opportunities are either non-existent or very limited.

Wildfowl preparing for migration, therefore, increase their food intake in order to lay down that vital fat and this shows itself in increased time spent feeding. Conveniently, for plant-eating species such as the grazing geese and wigeon, the onset of spring growth in the plants means higher levels of nutrients in the growing tips on which the birds feed.'

[From **Wildfowl**, Ogilvie and Pearson, 1994 Hamlyn Limited]

- (i) What is the stimulus for spring migration?
- (ii) Suggest **two** reasons why birds migrate.
- (iii) What is the 'vital fuel' used by migrating birds?
- (iv) Give **two** locations in the body in which this vital fuel may be found.
- (v) Suggest what happens to this fuel in the body tissues of the birds.
- (vi) In which part of plants do wigeon find the highest level of nutrients?
- (vii) Suggest a reason for the nutrient levels being highest in this part of the plant. **(27)**

(c) (i) Give an account of how you carried out a quantitative survey of a named plant species in an ecosystem that you have studied. In your answer describe how you recorded the results of your survey.

(ii) As a result of a disease, a species of plant disappeared from an ecosystem. Suggest **three** possible effects of the disappearance of this plant on the populations of other plants and animals in the ecosystem. **(24)**

13. (a) (i) Where is testosterone secreted in the body of the human male?
(ii) Give a brief account of the role of testosterone. **(9)**

(b) (i) Draw a large labelled diagram of the reproductive system of the human male.
(ii) Where are sperm produced?
(iii) State **two** ways in which sperm differ from ova (eggs).
(iv) Name a gland that secretes seminal fluid.
(v) State a function of seminal fluid. **(27)**

(c) (i) What is meant by contraception?
(ii) Give an example of a surgical method of male contraception. Suggest an advantage and a disadvantage of the method that you have named.
(iii) List **three** methods of contraception other than surgical. In your answer you may refer to either or both sexes.
(iv) Suggest a possible effect on a human population that may result from an increased availability of contraception. **(24)**

14. Answer any **two** of (a), (b), (c). **(30, 30)**

(a) The passage of water through a plant is known as the transpiration stream. Answer the following questions in relation to the transpiration stream.
(i) Explain how water enters the plant at the root hair.
(ii) Do minerals enter the plant by the process that you have indicated in (i)? Explain your answer.
(iii) How is xylem adapted for its role in water transport?
(iv) Strong forces of attraction exist between water molecules. Give an account of the importance of these forces in raising water to great height in trees.

(b) The graph shows the effect of varying auxin concentration on the root and shoot of a plant.

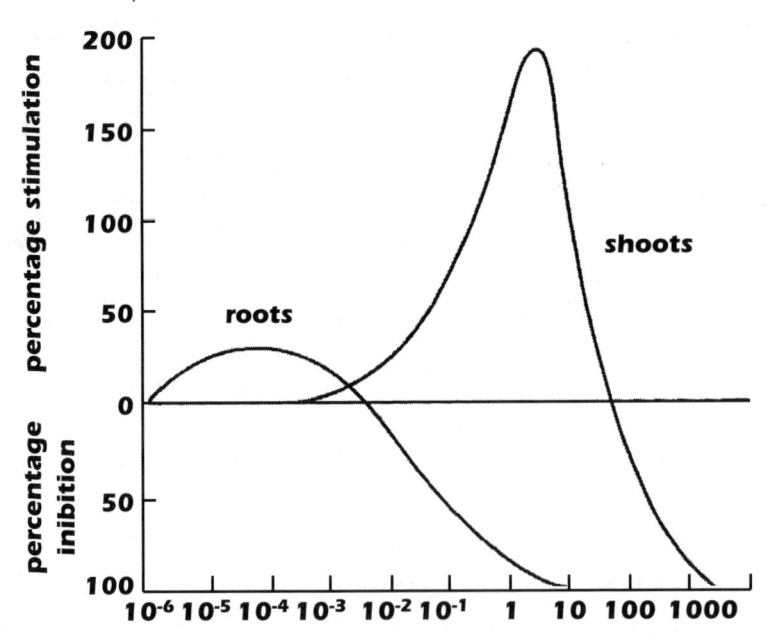

auxin concentration (parts per million)
NB logarithmic scale for auxin concentration

(i) What is an auxin?

(ii) At what approximate auxin concentration does the root receive maximum stimulation?

(iii) At what approximate auxin concentration does the shoot receive maximum stimulation?

(iv) What is the effect on the root of an auxin concentration of 10^{-2} parts per million?

(v) Give **two** examples of uses of synthetic (man-made) auxins.

(vi) Describe **three** methods used by plants to protect themselves from adverse external environments.

(c) Answer the following questions in relation to systems of response to stimuli in the human body.

(i) The pancreas is both an <u>exocrine</u> gland and an <u>endocrine</u> gland. Explain the underlined terms.

(ii) Name a product of the endocrine portion of the pancreas and state one of its functions.

(iii) Name a disorder other than cancer for each of the following and indicate a possible cause and a means of treatment:
1. musculoskeletal system
2. nervous system.

15. Answer any **two** of (a), (b), (c). (30, 30)

(a) (i) Comment briefly on the difficulty in classifying viruses as living organisms.

(ii) Name **two** diseases of humans caused by viruses.

(iii) Name **two** types of lymphocyte and state a role of each when viruses or other microorganisms enter the blood.

(iv) 'Immunity that results from vaccination is effectively the same as the immunity that develops following an infection.' Do you agree with this statement? Explain your answer.

(b) (i) Draw and label a diagram to show the basic structure of a typical bacterial cell.

(ii) Other than being prokaryotic, state **two** ways in which a typical bacterial cell differs from a typical human cell (e.g. cell from cheek lining).

(iii) Describe how some bacteria respond in order to survive when environmental conditions become unfavourable.

(iv) What is meant when a bacterium is described as being pathogenic?
(v) What are antibiotics? Use your knowledge of the theory of natural selection to explain the possible danger involved in the misuse of antibiotics.

(c) <u>Saprophytic</u> and <u>parasitic</u> fungi are widespread in nature.
(i) Explain each of the underlined terms.
(ii) State a role of each of these types of fungus in the overall scheme of nature.
(iii) Give **one** example of a beneficial fungus and **one** example of a harmful fungus.
(iv) State a function for each of the following structures that are found in fungi: rhizoid, sporangium, gametangium, zygospore.

MARKING SCHEME

LEAVING CERTIFICATE EXAMINATION, 2005

BIOLOGY – ORDINARY LEVEL

SECTION A

Any <u>five</u> questions from this section. Each question carries 20 marks.

1. **any four**   2(7) + 2(3)
    - (a) Biosphere – (part of earth) where life exists
    - (b) Habitat – (part of environment) where organisms/plants/animals live
    - (c) Consumer – organism that consumes another organism/heterotroph/end of food chain
    - (d) Producer – organism producing food (organic material)/autotroph/bottom of food chain
    - (e) Niche – position of an organism in its ecosystem/functional role of organism

2.   5 + 5(3)

    N.B. One wrong cancels one right for Cell Wall and Chloroplast.

3.

Structure	Cytoplasm	Cell Wall	Chloroplast	Nucleus	Vacuole
Animal Cell				✓	✓
Plant Cell		✓	✓	✓	✓

   7 answers   2(5) + 5(2)
   - (a) A = Anther   B = Filament
   - (b) A
   - (c) carpel/stigma/female/ovary/style/ovule
   - (d) Transfer of pollen from one flower/plant to another
   - (e) Wind/animal/named animal   **any two**

4. **5 answers**   2(7) + 3(2)

    (a)   A = chromosome (chromatid)   B = spindle (fibre)/thread/cord
    (b)   Chromosomes (chromatids) being pulled apart (going to opposite ends of cell)/anaphase
    (c)   2
    (d)   Reproduction/growth/multiply

5. **10 answers**   2(6) + 8(1)

	Carbohydrate	Protein	Fat
Oxygen	Done	✓	✓
Nitrogen	Done	✓	✗
Hydrogen	✓	✓	✓
Carbon	✓	✓	✓

6. **10 answers**   2(6) + 8(1)

    (a)   (i)   A = contractile/vacuole   B = cytoplasm/endoplasm
                        C = pseudopod/false foot   D = nucleus/organelle
        (ii) Protista/Protoctista
    (b)   (i)   A = flagellum   B = DNA/chromosome/nucleoid
                                                  not nucleus
                    C = cell wall/membrane   D = capsule (slime layer)
        (ii) Monera (Prokaryotae)

SECTION B

Answer any <u>two</u> questions from this section.

Each question carries 30 marks.

7. (a) (i)   Movement or diffusion of water   3
          (ii) Allows some molecules through/Visking tubing/cell membrane   3
    (b) (i)   Diagram (minimum = 2 solutions & membrane)   6, 3, 0
               Label - (title may be considered a label)   3
          (ii) water/water plus solute/membrane or tissue/observe or result/time   4(3)
               (If 'set up as above' – then diagram must be fully labelled accordingly)
          (iii) tissue or membrane swollen/water movement   3

8.	(a)	(i)	organic/biological/protein catalyst	3
		(ii)	fits (substrate)/active site/folded/can change shape	3
	(b)	(i)	name of enzyme ⎫ matching	3
		(ii)	name of substrate ⎭	3
		(iii)	Diagram (minimum = beaker, solution, temp. reference)	6, 3, 0
			Label – (title may be considered a label)	3
		(iv)	no more product/colour change/no more bubbles/no more foam	3
		(v)	water bath/different temperature treatments/Bunsen/thermostat	3
		(vi)	graph (horizontal line or multi-peaked graph not acceptable)	3
9.	(a)	(i)	growth/sprouting	3
		(ii)	chemical (enzyme) reactions/dissolve stored food/swell testa/ a condition of germination	3
	(b)	(i)	Diagram (minimum = test tube, seeds, variable)	6, 3, 0
			Control	3
			Label – (title may be considered a label)	3
		(ii)	presence of variable/absence of variable	2(3)
		(iii)	results of experiment	3
			results of controls	3

SECTION C

Answer any <u>four</u> questions from this section.

Each question carries 60 marks.

10.	(a)	(i)	organisms and their (non-living) environment	3
		(ii)	any 2 named ecosystems (e.g. seashore/hedgerow/forest/grassland/ lake/terrestrial/land/aquatic)	2(3)
	(b)		A = Diving beetle B = Water mite C = **Hydra** D = Pond snail E = Nematode F = Planarian G = Leech	7(3)
			(N.B. – Check exam book for answers)	
	(c)	(i)	an <u>undesirable</u> change in the environment	6
		(ii)	any valid activity	6
			prevention	3
		(iii)	conservation – protection/preservation/management of the environment	6

(iv) food source/balance of nature/biodiversity/prevention of extinction/ health of planet/aesthetic/recreational/O_2/CO_2 (not 'for clothes')
any three 3(3)

11. (a) (i) $C_6H_{12}O_6 + (6)O_2$ (or words) 2(3)
(ii) chloroplast 3
(b) (i) hydrogen (proton)/oxygen/electron or energy or ATP 3(3)
(ii) Hydrogen/protons (released into pool & combine with CO_2) to form glucose/oxygen used in respiration OR released/electrons are passed to chlorophyll 3(3)
(iii) stoma/guard cells 3
(iv) increase day length/artificial light/increase carbon dioxide level/ increase in temperature level 3
(c) (i) release of energy/oxidation of food 6
(ii) to provide energy or named metabolic activity 6
(iii) respiration in presence of oxygen 6
(iv) aerobic 3
(v) allow <u>any example</u> of 'industrial fermentation' 2(3)

Organism 3 marks	Product 3 marks
bacteria	beer/wine/yoghurt/enzymes/drugs/hormones/ antibiotics/methane (biogas)/etc.
fungus/yeast	carbon dioxide/wine/beer/single cell protein/ antibiotics

12. (a) (i) 1. Pulmonary artery 3
2. Pulmonary vein 3
(ii) carbon dioxide 3
(b) (i) A = larynx (voice box) B = trachea (wind pipe)
C = bronchus   D = bronchiole 4(3)
(ii) Alveolus 3
(iii) To produce sound or speech 3
(iv) To keep trachea open/prevent collapse of trachea/protection of trachea 3
(v) At the back of the throat/top of windpipe/oesophagus 3
To prevent food entering trachea/wrong way/prevent choking 3
(c) (i) diaphragm/intercostal 6 + 3

		(ii)	diaphragm contracts (lowers)/intercostal muscles contract/ribs move up and out/increased volume of thoracic cavity/pressure decreases/ intercostals relax/air rushes in/diaphragm relaxes/volume decreases/ pressure increases/air pushed out/inhale/exhale **any two**	2(3)
		(iii)	name/cause/prevention or treatment	3(3)
			<u>asthma</u>/allergic response or genetics or smoking or narrowing of bronchioles or infection or anxiety/use of inhaler or avoidance of allergens/exercise.	
			<u>bronchitis</u>/infection or narrowing of bronchi/antibiotics (for bacterial infection)/cancer of the lungs/MS effecting diaphragm.	
13.	(a)	(i)	A and a ⎫ **any two**	6 + 3
		(ii)	AB Ab aB ab ⎭ **points**	
	(b)	(i)	adenine, thymine, guanine, cytosine or letters A,T,G,C	4(3)
		(ii)	three bases/code for one amino acid	3
		(iii)	information (code) is copied to RNA molecule	3
		(iv)	ribosome	6
	(c)	(i)	organisms now existing/have descended from previous types/by (genetic) change/natural selection/response to environmental change/over time **any two**	2(3)
		(ii)	organisms best suited to environment/have greater chance of breeding/ and survive ['survival of the fittest' = 2(3)] **any two**	2(3)
		(iii)	Darwin/Wallace	3
		(iv)	▪ Fossil/series showing change or example/change related to environment/common descent or ancestry or explained **OR**	
			▪ Anatomy/homologous structure or bones (or explained)/example of/adaptive radiation (or explained)/example of/common descent or ancestry **OR**	
			▪ Embryology/similarity between embryos/two examples from fish, amphibians, reptiles, birds, mammals/adult forms different/ common descent or ancestry	
			any two points from one of the above	6 + 6
14.	Any two of (a), (b), (c).			
	(a)	(i)	A = cortex B = medulla/pyramid C = pelvis D = ureter	4(3)
		(ii)	bladder	3
		(iii)	cortex (A)/nephron/glomerulus/Bowman's capsule	3
		(iv)	cortex (A)/medulla (B)/nephron/convoluted tubule/loop	3
		(v)	urea/water/salt	3
		(vi)	skin/lungs/liver	3
			water/carbon dioxide/urea/salt/bile/sweat (not mentioned in (v))	3

	(b)	(i)	diagram (ovaries/oviducts/uterus/vagina)	**6, 3, 0 + 2(3)**
		(ii)	fertilisation located in oviduct } **pointed or**	**3**
			implantation indicated in uterus } **mentioned**	**3**
		(iii)	monthly cycle in female/menstruation or lining of uterus (endometrium)shed/blood discharged/F.S.H./Graffian follicles with eggs/secrete oestrogen/endometrium thickens/L.H./ovulation/ corpus luteum/progesterone/(if no fertilisation then) lining breaks down **any four**	**4(3)**
	(c)	(i)	to prevent back flow of blood	**6**
		(ii)	blood is under pressure/blood from heart/blood pumped	**6**
		(iii)	vein	**6**
		(iv)	substances can diffuse easily/in and out of blood/tissues/less fat content	**3**
		(v)	capillaries at both ends/joins two organs/two named organs	**3**
		(vi)	1. renal (arteries)	**3**
			2. coronary or cardiac (arteries)	**3**
15.	(a)	(i)	2	**3**
		(ii)	single or central vascular bundle (xylem)/root hairs/endodermis	**2(3)**
		(iii)	A = ground tissue B = vascular tissue C = dermal tissue	**3(3)**
		(iv)	xylem/phloem	**2(3)**
			Xylem – lignified/transports water/vessels/tracheids/dead	
			Phloem – transports food/sieve tubes/companion cells/living	
			any one difference	**3**
		(v)	food storage/storage of waste/photosynthesis/strength/support	**3**
	(b)	(i)	asexual reproduction (in plants)/cloning	**6**
		(ii)	'Seed' potatoes - stem	
			Runners of strawberries etc. - stem	
			Tuber of **Dahlia** - root	
			Bulb of onion - stem/leaf/bud	
			New plants from leaf - leaf	
			Artificial examples	
			Cuttings/grafts/layers - stem, bud, stem	
			any one example	**3 + 3**
		(iii)	One parent/less variation in offspring/no pollination/ no sexual reproduction	**6**
		(iv)	cutting/grafting/layering/micropropagation **any two**	**2(3)**
		(v)	Advantage – simple/fast/same as parent/avoids competition	**3**
			Disadvantage – lack of variation/diseases inherited	**3**

(c) (i) A = stolon/hypha B = rhizoid C = sporangium   3(4)
    (ii) anchorage/absorption/digestion/secretion of enzymes/nutrition/feeding   3
    (iii) (produces) spores/reproduction   3
    (iv) heterotrophic/saprotrophic/saprophytic/saprobic   3
          decomposes/recycling   3
    (v) Fungi   3
    (vi) yeast/mushroom/etc.   3

MARKING SCHEME

LEAVING CERTIFICATE EXAMINATION, 2005

BIOLOGY – HIGHER LEVEL

SECTION A

Answer any five questions.

1. Any five   5(4)
 - (a) Carbohydrate/polysaccharide
 - (b) Fat
 - (c) Carbon/C
 - (d) Starch
 - (e) Disaccharide
 - (f) Excretion

2. (a) A (possible) explanation (for an observation) or explained,   3(2) + 2(7)
        e.g. assumption
 - (b) (Set up for) comparison or explained
 - (c) Measurements or observations or information gathered
 - (d) A repeat of an experiment or procedure or explained
 - (e) A supported hypothesis or explained

3. (a) False   5(1) + 5(3)
    (b) False
    (c) True
    (d) True
    (e) True
    (f) True
    (g) False
    (h) True
    (i) True
    (j) True

4. (a) Rate (or photosynthesis) is increasing   5(2) + 2(5)
    (b) Rate (or photosynthesis) is levelling off (is not increasing)
    (c) (Light or carbon dioxide) saturated or explained
    (d) Chloroplast or chlorophyll
    (e) Respiration/combustion or burning
    (f) Increased (artificial) lighting/increased carbon dioxide/heating

5. Diagram   (6, 0) + 7(2)
    (a) Diagram   Diag 6,0
         Labels   – spindle
                     – centromere
    (b) Reproduction
    (c) Growth/repair/reproduction (only if development of macrospore/microspore is given)
    (d) No reduction in chromosomes/no homologous pairing during process/resulting nuclei identical/two cells
    (e) Carcinogen/mutation/mutagen/example 1/example 2/radiation or named/virus **any two**

6. (a) A = villus B = lacteal or lymph vessel C = muscle or wall   5(2) + 2(5)
    (b) Large surface area/rich blood supply/microvilli/thin-walled/lacteal   **any two**
    (c) Diffusion (passive transport)
    (d) Fats/fatty acids/glycerol/lipids   **any one**

SECTION B

Answer any two questions.

7. (a) (i) A vessel/container/named industrial example, e.g. vat — **3**
　　　　(ii) (Enzyme) – can be recovered — **3**
　　(b) (i) Name of enzyme/yeast — **3**
　　　　(ii) Diagram of apparatus (2 pieces) + one label — **3**
　　　　(iii) Use of apparatus, e.g. beaker/stirrer/syringe
　　　　　　Names of solutions, e.g sodium alginate/calcium chloride
　　　　　　Purpose, e.g. to trap enzyme/form beads
　　　　　　Sodium alginate/calcium chloride are compulsory points
　　　　　　any four – at least one from each — **4(3)**
　　　　(iv) Named substrate or named product/comment on procedure — **2(3)**

8. (a) (i) Making a copy — **3**
　　　　(ii) (Matching) RNA production
　　　　　　(notion of both DNA and RNA must be given) — **3**
　　(b) (i) Name of plant — **3**
　　　　(ii) Break up of cell (walls) or release of cytoplasm — **3**
　　　　(iii) A few seconds only (max 6 secs) — **3**
　　　　(iv) To break down membrane(s) or membrane components — **3**
　　　　(v) Clumps (protects) DNA/to remove protein/separates DNA/separates protein — **3**
　　　　(vi) Breaks down (acts on) protein — **3**
　　　　(vii) Proteins are associated with DNA (histones or chromosomes) — **3**
　　　　(viii) (Ice) cold — **3**

9. (a) (i) (Possesses) nucleus/membrane-bound organelles or named — **3**
　　　　(ii) Fungi — **3**
　　(b) (i) Name of plant — **3**
　　　　(ii) Cut or pick/container or avoidance of contamination/prevent leaves being crushed or shaken — **3**
　　　　(iii) Storage details/cutting procedure/attach to lid/method of attachment/ avoidance of contamination　　**any two** — **2(3)**
　　　　(iv) Dishes (or agar) <u>with</u> additives (food or example) — **3**
　　　　　　To provide a medium or to allow growth — **3**
　　　　(v) Pink colonies (circles) or negative result qualified — **3**
　　　　(vi) Description of safe disposal — **3**

SECTION C

Answer any four questions.

10. (a) (i) Manipulation of genes or explained — 3

    (ii) Micro-organism – production of hormone or enzymes or named or interferon or other — 3

    Plant – slow ripening tomatoes/herbicide resistant plants/ freeze-resistant plants/other — 3

  (b) (i) Recessive – its expression is masked by dominant (allele)/expressed when homozygous only — 3

    Allele – form of a gene or explained — 3

    (ii) Dominant allele masks the expression of the recessive allele or explained — 3

    (iii) 25% — 3

    (Gametes)   N   n   x   N   n — 3

    (Offspring Genotypes)   NN   Nn   Nn   nn — 3

    (Offspring Phenotypes)   (Normal Normal Normal) Abnormal — 3

    (or cross explained 3(3))

    (iv) Testing (people) for the presence of a (specific) gene — 3

    (v) Selection of embryo or any valid role — 3

  (c) (i) (Genes) on the same chromosome — 3

    Gene located on a sex (or X) chromosome — 3

    (ii) They are transmitted/on the same chromosome or together — 2(3)

    (iii) 1. XXCc and XY c - — 2(3)

    2. XXcc and XY C - — 2(3)

    [In 1. and 2. if genes are correct in both parents – 3 marks

    If genes and chromosomes are correct in both parents – 6 marks]

11. (a) (i) Aerobic respiration requires oxygen or anaerobic respiration does not — 3

    (ii) $C_6H_{12}O_6 + 6O_2 \longrightarrow 6H_2O + 6CO_2$ — 6, 3, 0

  (b) (i) Cytoplasm — 3

    (ii) Uses energy/combines with phosphate/to form ATP/ATP stores energy/ high energy bond/energy transferred (by ATP) **any three** — 3(3)

    (iii) Pyruvic acid (Pyruvate) — 3

    (iv) Mitochondrion — 3

    (v) Lactic acid — 3

    (vi) Increased breathing (deeper or faster) or reference to oxidation of lactic acid or increased oxygen — 3

(c)	(i)	Diagram – vessel plus anaerobic conditions	3
		Label (comment) relating to anaerobic conditions	3
	(ii)	Sugar or named sugar or starch	3
	(iii)	First reagent(s) or test named/any procedural point/initial colour/ final colour **any three**	3(3)
		(Potassium) dichromate/add acid or warm/orange/to green Iodoform test or potassium iodide/add sodium hypochlorite or warm/colourless/to yellow	
	(iv)	Carbon dioxide	3
	(v)	No more bubbles given off	3
	(vi)	Alcohol kills yeast or yeast dies or sugar used up	3

12. (a) (i) Rivalry (fight) for resource or named resource/organisms requiring <u>limited resources</u> 3

(ii) True (stated or implied)/because requirements are the same or explained 2(3)

(b) (i) 'increase in day length' 3

(ii) food/climate (weather)/to breed **any two** 2(3)

(iii) 'fat' 3

(iv) '<u>beneath</u> skin'/'<u>inside</u> abdomen' or around organs or named organ 2(3)

(v) converted to carbohydrate/used for energy (respiration) 3

(vi) '(growing) tips' 3

(vii) meristematic tissue or explained/region of high metabolic activity 3

(c) (i) Named plant 3

Choose sample area or transect (line or belt)/quadrat/random throw or along transect/many times or at stations/count or observe **any three** 3(3)

Method of recording data/calculate percentage cover or frequency or density/presentation of results 3

(ii) Any three valid effects 3(3)

13. (a) (i) Testis 3

(ii) Development of secondary sexual characteristics or example named/development of sex organs/sperm production **any two** 2(3)

(b) (i) Diagram (testis, associated duct, penis) 6, 3, 0

labels 2(3)

(ii) Testis 3

(iii) Size comment/shape or structural comment/motile (only if 'tail' or 'flagellum' not given)/chromosomal difference/does not (usually) contribute mitochondrial DNA to zygote **any two** 2(3)

		(iv)	Cowper's gland/seminal vesicle/prostate gland	3
		(v)	Allows sperm <u>to swim</u>/provides nutrients/lubricant/protects sperm	3
	(c)	(i)	Prevention of fertilisation (conception) or implantation or pregnancy	3
		(ii)	Vasectomy or described	3
			Advantage – simple operation/avoids side effects of hormonal contraception/effective/single procedure	3
			Disadvantage – not easily reversed/medical complications/ no protection against STIs	3
		(iii)	Any three examples	3(3)
		(iv)	Decrease (no increase) in population/demographic imbalance/ improved social conditions/comment on STIs/health issues	3

14. Answer any **two** of (a), (b) (c)

(a)	(i)	Osmosis/reference to different concentrations/membrane partially (selectively) permeable/comment on surface area of root hair(s) or no cuticle present **any three**		3(3)
	(ii)	No		3
		Only water (solvent) moves by osmosis or other correct comment		3
	(iii)	Tubular or continuous lumen/reinforced (lignified) walls/end to end/ pits/ lateral movement of water/wettable lining/narrow (bore) **any two**		2(3)
	(iv)	(called) cohesion/water evaporates in leaf or transpiration/is replaced/upward pull or tension/continuous stream/ensures movement/water column hard to break **any three**		3(3)
(b)	(i)	growth regulator/in plants or named plant or plant part		2(3)
	(ii)	$10^{-5} - 10^{-3}$		3
	(iii)	$1 - 10$		3
	(iv)	Inhibition or explained		3
	(v)	Rooting powder/tissue culturing/weed killer/ripening of fruit/ seedless fruits/other		2(3)
	(vi)	Thorns/modified leaves, e.g. pine needles/stinging (cells)/deep roots/ heat shock proteins/phytoalexins, e.g. production of antimicrobial chemicals/use of seeds/leaf fall/perennating organs or examples/dormancy/succulent tissues/toxins/other **any three**		3(3)
(c)	(i)	**Exocrine**: ducted or explained		3
		Endocrine: ductless or hormone producing		3
	(ii)	Insulin or glucagon		3
		Regulates blood sugar or regulates sugar (level) or correct explanation		3

(iii) 1. **Name** 3
Arthritis/osteoporosis
Cause 3
Arthritis – injury/hormonal imbalance/genetic/immune response
Osteoporosis – hormonal imbalance/lack of exercise/genetic/dietary/menopause
Treatment 3
Arthritis – anti-inflammatory drugs/analgesics/rest/exercise/replacement of joint/steroids or named/immuno-suppressants
Osteoporosis – HRT/exercise/diet/dietary supplements or named

2. **Name** 3
Paralysis/Parkinson's disease
Cause 3
Injury/genetic/disease/lack of dopamine
Treatment
Physiotherapy/dopamine or drugs to promote neurotransmitter production/stem cell/implant 3

15. Answer any **two** of (a), (b) (c)

(a) (i) non-cellular/one nucleic acid/can <u>reproduce in host cell</u> only
or obligate parasite/do not possess organelles or named organelle
any two 2(3)

(ii) Cold/'flu/polio/rabies/mumps/measles/AIDS (HIV) **any two** 2(3)

(iii) B-cells/T-cells or two named T cells, e.g. helper/killer/suppressor/memory **any two** 2(3)
B-cells – produce antibodies/agglutination or lysis/memory
T-cells – recognise/destroy infected or damaged cells/memory/activation/suppress immune system
Helper T – stimulate B cells or stimulate killer T cells/recognise antigens
Killer T – Destroy infected or damaged cells
Suppressor T – Switch off immune system or explained
Memory T – memorise antigen **any two** 2(3)

(iv) yes 3
in <u>both</u> cases the result is the production of antibodies 3

(b) (i) Diagram (wall, membrane) 3, 0
Labels 2(3)

(ii) Cell wall/size/capsule/flagellum/plasmid 2(3)

(iii) Produce spores 3

	(iv)	Disease-causing	3
	(v)	Substances produced by micro-organisms/inhibit (growth or reproduction) of bacteria or fungi	2(3)
		Misuse: survival of resistant strains/build-up of resistant population	3
(c)	(i)	saprophytic – live on dead organisms (matter)	3
		parasitic – living in or on another organism <u>causing harm</u>.	3
	(ii)	saprophytes – recycling (of nutrients)/decay	3
		parasites – keep populations under control/natural selection	3
	(iii)	beneficial – yeast for brewing or baking/named edible fungus/other	3
		harmful – ringworm/athlete's foot/potato blight/thrush/dry rot/ death cap/other	3
	(iv)	**Rhizoid** – anchors/digestion/absorption	3
		Sporangium – produces spores/stores spores/asexual reproduction	3
		Gametangium – produces gametes/sexual reproduction	3
		Zygospore – survival/dispersal	3